Effe

Writing

A Handbook for Accountants

Fifth Edition

Claire B. May, Ph.D.
The Art Institute of Atlanta

Gordon S. May, Ph.D., CPA
University of Georgia

Prentice Hall, Upper Saddle River, NJ 07458

Acquisitions Editor: Diane de Castro
Editorial Assistant: Fran Toepfer
Marketing Manager: Beth Toland
Production Editor: Lynda P. Hansler
Manufacturing Buyer: Lisa DiMaulo
Senior Manufacturing Supervisor: Paul Smolenski
Manufacturing Manager: Vincent Scelta
Cover Art: Don Baker/ Kolea Baker, Artist Representative, Inc.
Cover Design: Lorraine Costellano
Composition: Pine Tree Composition, Inc.

Library of Congress Cataloging-in-Publication Data

May, Claire Arevalo.
Effective writing: a handbook for accountants / Claire May, Gordon S. May.—5th ed.
p. cm.
Includes bibliographical references and index.
ISBN 0-13-011897-4
1. Business report writing. 2. Communication in accounting. I. May, Gordon S. I. Title.
HF5719.M375 1998
808′.066657—dc21 98-55174
CIP

Printed in the United States of America

10 9 8 7 6 5 4 3 2 1

ISBN 0-13-011897-4

Prentice-Hall International (UK) Limited, *London*
Prentice-Hall of Australia Pty. Limited, *Sydney*
Prentice-Hall Canada Inc., *Toronto*
Prentice-Hall Hispanoamericana, S.A., *Mexico*
Prentice-Hall of India Private Limited, *New Delhi*
Prentice-Hall of Japan, Inc., *Tokyo*
Pearson Education Asia Pte. Ltd., *Singapore*
Editora Prentice-Hall do Brasil, Ltda., *Rio de Janeiro*

Brief Contents

Contents

3

The Flow of Thought: Organizing for Coherence 30

4

A Sense of Style: Writing with Conciseness and Clarity 51

5

Standard English: Grammar, Punctuation, and Spelling 79

Preface

Effective Writing: A Handbook for Accountants, fifth edition, is designed to help accounting students and practitioners improve their communication skills. It can be used as a supplementary text for regular accounting courses, as a text in an accounting communication course, or as a text in a business communication or technical writing course when these courses include accounting students. The handbook is also a useful desk reference or self-study manual for accountants in practice.

Effective Writing guides the writer through all the stages of the writing process: planning, including analysis of audience and purpose; generating and organizing ideas; writing the draft; revising for readable style and correct grammar; and designing the document for effective presentation. In addition to these basic writing principles, the book includes chapters on letters, memos (including e-mail), reports, and other formats used by accountants in actual practice. Throughout the text, *Effective Writing* stresses coherence, conciseness, and clarity as the most important qualities of the writing done by accountants.

To supplement the instruction on writing effectively, we have included a chapter on oral presentations. Chapter 14 discusses preparation of the presentation, including audience analysis and organization of materials as well as techniques of effective delivery including use of visual aids.

We have also included a special section on "Writing and Your Career." In this section you will find a chapter on writing essay examinations (including professional examinations), a chapter on writing resumes and letters of application, and a chapter on writing for publication.

A special feature of this book is the chapter on accounting research. Here you will find valuable reference material on such topics as:

- Where to find accounting information (including Internet sites)
- How to write citations of accounting sources (including Internet sources)

Exercises and assignments throughout *Effective Writing* reinforce the concepts covered in the text. Some exercises have answers within the text for independent review. The *Instructor's Manual* contains answers to many other exercises. Most chapters include topics for writing or speaking assignments. The assignments, like the illustrations in the text, are concerned with accounting concepts and situations and thus will seem relevant and familiar to those studying and practicing accounting.

Effective Writing can be used in conjunction with traditional accounting courses. Instructors can assign cases and topics for research based on the accounting concepts being studied in class, or they can use the assignments provided in this handbook. Students then analyze the accounting problem, research the literature if necessary, and prepare answers according to an assigned format such as a letter, technical memo, formal report, or oral presentation. The handbook guides students toward principles of effective writing and speaking. Instructors can then evaluate students' performance based on the criteria discussed in the text and the *Instructor's Manual.*

The *Instructor's Manual* contains suggestions for everyone wishing to improve the communication skills of accounting students, whether in a regular accounting course or in a course devoted to communication. It includes topics such as motivating students to improve their communication skills, designing assignments, and evaluating performance. It also contains chapter commentaries and masters for transparencies and handouts.

We would like to thank the following individuals who reviewed the manuscript for the fifth edition and provided helpful comments and suggestions: James L. Dodd, Drake University; Jack R. Fay, Pittsburgh State University; Sridhar Ramamoorti, University of Illinois at Urbana—Champaign; Diane Roberts, University of San Francisco; and Diane Tanner, University of North Florida. Their input was greatly appreciated.

We hope that this book will help both those preparing to enter the profession and those already in practice to achieve greater success through effective communication.

Claire B. May
Gordon S. May

1

Accountants as Communicators

The ability to communicate effectively, whether through speaking or in writing, is essential to success in the accounting profession. To be truly competent, accountants must be able to use words effectively. Yet time and again, studies show that a major criticism of college graduates is that they do not speak or write well.[1]

Multinational accounting firms offer special courses to help their accountants write better. Various accounting organizations—the American Institute of Certified Public Accountants (AICPA) and many state societies, for example—offer continuing education courses in writing. Many colleges and universities now stress effective writing in accounting coursework.[2] The AICPA also evaluates candidates' writing skills as one component of the CPA exam.

A few years ago the managing partners of the nation's largest public accounting firms issued a jointly authored paper that stressed the importance of both written and oral communication skills to the practice of accounting. The following excerpt details some of the major issues discussed:

> Public accounting requires its practitioners to be able to transfer and receive information with ease.
>
> Practitioners must be able to present and defend their views through formal, informal, written, and oral presentation. They must be able to do so at a peer level with business executives.
>
> . . . Practitioners must be able to listen effectively to gain information and understand opposing points of view. They also will need the ability to locate, obtain, and organize information from both human and electronic sources.[3]

The American Accounting Association's Committee to Prepare a Statement of Basic Accounting Theory also identified the importance of communication in the practice of accounting: "Communication is a vital link in accounting activity. It is of no less importance than that of developing the information itself."[4]

The ability to communicate effectively, whether through speaking or writing, is essential to success in the accounting profession. Unfortunately, some students and accountants lack the skills they need to be effective communicators. Several years ago *The Wall Street Journal* reported that one-third of the accounting firms surveyed were dissatisfied with the communication skills of entry-level accountants.[5] In another study to determine why entry-level accountants lose their jobs, a high percentage of firms reported poor writing skills as a major reason for job terminations.[6]

A recent study of 1,400 chief financial officers indicated why they rank communication skills for accountants so highly. According to the study's report, "[I]ncreasingly, accountants are relied upon for their business interpretation of numbers and data, which requires strong verbal and written competencies."[7]

Because the ability to communicate effectively plays an important part in an accountant's success on the job, many employers screen prospective accountants for skills in oral and written communication. In fact, one study has shown communication skills to be the most important factor in decisions to hire new accountants. Employers view the ability to write and speak effectively as even more important than a prospective employee's grade point average.[8]

In 1997, an AICPA subcommittee issued the *AICPA Competency Model for the New Finance Professional*. This report lists competencies "that position the CPA to assume the role of a strategic business partner and to remain current and a relevant, forward-thinking member of the workforce of today and the future."[9] Among the personal attributes listed for competency is "effective business writing." The report says that the writing of entry-level professionals should exhibit proper grammar, appropriate style and tone, logical organization, clarity, and conciseness.[10]

Accountants need good communication skills to get a good job and to keep that job after they are hired. Of course, "communication skills" is a broad area. It includes formal and informal oral presentations, interpersonal communication, reading and listening, and many other skills. Because this book is primarily about writing, let's look further at some of the kinds of documents accountants write on the job.

WHAT DO ACCOUNTANTS WRITE?

No matter what kind of practice accountants have, writing is an essential part of the job. Whether in public accounting, management accounting, not-for-profit accounting, or government accounting, and whether specializing in tax, auditing, systems, or some other area, accountants write every day.

Examples in three areas—tax, auditing, and systems—suggest a few of the many occasions that require accountants to write. A tax accountant in a CPA firm often writes memos to other members of the firm that describe the results of his or her research. These memos become part of the clients' files. Then the accountant may write a letter advising the client about the best way to handle the tax problem. Tax accountants must also write letters to the Internal Revenue Service on behalf of clients.

Auditors write memos to be filed with the audit working papers describing the work done on an audit. Auditors may also write memos to their colleagues to request advice or to report research results. After the audit engagement, auditors often write advisory letters to management. The purpose of these letters is to suggest ways to improve accounting and internal control procedures.

Systems specialists write documents for readers with varying degrees of computer expertise. They may write a primer to explain how to use a software package, or they may write a highly technical report on a complex accounting system application.

No matter what their specialty, all accountants write memos to their supervisors, subordinates, and coworkers to request or provide information. They also write letters to clients, agencies, and a variety of other readers.

Technical reports and memos, both formal and informal, are also important ways in which accountants communicate. For instance, an accountant working for a corporation might write a report for management on alternative accounting treatments for a particular kind of business transaction. An accountant working for a CPA firm may write a technical memo on how best to handle an unusual accounting problem of a client.

To be effective, letters, memos, and reports must be well written. How will clients react if, after reading a letter from their CPA, they are still confused about their income tax problem? How will management or one's supervisors react to a report that is poorly organized and hard to follow?

Yet another kind of writing prepared by accountants is the narrative portion of a financial statement. Footnote disclosures, for instance, communicate information that users may need to interpret the statements accurately. Here is an example of a footnote disclosure in Pfizer's 1997 annual report:[11]

Savings and Investment Plans

> We have savings and investment plans for most employees in the U.S., Puerto Rico, the U.K., and Ireland. Employees may contribute a portion of their salaries to the plans and we match a portion of the employee contributions. Our contributions were $41 million in 1997, $36 million in 1996, and $33 million in 1995.

This footnote is fairly easy to understand. Unfortunately, the meaning of some footnote disclosures is not always clear to many financial statement readers. Arthur Adelberg and Richard Lewis, in an article in the *Journal of Accountancy*, note the need for more clearly written footnotes. They suggest that accountants use shorter sentences, active verbs, and definitions of technical terms when writing footnotes and other narrative portions of financial statements.[12*]

In 1997, the Securities and Exchange Commission (SEC) proposed a regulation requiring companies to write their disclosure documents in "plain English." In announcing this proposal, Arthur Levitt, chairman of the SEC, said, "Disclosure is not disclosure if it does not communicate."[13] This proposed regulation would require clearer and more concise communication.

HOW WELL DO ACCOUNTANTS WRITE?

The answer to this question—how well accountants write—has already been suggested by the study reporting the large numbers of entry-level accountants who lose their jobs because of poor writing skills. Some employers believe the problem is getting worse. One study suggests that almost half of all practitioners in large CPA firms believe that writing skills of their newly hired staff have declined.[14]

A letter to *The Wall Street Journal* points out the high costs to employers when accounting employees lack adequate writing skills, including the costs of quality control measures to correct faulty writing. In addition, "The expense of hiring and training those who are subsequently fired for [poor writing ability] must surely represent a tremendous waste of resources."[15]

*Copyright © 1980 by the American Institute of Certified Public Accountants.

WHAT MAKES WRITING WORK?

What is good writing? The list of tips for writers in Figure 1–1 summarizes many qualities of effective business writing, including writing by accountants. These qualities are stressed throughout this book; they are also very similar to the criteria the AICPA uses to evaluate writing skills on the CPA exam. Let's examine these tips in a little more detail.

The first tip concerns the *content* of the document. You must know what you are talking about, and the information you give should be accurate and relevant. The second tip for effective writing is to *write appropriately for your readers*. Your writing should be suitable for the readers in a number of ways: It should be written on a level they understand and find meaningful, and it should anticipate and answer their questions.

FIGURE 1–1 ***Tips for the Effective Writer***

1. *Content:* Be sure that the accounting content is correct and complete. Have you addressed all relevant accounting issues?
2. *Appropriateness for Readers:* Write the document with a particular reader in mind. Check that issues are discussed on a level the reader can understand. For most documents, it is better to focus on practical, explicit information and advice related to the case you are discussing rather than on general accounting theory.
3. *Conciseness:* Write as concisely as possible, given the reader's needs and the issues to be addressed.
4. *Clarity:* Develop a style that is clear and readable. Choose words that convey your meaning with precision and clarity.
5. *Coherence:* Structure the document so that it is coherent. The organization should be logical and the train of thought easy to follow. Summarize main ideas near the beginning of the document, and begin each paragraph with a topic sentence.
6. *Revision:* Revise the document so that it is polished and professional. It should be free of all spelling errors and typos; grammatical errors should not detract from the message.

The third tip is *conciseness.* Say what needs to be said in as few words as possible. To keep your writing concise, avoid digressions, unnecessary repetition, and wordiness.

Clarity is the next tip. Write as simply as possible, using words and phrases with which the reader is familiar. To improve the clarity of your writing, choose words that mean precisely what you intend so that your sentences convey only one meaning: the meaning you want to convey. Well-structured sentences also contribute to clear writing.

Coherence is the logical, orderly relationship of ideas. Coherent writing is, quite simply, writing that is well organized. The flow of thought is easy to follow, and important ideas stand out. To write coherently, you must carefully think through the ideas you wish to convey. The ideas must be arranged logically and then written in a way readers can comprehend. Coherence is the fifth tip for effective writers.

The final tip is to *revise* your writing so that it is polished and professional. Documents should look attractive and be free of grammatical and mechanical errors.

YOU CAN BECOME A GOOD WRITER

With all this talk about the importance of good writing to a successful career in accounting, you may feel overwhelmed or discouraged. Many people believe that they can never become good writers.

A word of encouragement is in order. Virtually anyone who succeeds in college work has the education and the ability to become at least an adequate writer, and probably even a good one. Problems with writing are often the result of two factors, both of which can be corrected: lack of adequate training in writing skills and lack of self-confidence.

Let's address the latter problem, the poor image some people have of themselves as writers.

One reason to be optimistic about your writing ability is that you've already learned quite a bit about how to write from English courses and other writing classes, as well as from your own experience. Most people are better writers than they realize. They have the potential to become even more effective after they've mastered a few strategies such as the ones we'll cover in this book. As you read this book, note the techniques and principles you already use in your writing. Don't lose sight of your strengths while you work to improve the areas that could be better.

Another reason you should be able to write well as an accountant is that you will be writing about topics you understand and find interesting. If you have had unpleasant experiences with writing in courses other than accounting, the problem may have been that you were writing about topics you weren't particularly interested in or didn't feel qualified to discuss. When we write about subjects we like and understand, it's much easier to write clearly and persuasively.

Finally, you may find it much easier to do the kind of writing recommended in this book because it will be simple, direct writing. Some people believe that they must write in long, complicated sentences filled with difficult, "impressive" vocabulary. In fact, just the opposite is true: Effective business writing is written as simply as possible. It is thus easier to do.

WRITING AND OTHER FORMS OF COMMUNICATION

Writing is only one of several forms of communication, along with such skills as reading, listening, speaking, and interpersonal communication. In fact, all these forms of communication work together to determine how well a person gives and receives information. Let's look at how reading, listening, and speaking skills can help you improve your writing.[16]

Reading

Reading affects writing in several ways. Often you will write a memo or letter in response to a written communication from someone else. In public practice, for example, you may write a letter to clients to answer questions they have posed in a letter to your firm. The ability to read the earlier correspondence carefully is essential to an effective response.

Careful reading is also important when you research accounting literature as background for the documents you write. The tax code, government regulations, Financial Accounting Standards Board (FASB) pronouncements, articles in professional journals, and *The Wall Street Journal* are examples of the material you must read to stay informed on accounting issues and procedures. You will need to understand this material and be able to apply it to particular situations.

You will also read information circulated and stored within your own firm or company, such as client files and memos from colleagues. Reading this material carefully will provide many of the insights and facts you need to deal effectively with situations for which you are responsible.

Thus, careful reading, with an understanding of important ideas and key facts, can contribute to effective writing.

Listening

Along with reading, the ability to listen carefully determines how well we receive information from others. On the job, you interact with colleagues, supervisors, subordinates, or clients; at school, you interact with professors and other students. Listening carefully to these people will provide important information you can use as the basis of your writing. It will provide facts about projects you are working on, along with insights into other people's expectations and concerns.

In many situations, listening skills contribute to effective writing. Instructions given by the professor in class, interviews with clients, requests from supervisors, and phone conversations with colleagues are a few examples. In all these situations, attentive listening is necessary to hear what people are saying. It's often a good idea to take notes and, when necessary, ask questions for clarification or additional information.

Careful listening to what others say is often a key ingredient in effective writing. By listening carefully, you will learn much about what others know about a situation, what their concerns are, and what they expect from you.

Speaking

What you write also affects what you say to others. Informally, you may have meetings and conversations to discuss reports or memos you've written. What you write may also be the basis for formal oral presentations before a group. You might make a presentation to a board of directors, senior managers, or members of a professional organization.

WRITING AND PROBLEM SOLVING

In the introduction to this chapter, we saw that the nation's largest public accounting firms are unanimous in calling for improved communication skills for those entering the profession. These firms also identify problem-solving skills as essential to successful accounting practice:

> Individuals seeking to be successful in the diverse world of public accounting must be able to use creative problem-solving skills in a consultative process. They must be able to solve diverse and unstructured problems in unfamiliar settings. They must be able to comprehend an unfocused set of facts; identify and, if possible, anticipate problems; and find acceptable solutions.[17]

Problem solving requires many skills, such as the identification of key issues, research into relevant literature, and the ability to think critically and analytically. At each step of the problem-solving process, writing can help you reach sound conclusions.

You can generate ideas on a topic by writing down what you know about that topic, as well as what you have yet to find out. The act of writing about a subject can actually help you clarify your thinking. As one wit has put it, "How do I know what I think until I see what I say?" There's more truth in this quip than might at first be apparent. Research into how people think and learn has shown that writers often generate ideas and improve their insights into a subject as they write down their thoughts.[18]

Writing can help you solve problems in other ways as well. For example, as you research accounting literature, you take notes. You may also write requests to other people for additional information you need in order to solve the problem.

Writing that you use to solve problems and make decisions is writing for yourself. Once the problems have been solved, or at least clearly defined, you can put your insights and conclusions into writing that will help you and others make decisions. Writing, problem solving, and decision-making are often inseparable, interactive processes that are essential to the practice of accounting.

In conclusion, remember that accounting is a process of both measuring and *communicating* information. Accountants need writing skills for many of their routine professional tasks, whether communicating with investors, management, clients, or fellow professionals. They need to use words effectively and to combine those words into good sentences and paragraphs.

Communication skills pay off in professional advancement as well. As Zane Robbins of Arthur Andersen & Co. has noted,

> All other things being equal, the professional accountant who can communicate best is likely to progress fastest. Those who are unable to write and communicate effectively often find themselves consigned to the purgatory of technician with little hope for long-term growth.[19]

To be a successful accountant, you must master many skills. You must understand and be able to apply accounting principles, of course, but you must also be able to communicate effectively. A competent accountant who is also an effective communicator will usually be rewarded with professional success.

EXERCISES

Exercise 1–1

Look for examples of effective and ineffective writing in the material you read regularly. Consider letters and memos as well as published professional material such as textbooks, professional articles, and FASB pronouncements. Then think about and answer the following questions:

1. What kind of material do you find easiest to read? What are some of the qualities that make this writing readable?
2. Examine closely the writing you find difficult to read. How do you think the writing could be improved?

3. Review the tips for effective writing summarized in Figure 1–1. Do the writing samples you have collected illustrate these qualities of good writing?

Exercise 1–2

Look at some recently published corporate annual reports and evaluate the financial statement disclosures they contain. Find examples of disclosures that are clear and concise and other examples that are not written as clearly or concisely as they could be. List the qualities that make some examples more clear and concise than others. (Hint: You can access many financial statements on the Internet by following links to listed companies at the New York Stock Exchange Web site at http://www.nyse.com.)

Exercise 1–3

Collect samples of your own writing. Analyze your writing, considering the following questions:

1. What kind of response do you usually get from your supervisors, peers, clients, and subordinates? Are readers sometimes uncertain of your meaning?
2. Review the qualities of effective writing summarized in Figure 1–1. Using this list as a benchmark, identify some of the strengths and weaknesses of your own writing.
3. Write a two-paragraph analysis of your writing. The first paragraph should identify the qualities of your writing that make it effective; the second paragraph should discuss what you need to improve. Begin each paragraph with a topic sentence that states the main idea of the paragraph. The first paragraph could begin this way:

   My writing is effective in several ways. For example, . . .

Exercise 1–4

Ask some accounting professionals about their experiences with writing on the job. Your questions might include some of the following questions:

- How much writing do they do in a typical day or week?
- What kinds of documents do they write? Who are their readers?
- What kinds of material do they read for their jobs?
- What specific writing skills do they believe are important for accountants?
- What are their pet peeves in the writing done by others?

During your conversations with these accountants, listen carefully to their responses and ask any questions you need for clarification. Later, write notes based on your conversations. Share your notes with your classmates during class discussions.

Exercise 1–5

Assume you are a staff accountant in a CPA firm. One of the firm's partners, Elaine Peters, has complimented you on the memos you have written. However, Ms. Peters has noticed that some of the firm's other staff accountants do not write very good memos, nor do they believe that effective writing is important.

Write a memo to the other staff accountants in your firm. Discuss why well-written memos are important and suggest some qualities that make the writing effective. Be sure that your own memo illustrates those qualities.

You will find suggestions on how to write a memo in Chapter 9.

NOTES

1. Lyman W. Porter and Lawrence E. McKibben, *Management Education and Development: Draft or Thrust into the 21st Century?* (New York: McGraw-Hill, 1988). Cited by Julie R. Dahlquist in "Writing Assignments in Finance: Development and Education," *Financial Practice and Education* 5, no. 1 (Spring/ Summer 1995): 107.
2. Gordon S. May and Claire B. May, "Communication Instruction: What Is Being Done to Develop the Communication Skills of Accounting Students?" *Journal of Accounting Education* 7 (Fall 1989): 233–44.
3. Duane R. Kullburg, William L. Gladstone, Peter R. Scanlon, J. Michael Cook, Ray J. Groves, Larry D. Horner, Shaun F. O'Malley, and Edward A. Kangas, *Perspectives on Education: Capabilities for Success in the Profession* (Big Eight Accounting Firms, 1989), 6.
4. Committee to Prepare a Statement of Basic Accounting Theory, *A Statement of Basic Accounting Theory* (Evanston, Ill.: American Accounting Association, 1966), 13.
5. *The Wall Street Journal*, 16 July 1986, "Words Count," 1.
6. Alan A. Cherry and Lucy A. Wilson, "A Study of the Writing Skills of Accounting Majors in California" (unpublished study, 1987).
7. *electronic accountant newswire*, (15 January 1998) [on-line], "Accountants' People Skills Given More Weight." Available from <http://www.electronicaccountant.com>; accessed 21 January 1998.
8. *New Accountant*, September 1986, "Popularity Poll Results," 20.
9. American Institute of Certified Public Accountants, Invitation to Comment, *AICPA Competency Model for the New Finance Professional*, Executive Summary (New York: AICPA, 7 October 1997).
10. American Institute of Certified Public Accountants, Invitation to Comment, *AICPA Competency Model for the New Finance Professional* (New York: AICPA, 7 October 1997), 5.
11. Pfizer, Inc., "Notes to Consolidated Financial Statements," *1997 Annual Report: Setting the Pace.* (New York: Pfizer, Inc., 1998), 52.

12. Arthur Harris Adelberg and Richard A. Lewis, "Financial Reports Can Be Made More Understandable," *Journal of Accountancy* 149 (June 1980): 44–50.
13. Mark H. Anderson, "SEC Proposes Rules for Plain-English Disclosure Documents," *The Wall Street Journal Interactive Edition* (13 January 1997) [online]. Available from <http://www.wsj.com>; accessed 13 January 1997.
14. Daniel P. Murphy, "An Analysis of the Application Skills Needed by Undergraduate Accounting Students Planning to Enter Tax Practice in the Southeastern United States: A Practitioner's Perspective," *Collected Papers of the American Accounting Association's Southeast Regional Meeting* (Atlanta, 1987), 120.
15. Gordon S. May, "No Accounting for Poor Writers," *The Wall Street Journal*, Letter to the Editor, 29 May 1987, 27.
16. See Elizabeth E. Orem and Jane O. Burns, "The Problems and Challenges of Teaching Accounting Students to Communicate," *Georgia Journal of Accounting* 9 (Spring 1988): 9–24.
17. Kullburg et al., 6.
18. Lee Odell, "The Process of Writing and the Process of Learning," *College Composition and Communication* 31, no. 1 (February 1980): 41–50.
19. Zane Robbins, "How to Develop Basic Writing Skills," *The Arthur Andersen Chronicle* 40, no. 1 (1981): 9.

2

The Writing Process: An Overview

Effective writing, like accounting, is a process. One step in the accounting process is to analyze transactions to determine how to record them. You decide what accounts to use and how detailed the entry description must be in order to be useful.

Several questions basic to the accounting system underlie your analysis of financial transactions and their treatment. What is the purpose of the information recorded and ultimately reported? Who are the users of this information and what are their needs? Do the readers expect this information to be presented in a certain form, such as the typical presentations found in annual reports? How can the information be most fairly and effectively presented?

These questions are as important to good writing as they are to good accounting. Planning, which emphasizes both the purpose of the writing and the needs and expectations of the readers, is the first step in the writing process.

This chapter discusses the writing process from beginning to end: planning for purpose and audience, gathering information, generating and organizing ideas, drafting, revising, and proofreading. (Figure 2–1 summarizes the steps of the writing process.) The chapter shows you how to apply this process to overcome much of the anxiety you may feel about writing, including the problem of writer's block. Throughout the chapter,

FIGURE 2–1 *The Writing Process*

Plan

- Read the assignment or consider the task carefully.
- Analyze the purposes of the document.
- Identify the accounting issues.
- Analyze the reader's interests, needs, and expectations.
- Gather and organize material.

Draft

- Put the ideas down on paper.
- Don't stop to edit.
- Write the parts of the paper in whatever order you wish.

Revise

- Revise the document so that it is clear, coherent, and concise.
- Proofread for grammatical, mechanical, and typographical errors.

we also discuss how computers, especially word processors, can help you at every stage of the writing process.

The previous chapter identified six tips for effective writing that focused on content, appropriateness for readers, conciseness, clarity, coherence, and revision (see Figure 1–1). In this and following chapters, we will discuss specific guidelines and techniques that will help you achieve these goals.

GETTING STARTED: IDENTIFYING PURPOSE

The first stage in the writing process—analyzing the purpose of the document—is easy to overlook. When you think about purpose, you decide what you want to accomplish with your letter, memo, or other document. Do you want to provide your readers with information about some topic, answer their questions, recommend a course of action, persuade them to do something, or agree with you on some point?

These are just a few of the purposes a document can have. What is important is to think carefully about the purpose *before* beginning to write. It might be helpful to think of purpose in terms of three categories: to give information about something, to propose a course of action, or to solve a problem. The purpose of most writing tasks falls into one of these categories, or perhaps a combination of two or three.

A report on leases, for example, could have numerous purposes. If you were writing such a report, you would first determine its primary purpose. Should the report simply compare and contrast operating and capital leases? Is the purpose of the report to recommend a particular kind of lease for a certain company in a given situation? Should the report analyze the income tax implications of a lease the company is evaluating?

Here is another example. Assume you are the controller for the Hamilton Art Supply Company. Hamilton is considering a purchase of stock in Colors Galore, one of Hamilton's major suppliers of crayons. A report on this possible purchase could have any of the following purposes:

- To inform management of the advantages (or disadvantages) of such a purchase
- To recommend that Hamilton purchase (or not purchase) the stock
- To suggest a way to finance the purchase

The purpose of the report, or of any writing, determines what material it should contain. Consider another example. Your client, White Manufacturing, is faced with a lawsuit that could result in a large loss. You might write a letter to White Manufacturing's controller about the disclosure requirements for contingent loss liabilities due to pending litigation. In such a letter, you would not discuss gain contingencies or loss contingencies from bad debts. You would analyze the specific purpose of the letter to decide what information was relevant for this situation.

Another way to think about the purpose of a document is to identify the accounting issues it will address. Sometimes these issues are obvious, but at other times you must analyze the situation carefully before all the issues become apparent. For example, a client may seek your help on the best way to record a transaction to minimize the income tax liability. As you analyze the transaction, you may become aware of accounting issues that would never occur to the client, such as the need to record the transaction consistently with generally accepted accounting principles.

Identifying the issues may help you to define the purposes of the document you are writing, because one purpose may be to explain the accounting issues in a way your reader can understand.

Once you have analyzed your purposes carefully, it's a good idea to write them down. Be as specific as possible and try to define the purposes in a sentence. This sentence may later become part of the introduction of the letter, memo, or report.

Two final words about purpose: *be specific*. Remember that you are writing to particular individuals in a particular situation. Relate the purpose of your writing to these people and their concerns. That is, state the purpose in the context of this specific situation rather than in broad, general terms. In the Hamilton Art Supplies example, suppose you were writing a report on how to finance a purchase of Colors Galore stock. You would limit your discussion to the financing alternatives available to Hamilton and those that are practical for it to consider.

Sometimes, to determine the purpose of a document you will need to read previous correspondence on the subject, such as a letter from a client. Be sure to read this correspondence carefully, underlining important information and noting what questions you've been asked to address. You may also be asked orally to write something, perhaps by your supervisor. If you receive an oral request to write, listen carefully to the directions. If the purpose of the document is not clear, ask questions until you're sure what the document should include.

ANALYZING THE READERS

Another important consideration in the planning of a writing task is who the readers will be. A memo on a highly technical accounting topic would be written one way for an accounting colleague, but another way for a client or manager with only limited knowledge of accounting procedures and terminology.

Effective writers analyze the needs and expectations of their readers before they begin to write. In writing a letter or memo, you will probably be writing to a limited number of people, perhaps to only one person. You also know, or can find out, important information about the readers. Again, you must ask certain questions. How much do the readers know about the subject being discussed? What else do they need to learn? The answer to these questions will suggest the terms that should be defined, the procedures that should be explained, or the background information that should be provided.

Accountants who deal with the public should be particularly careful in analyzing the needs of their readers. For example, a tax specialist might have clients with widely varying experience and knowledge of tax terminology. A corporate executive would probably understand such concepts as depreciation and accruals, but a small shopkeeper might not be familiar with them. Business letters to these two clients, even on the same topic, would be written differently.

Consider the readers' attitudes and biases. Are they likely to be neutral to your recommendations, or will they need to be convinced? Remember to write with the readers' interests, needs, and concerns in mind. How will the readers benefit, directly or indirectly, from what you propose? How can you present your arguments to overcome readers' objections and biases? To answer this last question, you must anticipate readers' questions, research the issues, and then organize your arguments into a convincing sequence.

Other important considerations when analyzing readers' needs and expectations are tone and style. What are their attitudes and biases?

Some readers react well to an informal, friendly style of writing, but other readers believe that professional writing should be more formal. Whoever your readers are, remember always to be courteous. Whether you write in a technical or simplified style, all readers appreciate (and deserve!) consideration, tact, and respect.

Word choices also contribute to an effective writing style. Many readers might find the following sentence troubling:

> An efficient accountant dictates letters to his secretary; she then types the letters for his signature.

Some readers might argue that the choice of pronouns (accountant/he, secretary/she) implies a gender bias. Use plural nouns and pronouns to avoid gender bias:

> Efficient accountants dictate letters to their secretaries, who then type the letters for their supervisors' signatures.

Sometimes your readers will have additional expectations about your documents. In a classroom situation, the instructor will usually give directions about different aspects of your papers, such as style, format, and due date. The instructor expects you to follow these directions. How well you do so usually affects your grade.

Readers' expectations are also important when you write on the job. Managers in some firms expect in-house memos and reports to follow certain conventions of format, organization, and style. If you work for such a firm, your memos and reports will seem more professional—and will be more effective—if they are consistent with these expectations.

In fact, meeting readers' expectations may actually be a matter of company policy. Policies may govern how certain documents are written and what procedures they must go through for approval. Many public accounting firms do not let new staff send letters to clients unless they are first approved by a manager or partner. If you were a new staff member in such a firm, you might draft the client letter, but the manager or partner would review it and possibly ask you to make revisions. Moreover, for certain documents, such as some engagement letters, the actual language used in the letter might be determined by company policy. The partner will expect you to follow these policies with great care.

In the example of the client letter just discussed, there are actually two or three readers: the manager and/or partner who reviews and approves the letter, and the client who receives it. This letter should be written on a technical level that is appropriate for the client, and it should address the client's concerns, but it should also meet the expectations of the manager and partner. Analyzing readers' needs, interests, and expectations is obviously more complex when there are several readers. Think carefully about the different readers and use your best judgment to meet the expectations of them all.

FIGURE 2–2 *Planning a Paper*

Consider these questions as you plan the documents you write:

1. Answer after you read and analyze the assignment or consider the task:
   - What are the accounting issues in this case?
   - What literature will I research to resolve these issues?
   - Who will be the readers of this document?
   - What are the readers' concerns?
   - What are the purposes of this document?
2. Answer after you research and analyze the case:
   - What are the main points (conclusions) I need to make in this document?
   - What material should I include to make these conclusions clear and meaningful to the reader(s)?

Analyzing readers' needs and expectations is an important part of the preparation for writing. Planning, which considers both your audience and your purpose, is the first guideline for effective writing.

1. **Analyze the purpose of the writing and the needs and expectations of the readers.**

Figure 2–2 summarizes questions you can ask yourself to help you plan your writing.

GETTING YOUR IDEAS TOGETHER

Once you have evaluated the purpose of the writing and the needs of the readers, you are ready for the second stage in the writing process: gathering information and organizing the ideas you want to present. This step may be quick and simple. For a short letter, you may not need to do further research; organizing your ideas may involve only a short list of the main topics you wish to include in the letter—perhaps one topic for each paragraph.

For much of the writing you do, gathering information and organizing may be a more complicated process, one involving a great deal of thought and perhaps some research as well. Let's look at some techniques you can use.

Gathering Information

Before you begin to write the document, be sure that you have all the information you need and that this information is accurate. Two useful ways to gather this information are to check the work that has already been done and to find new information.

For many projects, some information may already be available. If you're working on an audit, for example, information may be available from other members of the audit team as well as from the files from the previous years' audits. Explore these sources of information fully: Review the files carefully and, when necessary, talk with the people who have already worked on the project.

Sometimes you may need to do additional research. This task may involve background reading on a technical topic or a careful review of accounting pronouncements, such as FASB statements or the Internal Revenue Code. As you read this material, take notes carefully and be alert for information that will help you when you write.

This research may also require you to interview people who will be affected by the project that you are working on. Suppose that you intend to write a report to propose a new accounting information system for your company. You can gain important insights into topics your report should cover by talking with the people who would be affected by the proposed system. You can learn what they want the system to accomplish or what they need to know about it.

Generating Ideas

Once you have gathered the information you need, you will be ready to begin the next phase of the writing process: deciding exactly what to say.

If you have not already written your statement of purpose, now is the time to do so. Try to break up the purpose into several subtopics. Suppose the purpose of a client letter is to recommend that the client update her computerized accounting system. The statement of purpose for this letter could specify the different accounting jobs for which the expanded system would be useful, and it could also outline its major advantages.

Another useful technique for generating ideas is brainstorming. With this technique, you think about your topic and write down all the ideas that come to you. Write them down in whatever order they come to you; don't worry about organizing the ideas or evaluating them. Later you can consider how these ideas fit into the skeletal outline you developed when you analyzed the purposes of the document.

You may find brainstorming easier to do at the computer using a word processor. As you type in the key words and phrases that occur to you, it's possible that the phrases will start to become sentences and the sentences will flow together to become paragraphs. Most people can type faster than they can write with a pencil or pen. You may find that the faster you record your ideas, the more freely the ideas flow. Thus, a word processor can be a valuable tool for generating ideas.

Some writers also find that computerized outlining programs help them generate ideas at the computer. These programs can help you organize your thoughts into a structure. They put details in the proper places and give you a bird's-eye view of the paper's overall organization.

Arranging Ideas: Organization

Once you've decided what you want to say, it's important to consider how best to arrange these ideas so that the readers will find them easy to follow. In other words, it's time to think about how the document will be organized.

Much of the work you've already done will help you decide on the best pattern of organization. If you've used an outlining program to generate ideas, the outline you've produced may provide the structure you need. Keep in mind, though, that you may need to rearrange the sections of the outline so that they will be presented in the most effective order.

Even if you haven't arranged your ideas in the form of an outline, other work you've done to prepare your paper may help you decide on an effective organization. You may be able to use your statement of purpose as the basis of your organization, or your paper may be structured so that the reader's major concerns will be your principle of organization—that is, each concern might be a major division of your paper. Some documents can be organized according to the accounting issues they address.

When considering all these approaches to organization, and possibly deciding among them, remember this principle: The document's organization should be determined by the needs and interests *of your readers.* Arrange your ideas in the order that they will find most helpful and easiest to follow.

There are a few other points of organization to consider. First, most writing has the same basic structure: an introduction, a concise statement of ideas, development of the main ideas, and a conclusion. This structure is shown in Figure 2–3. Later chapters of this handbook will discuss more fully this basic structure as it is used for particular kinds of writing.

Another point is that ideas should be arranged in a logical order. To describe the process of reconciling bank statements, for instance, you would discuss each step of the procedure in the order in which it is performed.

Finally, you can often organize ideas according to their importance. In business writing, always arrange ideas from the most to the least important. Note that this principle means you start with the ideas that are most important *to the reader.*

Suppose you are writing a report to recommend that your firm purchase a new computer system for maintaining its accounting records. Naturally, you will want to emphasize the advantages of this purchase, de-

FIGURE 2–3 ***Basic Writing Structure***

- *Introduction:* identifies the subject of the document and tells why it was written. Sometimes the introduction also provides background information about the topic or stresses its importance. You may also use the introduction to build rapport with your reader, perhaps by mentioning a common interest or concern or referring to previous communication on the topic.
- *Concise statement of the main ideas:* summarizes explicitly main ideas, conclusions, or recommendations. This part of a document may be part of the introduction or a separate section. It can be as short as a one-sentence statement of purpose or as long as a three-page executive summary.
- *Development of the main ideas:* includes explanations, examples, analyses, steps, reasons, and factual details. This part of an outline or paper is often called the body.
- *Conclusion:* brings the paper to an effective close. The conclusion may restate the main idea in a fresh way, suggest further work, or summarize recommendations, but an effective conclusion avoids unnecessary repetition.

scribing them in the order that is likely to be most convincing to the readers of the report. However, this investment might also have drawbacks, such as the cost to purchase and install the equipment and the problems involved in converting from the old system to the new one. For your report to appear well researched and unbiased, you need to include these disadvantages in your discussion. You might use the following structure:

I. Introduction, including your recommendation
II. Body
   A. Advantages, beginning with those most appealing to the readers
   B. Disadvantages, including, when possible, ways to minimize or overcome any drawbacks
III. Conclusion

One final word about organization: Once you've decided how to arrange your ideas, it's a good idea to actually write an outline, if you haven't already done so. Having an outline before you as you draft your paper will help you keep the paper on track. You'll be sure to include all the information you had planned and avoid getting off the subject.

The guidelines for effective writing can now be expanded:

1. **Analyze the purpose of the writing and the needs and expectations of the readers.**
2. **Organize your ideas so that readers will find them easy to follow.**

WRITING THE DRAFT

The next major step in the writing process is writing the draft. The purpose of this step is to put your ideas in writing. Spelling, punctuation, and style are not important in the draft. What is important is to write the ideas so that you can later polish and correct what you have written.

If you did your brainstorming at the computer, you may already have parts of your draft if the list of ideas you began with evolved into sentences or paragraphs as you typed.

If you have not already begun to work at a word processor, the draft stage of the writing process is an excellent place to start. As we've pointed out, most people find that they can type at a keyboard faster than they can write with a pencil or pen. Composing the draft at a word processor may thus be faster than composing by hand. It may also be easier because your ideas will flow more quickly. Your stream of thought won't be impeded by the mechanics of writing.

The outline you have prepared will guide you as you write. However, you may decide to change the outline as you go, omitting some parts that no longer seem to fit or adding other ideas that now seem necessary. Changing the outline is fine, because when you revise the draft later you can make sure your thoughts are still well organized.

Although you will use your outline as a guide to the ideas you want to include in your draft, you may find it easier to write the various parts of the document in a different order from the one in the outline. Some people find introductions hard to write, so they leave them until last. You may also choose to write the easiest sections of your draft first, or you may start writing some parts of the draft while you are still getting the material together for other parts. If you're composing at a computer, rearranging the parts of your paper is particularly easy because word processing programs enable you to move blocks of text.

One final word of advice on the draft stage: Don't allow yourself to get stuck while you search for the perfect word, phrase, or sentence. Leave a blank space, or write something that is more or less what you mean. You'll probably find the right words later.

REVISING THE DRAFT

The next stage in the writing process is the revision of the draft. In this step, you check your grammar, polish your style, and make a final check to see that the ideas are effectively and completely presented. As you revise, read the document from the reader's point of view.

You'll need to revise most of your writing more than once—perhaps even three or four times. The key to revising is to let the writing get cold between revisions; a time lapse between readings enables you to read the draft more objectively and see what you have actually said, instead of what you meant to say. Ideally, revisions should be at least a day apart.

Another technique is to have a colleague review the draft for both the content and the effectiveness of the writing. Choose a reviewer who is a good writer and evaluate the reviewer's suggestions with an open mind.

If you've put your draft on a word processor, check the text with an editing program or grammar checker. These programs identify certain errors in style, such as sentences that are too long and paragraphs that use the same word too often. Programs are also available that identify some mistakes in punctuation and grammar as well as most misspelled words.

A word of caution is in order about these style analyzers and grammar checkers—they're not infallible. They can't catch all the weaknesses in your text, and sometimes they flag problems that aren't really there. If you use these programs to analyze your writing, you still have to use your own judgment about what changes to make. The poem shown in Figure 2–4 illustrates these points!

FIGURE 2–4 ***Spelling Checkers Don't Catch Everything!***

A Tribute to Spelling Checkers

I have a spelling checker, it came with my PC
It plane lee marks four my revue miss steaks aye can knot sea.
Eye ran this poem threw it. Your sure reel glad two no
Its vary polished in it's weigh. My checker tolled me sew.
A checker is a bless sing. It freeze yew lodes of thyme.
It helps me right awl stiles two reed, and aides me when aye rime.
Each frays come posed up on my screen eye trussed too bee a joule.
The checker pours o'er every word, to cheque sum spelling rule.
Be fore a veiling checkers, hour spelling mite decline.
And if were lacks or have a laps, we wood be maid to wine.
Butt now bee cause my spelling is checked with such grate flare
Their are know faults with in my cite. Of non eye am a wear.
Now spelling does not phase me. It does not bring a tier.
My pay purrs awl due glad den with wrapped words fare as hear.
To rite with care is quite a feet of witch won should be proud.
And wee mussed dew the best wee can sew flaws are knot aloud.
Sow eye can sea why aye dew prays such soft ware four pea seas
And why I brake in two averse by righting want too pleas.

(Written by Jerrold H. Zar, Dean of the Graduate School, Northern Illinois University. Reprinted with permission from the *Journal of Irreproducible Results*.)

Another revision technique that works with a word-processed text is to print the document and edit the hard copy by hand. Then make the revisions on your disk the next time you work at the computer. Some writers find that they revise more effectively if they work with a hard copy rather than text on a screen.

In sum, if you've put the draft on a word processor, the revision will be much easier and quicker than if you have to revise by hand and then retype the entire manuscript. With a few commands to the computer, you can add text, delete it, or rearrange it. You can insert sentences, change wording, and move paragraphs around. You can make minor changes to your draft or major ones, all the time preserving the remainder of your draft without retyping.

The next four chapters of the handbook discuss what to look for when putting your writing in final form.

We now have three guidelines for effective writing:

1. **Analyze the purpose of the writing and the needs and expectations of the readers.**
2. **Organize your ideas so that readers will find them easy to follow.**
3. **Write the draft and then revise it to make the writing polished and correct.**

THE FINAL DRAFT

After you have polished the style and organization of the paper, you will be ready to put it in its final form. Consider questions of document design, such as the use of headings, white space, and other elements of the paper's appearance.

Proofreading is also an important step. Here are some suggestions for effective proofreading:

1. Proofreading is usually easier if you leave time between typing and looking for errors. You will see the paper more clearly if you have been away from it for a while.
2. If you've drafted your paper on a word processor, use a spell-check program to eliminate spelling and typographical errors. Remember that a computer may not distinguish between homonyms such as *their* and *there* or *affect* and *effect.*
3. If you don't have access to a word processor, use a dictionary to look up any word that could possibly be misspelled. If you are a poor speller, have someone else read the paper for spelling errors.
4. If you know that you tend to make a certain type of error, read through your paper at least once to check for that error. For example, if you have problems with subject-verb agreement, check every sentence in your paper to be sure the verbs are correct.

5. Read your paper backwards, sentence by sentence, as a final proofreading step. This technique will isolate each sentence and should make it easier to spot errors you may have overlooked in previous readings.

DEALING WITH WRITER'S BLOCK

Writer's block is a problem all of us face at some time or another. We stare at blank paper or at a blank screen with no idea of how to get started. The ideas and the words just don't come.

Many of the techniques already discussed in this chapter will help you overcome writer's block. Thinking of writing as a process, rather than a completed product that appears suddenly in its final form, should help make the job less formidable. Any difficult task seems easier if you break it down into manageable steps.

The discussions of the steps in the writing process, especially the section on writing the draft, have included suggestions that will help you overcome writer's block. Here is a summary of these techniques:

1. Plan before you write so that you know what you need to say.
2. Write with an outline in view, but write the paper in any order you wish. You can rearrange it later.
3. Don't strive for perfection in the draft stage. Leave problems of grammar, spelling, style, and so forth to the revision stage.
4. Begin with the easiest sections to write.
5. Don't get stuck on difficult places. Skip over them and go on to something else. You may find that when you come back to the rough spots later they will not be as hard to write as you had thought at first.

WRITING UNDER PRESSURE

Throughout this chapter, we've seen how writing is easier if you break the project down into steps. It's easy to manage these steps when you have plenty of time to plan, research, draft, revise, and polish.

But what about situations where you don't have the luxury of time? What about writing essay questions on an exam, or on-the-job writing tasks where you have only a little while to produce a letter or memo?

The truth is that any writing project, no matter how hurriedly it must be done, will go more smoothly if you stick with the three basic steps of the writing process: plan, draft, and revise. Even if you have only a few minutes to work on a document, allow yourself some of that time to think about who you're writing to, what you need to say, and the best way to organize that material. Then draft the paper.

Allow yourself some time to revise as well. If you have access to a word processor, revision will be much quicker and easier to do. Using a spell-check program, which takes only a few minutes for a short memo or letter, can help eliminate embarrassing spelling and typographical errors.

WRITING AT THE COMPUTER

This chapter has discussed how a word processor can help you write. We've mentioned outlining and spell-check programs, and you may want to investigate other types of computerized writing aids. Some writers find these supplementary programs helpful; others find that a good word processor with a spell-check program is the only computer help they need.

But what if you don't have ready access to a computer? Of course, people wrote well for centuries before computers were ever invented. If you must compose with pencil and paper, you can still write effectively, especially if you follow the steps of the writing process we've been discussing, but writing by hand will take you longer, especially when you revise and polish your draft.

With the widespread availability of computers, both on college campuses and in the workplace, most people can use word processors for their writing.

It is beyond the scope of this book to discuss particular word processing programs or other computerized aids to writing. Whether you're still at school or already on the job, find out what computer programs are available and learn the features of the programs that will help you to write well. Time spent learning these programs will pay off as you begin to write more effectively and quickly.

EXERCISES

Exercise 2–1

Among your business correspondents are the following people:

1. The controller of a large corporation (an accountant).
2. Another CPA.
3. A financial analyst.
4. A manager in a large corporation (educated and experienced in business, but not an accountant).
5. The owner/president of a recently opened small business (little business education or experience).
6. A bookkeeper under your supervision.
7. An IRS agent.

For each correspondent, which of the following terms or procedures would you *probably* need to explain?

a. GAAP
b. historical cost
c. the latest IRS regulations governing depreciation
d. equity
e. the matching concept
f. capital leases
g. fair market value
h. present value
i. current asset
j. asset
k. mark to market
l. APB 17

Exercise 2–2

You want the local CPA firm for which you work to pay your expenses to attend a two-day seminar on "Effective Writing." You expect your expenses will total $1,000, and with travel time you will be absent from your job for three days if you attend. Your supervisor, Joan Smith, is unfamiliar with the seminar; you need to convince her that your attendance would benefit your firm by making you a more effective employee.

Study chapter 9 for suggestions on memo organization and format and then write a memo to Ms. Smith making your request and persuading her to give her approval.[1]

Exercise 2–3

Write a memo to your classmates to tell them what computer equipment and software packages are available on your campus to help them with their writing. Consider what information your classmates need and what questions they may ask. For example, if you describe the computer lab on campus, readers will want to know the hours of the lab, the number and types of computers and software packages available, and whether lab assistants are available for help. If you're describing a word processing or editing package, readers may want to know how these programs can make their writing easier and more effective.

Chapter 9 provides advice on how to write a memo.

Exercise 2–4

Analyze the letter in Figure 2–5. How would you react if you received this letter?

1. Think about and then discuss with your classmates these questions:
   - What are the weaknesses of the letter? (Hint: The letter has many typos and spelling errors. Can you find them all? In addition to these problems, the letter has a number of less obvious weaknesses. What are they?)
   - What are the strengths of this letter? (It does have some strengths!)

FIGURE 2–5 ***Letter for Exercise 2–4: What Is Wrong with This Letter?***

Wright and Wrongh, CPAs
123 Anystreet
Anytown, US 12345

Corner Dress Shop
123 Anyother Street
Anytown, US 12345

Gentlemen

We are in receipt of your correspondence and beg to thank you.

After extensive research we have found what we hope will be a satisfactory reponse to your questions, we hope you will find our work satisfactory.

There were two possibilities for the resolution of this issue that we considered after a careful analysis of the applicable IRC sections to your situation. If the first possibility proved relevant, then you would be subject to a fine of $5500, plus penalties and interest. If athe other possibility was the best solution, then you would receive a $4400 credit because of a loss carryforard to your current year returns.

As you no doubt know, IRC Sec.341(6)a [paras. 5-9] stipulate the regulations we must follow. Thus, to be in compliance with the rules and regs. you must follow the provisions of the pertinent sections.

As your CPAs, we are most concerned that we be in compliance with all standards of professional ethics, and we always keep this in mind when we advise you on your tax and accounting questions.

After extensive research, we advise you to file an amended return immediately because the first possibility enumerated in the above paragraph proves to be the correct solution to your problem.

Thanking you in advance, we remain

Yours with highest regards,

M. Ostley Wrongh

M. Ostley Wrongh
Wright and Wrongh, CPAs

2. Revise the letter so that it is more effective. Invent any details you need for your revision.

   Chapter 8 provides information on letter writing.

NOTES

1. Adapted from Gadis J. Dillon, "Writing Assignment for Intermediate Accounting" (unpublished class assignment, University of Georgia, 1982).

3

The Flow of Thought: Organizing for Coherence

Coherence is one of the six tips for effective business writing discussed in chapter 1 (see Figure 1–1). Coherent writing is organized so that important ideas stand out. The flow of thought is logical and easy to follow.

Chapter 2 introduced several techniques to help you make your writing more coherent: analyzing your purpose and the reader's needs, then planning and outlining before you begin to write. This chapter discusses additional ways to ensure that your writing is coherent. It explores how to write with unity, use summary sentences and transitions, and structure effective paragraphs and essays.

WRITING WITH UNITY

The key to unified writing is to establish the main idea of each document. An office memo may contain only one paragraph, but that paragraph has a central idea. A report may run to many pages, but it still has a central idea or purpose, and probably secondary purposes as well. It's important to decide on your main ideas before you begin writing, preferably before beginning your outline. Deciding on the main idea of a document is similar to analyzing its purpose, as discussed in chapter 2.

You should be able to summarize a main idea in one sentence. In a paragraph, this sentence is called the topic sentence. In longer documents involving more than two or three paragraphs, this sentence may be called the thesis statement or a statement of purpose.

The main idea is the key to the entire document. Every other sentence should be related to it, either directly or indirectly. The central idea is like the hub of a wheel or the trunk of a tree. All other ideas branch off from the central idea—they explain it, analyze it, illustrate it, or prove it. Any sentences or details that are unrelated to the main idea, either directly or indirectly, are irrelevant and should be omitted. In longer documents, entire paragraphs may be irrelevant to the main purpose. These irrelevant paragraphs are called digressions.

When you remove digressions and irrelevant sentences, your writing becomes unified: every sentence is related to the main idea.

The paragraph below is not unified. Which sentences are irrelevant to the topic sentence?

> (1) Incorporation offers many advantages for a business and its owners. (2) For example, the owners are not responsible for the business's debts. (3) Investors hope to make money when they buy stock in a corporation. (4) Incorporation also enables a business to obtain professional management skills. (5) Corporations are subject to more government regulation than are other forms of organization.

Sentence 1, the topic sentence, identifies the main idea of the paragraph: the advantages of incorporation. Sentences 3 and 5 are off the subject.

Writing with unity is an important way to make your writing coherent.

USING SUMMARY SENTENCES

In coherent writing, the main ideas stand out. You can emphasize your main ideas by placing them in the document where they will get the reader's attention.

First, as chapter 2 suggested, it's usually a good idea to summarize your main ideas at the beginning of the document. A long document, especially a report, should have a separate summary section at or near the beginning of the paper. This formal summary may be called an abstract, an executive summary, or simply a summary.

When writing these summary sections, be specific and remember the reader's interests and needs. Let's say you are writing a memo to the bookkeepers at Winston Sales Company to explain the advantages of using a particular accounting software package. Summarize those advantages specifically and relate them to Winston Sales. One of these advantages might be stated this way: "This software is particularly easy to use because of the additional on-line help it provides that competing software doesn't provide."

The summary at the beginning of a document may be several sentences or even pages long, depending on the length of the document and the complexity of the main ideas or recommendations. Here is an example:

> The following procedures will ensure a smooth transition to the new computerized system:
>
> - Management should designate a representative from each department to attend the three-week workshop at company headquarters.
> - Each department should plan a training session for its employees to emphasize the department's use of the system.
> - A two-month transition period should be allowed for converting from the old system.
> - Troubleshooters should be available to all departments to solve any problems that occur.

Summary sentences are important in other places besides at the beginning of a document. They are also important at the beginning of each section of the paper in the conclusion.

Any paper that is longer than three or four paragraphs probably has more than one main idea or recommendation; each of these ideas is suggested in the introduction or in a separate summary section. Often, the logical way to organize the remainder of the document is to use a separate section of the paper to discuss each idea further. Each section begins with a summary statement to identify the main idea, or the topic, of that section. The reader will then have a clear idea of what that section is about. It's a good idea to use somewhat different wording from that used in the beginning of the paper.

The principle we've been discussing sounds simple: Begin with your conclusion and then give your support. However, many writers have trouble putting this advice into practice. The difficulty may occur because this order of ideas is the reverse of the process writers go through to reach their conclusions. The typical research process is to gather information first and then to arrive at the conclusions. A writer may try to take the reader through the same investigative steps as those he or she used to solve the problem or answer the question.

Think about your readers' needs. They're mainly interested in the findings of your research, not in the process you went through to get there. They may very well want to read about the facts you considered as well as your analytical reasoning; in fact, some readers will carefully evaluate the soundness of your data and methodology. However, their first concern is with the conclusions themselves.

When a paper is organized in the way recommended here, we say that it has a deductive structure: It begins with the conclusion and then gives the proofs. The opposite of deductive organization is an inductive structure, which gives the data and then presents the conclusions. Research is usually done inductively, but most readers prefer that the results be presented in a deductive organization.

Conclusions may be presented again in a concluding section, especially if the document is very long. Once again, you may need to remind the reader of your main ideas, but be careful not to sound repetitive. The length and complexity of the document determine how much detail to include in your conclusion.

TRANSITIONS

Transitions, which are another element of coherent writing, link ideas together. They can be used between sentences, paragraphs, and major divisions of the document. Their purpose is to show the relationship between two ideas: how the second idea flows logically from the first, and how both are related to the main idea of the entire document.

As an example of how transitions work, consider this paragraph. The topic sentence (main idea) is the first sentence; the transitional expressions are in italics:

> (1) Financial statements are important to a variety of users. (2) *First*, investors and potential investors use the statements to determine whether a company is a good investment risk. (3) These users look at such factors as net income, the debt-to-equity ratio, and retained earnings. (4) *Second*, creditors use financial statements to determine whether a firm is a good credit risk. (5) Creditors want to know whether a firm has a large enough cash flow to pay its debts. (6) *Third*, government agencies analyze financial statements for a variety of purposes. (7) *For example*, the Internal Revenue Service wants to know whether the company has paid the required amount of taxes on its income. (8) These examples of financial statement users show how diverse their interests can be.

The sentences beginning *first* (2), *second* (4), and *third* (6) give three examples of the paragraph's main idea: the variety of financial statement users. These three sentences relate to one another in a logical, sequential way, which the transitions make clear. These sentences also relate directly to the topic sentence; they illustrate it with specific examples. Sentence 7, which begins with *for example*, relates only indirectly to the main idea of the paragraph, but it relates directly to sentence 6. Sentence 7 identifies one reason why government agencies need access to financial statements.

Transitions can express a number of relationships between ideas. In the sample paragraph, the transitions indicate an enumerated list (2, 4, and 6) and a specific illustration of a general statement (7). Transitions can also imply other relationships between ideas—conclusions, additional information, or contrasts, for example.

To see the importance of transitions within a paragraph, look at the following example, which lacks transitions:

> Incorporation offers several advantages to businesses and their owners. Ownership is easy to transfer. The business is able to maintain a continuous existence even when the original owners are no longer involved. The stockholders of a corporation are not held responsible for the business's debts. If the Dallas Corporation defaults on a $1,000,000 loan, its investors will not be held responsible for paying that liability. Incorporation enables a business to obtain professional managers with centralized authority and responsibility. The business can be run more efficiently. Incorporation gives a business certain legal rights. It can enter into contracts, own property, and borrow money.

Now see how much easier it is to read the paragraph when it has appropriate transitions:

> Incorporation offers several advantages to businesses and their owners. *For one thing*, ownership is easy to transfer, and the business is able to maintain a continuous existence even when the original owners are no longer involved. *In addition*, the stockholders of a corporation are not held responsible for the business's bad debts. If the Dallas Corporation defaults on a $1,000,000 loan, *for example*, its investors will not be held responsible for paying that liability. Incorporation *also* enables a business to obtain professional managers with centralized authority and responsibility; *therefore*, the business can be run more efficiently. *Finally*, incorporation gives a business certain legal rights. *For example*, it can enter into contracts, own property, and borrow money.

Transitional Words and Phrases

Here is a list of commonly used transitional expressions, their meanings, and example sentences showing how some of them work.

- **Adding a point or piece of information:** *and, also, in addition, moreover, furthermore, first/second/third, finally.*

  Accounting is a demanding profession. It can also be financially rewarding.

- **Making an exception or contrasting point:** *but, however, nevertheless, on the other hand, yet, still, on the contrary, in spite of . . ., nonetheless.*

  The use of historical cost accounting has many drawbacks. Nevertheless, it is still the basis of most accounting procedures.

- **Giving specific examples or illustrations:** *for example, for instance, as an illustration, in particular, to illustrate.*

  Financial statements serve a variety of users. For example, investors use them to evaluate potential investments. Other users include . . .

- **Clarifying a point:** *that is, in other words, in effect, put simply, stated briefly.*

  The basic accounting equation is *assets equal liabilities plus owners' equity*. That is, A = L + OE.

- **Conceding a point to the opposite side:** *granted that, it may be true that, even though, although.*

  Although generally accepted accounting principles are not perfect, their use may offer considerable assurance that financial statements are presented fairly.

- **Indicating place, time, or importance:**
  - Place: *above, beside, beyond, to the right, below, around.*
  - Time: *formerly, hitherto, earlier, in the past, before, at present, now, today, these days, tomorrow, in the future, next, later on, later.*
  - Importance: *foremost, most importantly, especially, of less importance, of least importance.*

  In earlier centuries there was no need for elaborate accounting systems. However, the size and complexities of today's businesses make modern accounting a complicated process indeed.

- **Indicating the stages in an argument or process, or the items in a series:** *initially, at the outset, to begin with, first, first of all, up to now, so far, second, thus far, next, after, finally, last.*

  The accounting process works in stages. First, transactions must be analyzed.

- **Giving a result:** *as a result, consequently, accordingly, as a consequence, therefore, thus, hence, then, for that reason.*

  Generally accepted accounting principles allow flexibility in their application. Therefore, accountants are able to meet the changing needs of the business world.

- **Summing up or restating the central point:** *in sum, to sum up, to summarize, in summary, to conclude, in brief, in short, as one can see, in conclusion.*

  In conclusion, transitions often make writing much easier to read.

Repetition of Key Words and Phrases

Another way to add coherence to your writing is to repeat key words and phrases. This repetition may be particularly useful in connecting paragraphs and major divisions of the document. These repetitions are typically located at the beginning of a new paragraph or section.

The following outline of a student's essay shows the structure of a discussion on alternatives to the historical cost basis of accounting. Notice how the combination of transitional expressions and repeated key phrases holds the report together. These techniques also tie the parts of the report to the main idea of the paper, which is summarized in the thesis statement. Notice also how summary sentences appear throughout the outline.

The Monetary Unit Assumption

I. Introductory paragraph
   A. Introductory sentences

One of the basic assumptions made by accountants is that money is an effective common denominator by which business enterprises can be measured and analyzed. Implicit in this assumption is the acceptance of the stable and unchanging nature of the monetary unit. However, the validity of this assumption has been questioned not only by academicians and theorists, but by practitioners as well.

- B. Thesis statement (main idea of entire paper)
  Several solutions have been proposed by accountants to correct for the changing value of the monetary unit.

II. Body

- A. Nature of the problem
  The unadjusted monetary unit system has been criticized because it distorts financial statements during periods of inflation.
- B. First solution to the problem
  1. One solution to overstating profits solely because of inflation is to adjust figures for changes in the general purchasing power of the monetary unit. (This paragraph describes the solution and its advantages.)
  2. However, the general purchasing power approach has been criticized for several reasons. (The paragraph describes the disadvantages of this approach.)
- C. Second solution to the problem
  1. Instead of the general purchasing power procedure, some favor adjusting for changes in replacement cost. (Paragraph describes this solution.)
  2. One of the major advantages of the replacement cost approach . . . (Paragraph discusses several advantages.)
  3. One authority has summarized the criticisms of replacement cost accounting: "Most of the criticisms . . . ." (Paragraph discusses the disadvantages of this approach.)

III. Concluding paragraph
Adjusting for changes in the general purchasing power and adjusting for changes in replacement cost represent attempts to correct the problems of the stable monetary unit assumption in times of inflation.

Pronouns Used to Achieve Coherence

Another tool you can use to achieve coherent writing is the pronoun. A pronoun stands for a noun or a noun phrase that has previously been identified. The noun that the pronoun refers to is called its *antecedent*. Consider this sentence:

> Firms usually issue their financial statements at least once a year.

In this sentence, the pronoun *their* refers to the noun *firms*. Put another way, *firms* is the antecedent of *their*.

Because pronouns refer to nouns that the writer has already used, pronouns help connect the thoughts of a paragraph. Look at how the pronouns work in this paragraph:

> The audit staff reviewed the financial statements of Toppo Industries to determine whether the statements had been prepared in accordance with generally accepted accounting principles. *We* found two problems that may require *us* to issue a qualified opinion. First, Toppo has not been consistent in *its* treatment of contingencies. Second, *we* identified several transactions that may violate the concept of substance over form. *We* suggest a meeting with Toppo's management to discuss these issues.

Pronouns require a word of warning, however. Unless a writer is careful, the reader may not be sure what noun the pronoun refers to. Look at the problem in this sentence:

> The managers told the accountants that they did not understand company policy.

Who didn't understand company policy—the managers or the accountants? This sentence illustrates the problem of ambiguous pronoun reference. Chapter 5 discusses this problem further.

Problems with Transitions

A few problems can occur with transitions other than the failure to use them when they are needed. One problem occurs when a writer uses transitional expressions too often. These expressions are necessary to make the relationship of ideas clear when there might be some confusion. Often this logical relationship is clear without the use of transitional expressions. Consider this paragraph:

> Accountants never finish their education. They work hard for their college degrees, but after college they must continue studying to stay current on the latest developments in the profession. They must be thoroughly familiar with changing government regulations and new pronouncements by professional organizations such as the FASB. To improve their professional competence, they participate in a variety of continuing education programs sponsored by such organizations as the AICPA and state accounting societies. Indeed, well-qualified accountants are lifetime students, always seeking better ways to serve their clients and the public.

Notice how easy this paragraph is to follow, even though it doesn't use a single transitional expression.

Another problem with transitions occurs when the writer uses the wrong expression, suggesting an illogical connection of ideas. Consider these examples:

FAULTY TRANSITION: GAAP are not established by federal law. For instance, organizations such as the FASB issue

	these standards, and the FASB is not part of the federal government.
REVISED:	GAAP are not established by federal law. Rather, organizations that are not part of the federal government, such as the FASB, issue these standards.
FAULTY TRANSITION:	If accountants do not follow GAAP, they may lose their CPA licenses. Therefore, they must follow GAAP to conform to their code of professional ethics.
REVISED:	If accountants do not follow GAAP, they may lose their CPA licenses. They must also follow GAAP to conform to their code of professional ethics.

Transitions, when used correctly, are a valuable tool for clarifying the relationship between ideas. If you use transitions carefully along with summary sentences and a logical organization, your writing will be easy to follow.

The next sections of this chapter show how to use these techniques to write coherent paragraphs, discussion questions, essays, and other longer forms of writing.

PARAGRAPHS

This section of the chapter is devoted to techniques of paragraphing: how to plan length, structure, and development so that your paragraphs are coherent.

Length

You may not be sure how long paragraphs should be. Are one-sentence paragraphs acceptable? What about paragraphs that run on for nearly an entire typed page?

One rule is that a paragraph should be limited to the development of one idea. Thus, the length of most paragraphs is somewhere between one sentence and an entire page. However, an occasional short paragraph, even of only one sentence, may be effective to emphasize an idea or to provide a transition between two major divisions of the writing.

Be wary of long paragraphs, which look intimidating and are often hard to follow. You may need to divide a long paragraph into two or more shorter ones. Appropriate transitions can tie the new paragraphs together and maintain a smooth flow of thought.

A good rule is to limit most of your paragraphs to four or five sentences.

Structure

Another feature of well-written paragraphs is an appropriate structure. We have already suggested that a strong topic sentence can contribute to a unified, coherent paragraph. A topic sentence states the main idea of the paragraph. It is usually the first sentence in the paragraph, and sometimes it contains a transition tying the new paragraph to the previous one. All other sentences in the paragraph should develop the idea expressed in the topic sentence.

Two patterns of paragraph organization are useful for accountants' writing tasks: the simple deductive paragraph and the complex deductive paragraph. The simple deductive arrangement states the main idea in the first sentence (topic sentence); all other sentences *directly* develop that idea by adding details. A concluding sentence is sometimes helpful. Look again at this paragraph, which illustrates a simple deductive organization:

> (1) Accountants never finish their educations. (2) They work hard for their college degrees, but after college they must continue studying to stay current on the latest developments in the profession. (3) They must be thoroughly familiar with changing government regulations and new pronouncements by professional organizations such as the FASB. (4) To improve their professional competence, they participate in a variety of continuing education programs sponsored by such organizations as the AICPA and state accounting societies. (5) Indeed, well-qualified accountants are lifetime students, always seeking better ways to serve their clients and the public.

In this paragraph, sentence 1 is the topic sentence, sentences 2 through 4 develop the main idea, and sentence 5 is the conclusion. A simple deductive paragraph has a simple structural diagram such as this one:

(1) Topic sentence—main idea
    (2) Supporting sentence
    (3) Supporting sentence
    (4) Supporting sentence
(5) Concluding sentence (optional)

A complex deductive paragraph has a more elaborate structure. This paragraph is complex deductive:

> (1) Financial statements are important to a variety of users. (2) First, investors and potential investors use the statements to determine whether a company is a good investment risk. (3) These users look at such factors as net income, the debt-to-equity ratio, and retained earnings. (4) Second, creditors use financial statements to determine whether a firm is a good credit risk. (5) Creditors want to know whether a firm has a large enough cash flow to pay its debts. (6) Third, government agencies analyze financial statements for a variety of purposes. (7) For example, the Internal Revenue Service wants to know whether the company has paid the required amount

of taxes on its income. (8) These examples of financial statement users show how diverse their interests can be.

In this paragraph, sentence 1 (the topic sentence) states the main idea. Sentence 2 directly supports the main idea by giving an example of it, but sentence 3 explains sentence 2. Thus, sentence 3 directly supports sentence 2, but only indirectly supports sentence 1. Complex deductive paragraphs have a structural diagram similar to this one:

(1) Topic sentence—main idea
  (2) Direct support
    (3) Indirect support
  (4) Direct support
    (5) Indirect support
  (6) Direct support
    (7) Indirect support
(8) Conclusion (optional)

Complex deductive paragraphs can have numerous variations. The number of direct supporting sentences can vary, as can the number of indirect supports. Sometime direct supports may not require any indirect supports.

Consider another example of a complex deductive paragraph:

(1) Two of the most popular inventory flow assumptions used by businesses today are FIFO (first-in, first-out) and LIFO (last-in, first-out). (2) FIFO assumes that the first goods purchased for inventory are the first goods sold. (3) Therefore, ending inventory under FIFO consists of the most recent purchases. (4) Because older, usually lower costs are matched with sales revenues, FIFO results in a higher net income and thus higher income tax liabilities. (5) The LIFO flow assumption, on the other hand, assumes that the most recent purchases are the first goods sold. (6) Cost of goods sold, however, is based on more recent, higher prices. (7) Thus, LIFO usually results in lower net income and lower income tax liabilities. (8) This advantage makes LIFO very popular with many businesses.

This paragraph can be outlined to reveal the following structure:

I. Topic sentence (1): Two popular inventory flow assumptions
  A. FIFO (2–4)
    1. Description (2)
    2. Effect on inventory (3)
    3. Effect on net income and taxes (4)
  B. LIFO (5–8)
    1. Description (5)
    2. Effect on inventory (6)
    3. Effect on net income and taxes (7)
    4. Popularity (8)

The descriptions of FIFO and LIFO in this paragraph are very condensed, probably too condensed for most purposes. Moreover, the paragraph is really too long. It would probably be better to divide it between sentences 4 and 5. The result would be two shorter but closely related paragraphs. Both would have simple deductive structures. However, the first paragraph would be a modified version of a simple deductive structure because the main idea of this paragraph would be the second sentence.

The important idea about both simple and complex deductive paragraphs is their unity: All sentences, either directly or indirectly, develop the main idea of the paragraph as expressed in the topic sentence.

Some writers may wonder about a third type of paragraph organization: paragraphs with an inductive structure. Inductive paragraphs put the main idea last. Supporting sentences lead up to the topic sentence, which is the last sentence in the paragraph.

For most business writing, inductive paragraphs are not as effective as simple or complex deductive paragraphs. Business readers like to identify main ideas from the start. They don't like to be kept in suspense, wondering "What's all this leading up to? What's the point?" Thus, it's a good idea to stick with deductive organization for most, if not all, of your paragraphs.

Paragraph Development

An effective paragraph is not only well organized; it is also well developed. That is, the idea expressed in the topic sentence is adequately explained and illustrated so that the reader has a clear understanding of what the writer wishes to say.

Several techniques are useful for paragraph development: descriptive and factual details, illustrations or examples, definitions, and appeals to authority.

Descriptive and factual details give a more thorough, concrete explanation of the idea expressed in a general way in the topic sentence. Factual details give measurable, observable, or historical information that can be objectively verified. Descriptive details are similar to factual details. They give specific characteristics of the subject being discussed.

When you use details with which your readers are familiar, they can better understand your observations and conclusions. In the following paragraph, the main idea is stated in the first sentence. The paragraph is then developed with factual details:

> Our net income for next year should increase because we've signed a contract with an important new customer. Flip's Frog Ponds, Inc., which last year had over $4 billion in revenue, has ordered a million lily pads from our horticultural division. This new business should increase our revenues by at least 15 percent.

Another useful technique of paragraph development is illustrations or examples—typical cases or specific instances of the idea being discussed. Illustrations can take a variety of forms. A paragraph may combine several brief examples, or it may use one long, extended illustration. The examples may be factually true, or they may be hypothetical, invented for the purpose of illustration.

Definitions are useful to explain concepts or terms that might be unfamiliar to the reader. A definition can be formal, such as the meaning given in a dictionary or an accounting standard, or it can be a more informal explanation of a term. Often a definition is more effective when combined with an illustration.

Here is a paragraph developed by definition and illustration:

> *Assets* can be defined as "economic resources—things of value—owned by a business."[1] For example, cash is an asset; so are the land, buildings, and equipment owned by a business. Sometimes assets are resources legally owned by a business, though not tangible. An example of this kind of asset is an account receivable.

Finally, some paragraphs are developed by appeals to authority—facts, illustrations, or ideas obtained from a reputable source such as a book, article, interview, or official pronouncement. Appeals to authority may be paraphrases—someone else's idea expressed in your own words—or direct quotations from the source being used. The paragraph above uses a direct quotation from an accounting textbook to provide an authoritative definition of *assets*. Chapter 7 gives more information on the correct use of quotations and paraphrases.

By using a variety of techniques, you can develop fully the ideas expressed in the topic sentences of your paragraphs. Factual and descriptive detail, illustration, definition, and authority all give the reader a clear understanding of what you wish to explain.

However you decide to develop your paragraphs, remember the importance of your reader's interests and needs. It's usually better to select supporting details and examples with which the reader is already familiar.

DISCUSSION QUESTIONS AND ESSAYS

A section about discussion questions and essays might seem too academic for a writing handbook for accountants, but many accounting students take exams with discussion questions, and essay questions may be an important part of professional certifications exams. In addition, many of the principles of organizing and developing an essay are applicable to memos, reports, and other types of writing used by accountants in practice.

Discussion Questions

The key to answering a short discussion question (one to three paragraphs) is to write well-organized paragraphs with strong topic sentences. Usually the question itself will suggest the topic sentence. Consider this question:

> Discuss who the users of financial statements are.

The answer to this question might begin with the following sentence:

> The users of an organization's financial statements are mainly external to the organization.

The first paragraph of the answer would discuss external users, such as investors, creditors, and government agencies. A second, shorter paragraph might then discuss internal users of financial statements, such as management and employees. The second topic sentence might be as follows:

> People in an organization are also interested in its financial statements.

Short paragraphs with strong topic sentences will help the exam grader identify your main ideas and thus will give you credit for what you know.

Essays

Before you read this section, review the discussion of paragraph development on pages 41–42. Pay particular attention to the complex deductive pattern of organization.

Complex deductive paragraphs have a main idea (topic sentence) supported by major and minor supports.

Essays—discussions of four or more paragraphs—are organized the same way, except that the main idea (thesis statement) has as its major supports paragraphs rather than sentences. In addition, the thesis statement may come at the end of the first paragraph, in which case it may be preceded by sentences that give background on the topic or otherwise interest the reader in what is being discussed. Here is the outline of a five-paragraph essay:

I. Introduction—first paragraph
   A. Attention-getting sentences (optional)
   B. Thesis statement—main idea of the essay, usually expressed in one sentence

II. Body of the essay—develops the thesis through analysis, explanation, examples, proofs, or steps
    A. Major support—second paragraph
        1.
        2. } Minor supports—sentences that develop the paragraph in a simple or complex deductive organization
        3.
    B. Major support—third paragraph
        1.
        2. } Minor supports
        3.
    C. Major support—fourth paragraph
        1.
        2. } Minor supports
        3.
III. Conclusion—fifth paragraph
    A. Repeats the essay's main idea (a variation of the thesis statement) or otherwise provides closure
    B. Forceful ending (optional)

Some of the parts of this outline need more discussion.

Attention-Getting Sentences Some essays begin with attention-getting sentences, which are intended to get the reader interested in the subject. Several techniques can be used:

- Give background information about the topic. Why is the topic of current interest?
- Pose a problem or raise a question (to be answered in the essay).
- Define key terms, perhaps the topic itself.
- Show the relevance of the topic to the reader.
- Begin with an interesting direct quotation.
- Relate a brief anecdote relevant to the topic.
- Relate the specific topic to a wider area of interest.

The following essay introduction uses two of these techniques. It poses a question and then suggests the relevance of the topic to the reader, assuming that the essay was written for accountants. The final sentence of the paragraph is the thesis statement.

> Do accountants need to be good writers? Some people would answer "No" to this question. They believe an accountant's job is limited to arithmetical calculations with very little need to use words or sentences. But this picture of an accountant's responsibilities is a misconception. In fact, good writing skills are essential to the successful practice of accounting.

Sometimes you may choose not to use attention-getting sentences, but decide instead to begin your essay with the thesis statement. This is a particularly good strategy to use for exam questions.

Thesis Statement The thesis statement summarizes the main idea of the essay, usually in one sentence. It may be a *simple* thesis statement, such as the one in the preceding example. Alternatively, the thesis statement may be *expanded*. That is, it may summarize the main supports of the discussion. Here is an example of an expanded thesis statement:

> In fact, successful accountants must have good writing skills to communicate with clients, managers, agencies, and colleagues.

Sometimes, to avoid a long or awkward sentence, you may want to use two sentences for the thesis statement:

> In fact, good writing skills are essential to the successful practice of accounting. For example, during a typical business day an accountant may write to clients, managers, agencies, or colleagues.

Conclusion The conclusion should provide the reader with a sense of closure—a feeling that the essay is complete, that the train of thought has come to a logical end. Sometimes you can give your essays closure by repeating the main idea, usually in some variation of the thesis statement. You may also want to end with a forceful statement that will stay in the reader's mind, thus giving the discussion a more lasting impact. For a strong ending, you can use several techniques, many of which resemble those used in the introduction:

- Show a broad application of the ideas suggested in the discussion.
- End with an authoritative direct quotation that reinforces your position.
- Challenge the reader.
- Echo the attention-getting sentences. For example, if you began by posing a question in the introduction, you can answer it explicitly in the conclusion.

If you're writing an essay on an exam, a concluding paragraph may not be necessary, but it's important that the essay seem finished. It will probably seem complete if you've developed your thesis statement fully.

Applying Essay Techniques to Other Kinds of Writing

If you are answering an essay question on an exam, you can use the techniques just discussed to organize and develop an effective discussion. Chapter 11, which discusses essay exams more fully, provides additional suggestions. But how do the techniques you use for essays work with the writing formats more typically used by accountants (letters, memos, and reports)?

Everything you write should have a main idea. In an essay this idea is called the thesis statement; in a memo or report the main idea might be included in the statement of purpose or recommendations. Whatever you're writing, it's a good idea to identify the main idea before you even begin your outline. Unless this idea is clear in your mind—or clearly written in your notes—your writing may be rambling and confusing. Your reader might then wonder, "What's this person trying to say? What's the point?"

Whatever you write should be organized around a central idea, just as an essay is organized. Letters, reports, and memos share other features of an essay as well: a basic three-part structure (introduction, body, conclusion), complex deductive organization, and the need for adequate transitions and concrete support.

If you understand the principles discussed in this chapter, you will find it easier to plan and organize the writing tasks that are part of your professional responsibilities.

Sample Essay

The following is an assignment for an essay given in an accounting class. Figure 3–1 shows a student's answer that illustrates some of the principles of good organization and development.

> *Assignment.* Several international organizations are encouraging the development of a set of international accounting standards. Explain in 300–500 words why the development of international accounting standards may be important.

This chapter has added four guidelines to our list of ways to make your writing more effective. We now have seven guidelines:

1. **Analyze the purpose of the writing and the needs and expectations of the readers.**
2. **Organize your ideas so that readers will find them easy to follow.**
3. **Write the draft and then revise it to make the writing polished and correct.**
4. **Make the writing unified. All sentences should relate to the main idea, either directly or indirectly. Eliminate digressions and irrelevant detail.**
5. **Use summary sentences and transitions to make your writing coherent.**
6. **Write in short paragraphs that begin with clear topic sentences.**
7. **Develop paragraphs by illustration, definition, detail, and appeals to authority.**

TEST YOURSELF

Is the following paragraph coherent? If not, revise it to improve its organization, using some of these techniques:

- Write a strong topic sentence stating the paragraph's main idea.
- Use transitional devices to show the relation between sentences.
- Eliminate sentences that don't fit.
- Divide long, disunified paragraphs into shorter, unified ones.

FIGURE 3–1 ***Example of an Essay***

The Importance of International Accounting Standards

The need for international accounting standards has received great attention over the past two decades. Increasing globalization of business and capital markets has been the major reason for this attention. When different countries have different business regulations and use different accounting methods, the increased complexity of conducting business and raising capital across national borders presents major challenges. By analogy, consider how difficult the reporting process in our own country would be if each of the 50 states employed different business regulations and a different set of accounting standards. Clearly, in such a case our capital markets as reflected by the activities of the New York Stock Exchange and the NASDAQ could not operate as efficiently or robustly as they now do.

If investors in international capital markets must make investment choices among corporations that use different accounting standards, competing investment opportunities become less comparable and much more risky. The result is likely to be that fewer investors will undertake the effort or assume the risk of investing in foreign corporations or in corporations that have a lot of foreign holdings. Consequently, fewer corporations may list their securities on a foreign exchange. Ultimately, such difficulties could seriously impede the expansion of international capital markets and the development of more healthy international economies.

The International Accounting Standards Committee (IASC) was organized in 1973 and currently includes professional accounting bodies from over 85 countries in its membership. Since its inception, the IASC has issued numerous International Accounting Standards (IASs). Through its efforts it hopes to encourage "harmonization" of accounting standards that will allow for variances in application of basic concepts and principles.

Although there is no mechanism for enforcing compliance with these IASs, there is widespread international support encouraging compliance. Most international accounting organizations, securities exchanges, and governments support the basic concept of harmonization. Several of the world's securities exchanges either permit or require compliance with IASs by their registrants. The International Organization of Securities Commissions (IOSCO) and the Organization for Economic Cooperation and Development (OECD) cooperate with the IASC in its development of international accounting standards. The European Union has accepted the IASC's international accounting standards for its member countries.

Although the prospect for *uniform* accounting standards among all countries is not realistic, reducing differences through the concept of harmonization is clearly a worthwhile goal.

- Rearrange sentences by grouping ideas together (add sentences if necessary).

Government accountants help national, state, and local governments control spending and budgeting. Government spending could run rampant. Governmental accounting is similar to industrial accounting in many of its functions. Government accountants help prevent the government from wasting taxpayers' money.

TEST YOURSELF: ANSWER

This paragraph needs revision. Here is one possibility:

> Government accountants help national, state, and local governments control spending and budgeting. Without controls, government spending could run rampant. Thus, one function of government accountants is to help prevent the government from wasting taxpayers' money.

EXERCISES

Exercise 3–1

Homer Baer is a junior staff accountant for a small CPA firm in Mobile, Alabama. The senior partners have asked him to investigate two computer systems for possible purchase by the firm. The partners have also asked him to recommend the system the firm should buy. Homer has drafted the following outline for his report and asked for your critique.

I. Introduction
II. The history of computer technology
III. Simple Sam Computer Model B-13
  A. General description of features
  B. Nearest service center in Atlanta, Georgia
  C. Can handle much of the firm's computer work
  D. Limited capacity for future expansion
  E. Takes up only a small amount of office space
IV. Whiz Kid Computer Model 1004
  A. Easily adaptable in the future to new programs and functions
  B. Slightly larger than the Simple Sam Model
  C. Service center in Mobile
  D. Can handle all the firm's current computer work
  E. General description of features
V. The need for accountants to have more training in computer science
VI. The role of computers in the future of accounting
VII. Conclusion

1. What is the purpose of Homer's report?
2. What do you think is the main idea of the report?
3. What material included in Homer's outline is irrelevant to his purpose?
4. What necessary information has he forgotten to include?
5. Are the ideas in the outline arranged logically? If not, rearrange the ideas into a more effective outline. Include only relevant material.
6. What kinds of transitional devices could Homer use when he writes his report? Rewrite the outline in sentence form, and include transitional devices.

Exercise 3–2

Are the following paragraphs effectively organized, or do they lack unity or coherence? Analyze the paragraphs to determine whether they need revision. Then revise the faulty paragraphs, using some of these techniques:

- Write a strong topic sentence stating the paragraph's main idea.
- Use transitional devices to show the relation between sentences.
- Eliminate sentences that don't fit.
- Divide long, disunified paragraphs into shorter, unified ones.
- Rearrange sentences by grouping relevant ideas together (add sentences if necessary).

1. One service that public accountants perform is auditing. Accountants examine clients' financial statements to see if they are in conformity with generally accepted accounting principles. Accountants give credibility to financial statements. Public accountants offer management consulting services. Management consultants suggest ways firms can improve such functions as information processing, budgeting, and accounting systems. Taxes are an increasingly complex area. Accountants prepare and file returns and advise clients how to incur the smallest tax liability on a transaction.
2. Although the purchase of our supplier's stock may offer us several advantages, there are also some potential problems we should consider. For one thing, we may not always need the supplier's raw material, because we may not always manufacture the product that requires this material. And even if we continue to manufacture our product, our research and development staff many develop a cheaper, synthetic raw material. Finally, if we do purchase the stock but later need to resell it, we cannot be assured that the stock will be marketable at that time.

Exercise 3–3

Discuss the following topics in well-organized and well-developed paragraphs or essays.

1. Historical cost
2. The matching concept
3. Retained earnings
4. LIFO

5. Lower of cost or market as applied to inventories
6. Revenue
7. Statement of cash flows

Exercise 3–4

Discuss the topics defined below, using the techniques covered in this and earlier chapters. Your answers might range from one to five paragraphs or more, depending on the topic.

1. Contrast financial and managerial accounting.
2. Explain what is meant by the term "generally accepted accounting principles."
3. Discuss the concept of the going concern.
4. Contrast cash-basis accounting with accrual-basis accounting.
5. Discuss the history of private sector standard-setting bodies for financial accounting in the United States.

NOTES

1. Jack E. Kiger, Stephen E. Loeb, and Gordon S. May, *Accounting Principles*, 2nd ed. (New York: Random House, 1987), 1062.

4

A Sense of Style: Writing with Conciseness and Clarity

So far we've looked at writing mainly as an organizational task: planning the structure and contents of the paper so that it achieves its purpose in a way readers will find meaningful. We have stressed the quality of coherence: writing that is easy to follow, with main ideas that stand out. Chapters 2 and 3 looked at writing in terms of large units. They discussed the structure of the paper as a whole and the organization of sections and paragraphs.

We turn now to a more detailed level of effective writing. This chapter looks at word choices and sentence structures that contribute to a vigorous, readable writing style. In this discussion of style, we emphasize two other important qualities of effective writing: conciseness and clarity, which are two of the tips for writing in Figure 1–1.

CONCISENESS

Conciseness is important because readers may tire of wordy writing, lose interest, and miss important ideas. Chapter 3 suggested several ways to make your writing more concise by eliminating digressions and irrelevant detail. In general, we can define concise writing as that which contains no unnecessary elements—no extra words, phrases, sentences, or paragraphs.

Be concise—make every word count.

Unnecessary Words

The easiest way to make every word count is to see how many words you can cross out of your writing, often with only a simple revision of the sentence. Beware of dead words (words that fill up space without adding meaning). Here are some examples of sentences littered with dead words:

WORDY:	To stay informed on the latest information, accountants must read a great number of published materials about accounting. [18 words]
CONCISE:	To stay current, accountants must read many accounting publications. [9 words]
WORDY:	This disclosure has the capacity of providing important information to creditors and investors. [13 words]
CONCISE:	This disclosure can provide important information to creditors and investors. [10 words]
WORDY:	For the sake of our tax liability reduction goals, we changed the way we accounted for the purchase. [18 words]
CONCISE:	To reduce our tax liability, we changed the way we accounted for the purchase. [14 words]
WORDY:	There is one organization that has been very influential in improving the profession of accounting—the AICPA. [17 words]
CONCISE:	The AICPA has improved the accounting profession significantly. [8 words]
WORDY:	We hope the entire staff will assist us in our efforts to reduce costs. [14 words]
CONCISE:	We hope the entire staff will help us reduce costs. [10 words]
WORDY:	The estimates range all the way from $100 to $350. [10 words]
CONCISE:	The estimates range from $100 to $350. [7 words]

Watch out for *there is* and *there are*. They can usually be eliminated. *The fact that, which is*, and *which are* can sometimes be left out:

WORDY:	There are several planning strategies that we can use to reduce our income taxes. [14 words]
CONCISE:	We can reduce our income taxes by using planning strategies. [10 words]
WORDY:	I would like to call your attention to the fact that our earnings last month were down 50 percent. [19 words]
CONCISE:	Remember that our earnings were down 50 percent last month. [10 words] or (even better) Our earnings dropped 50 percent last month. [7 words]
WORDY:	In spite of the fact that our costs rose by 10 percent, we still were able to keep our prices stable. [21 words]
CONCISE:	Although costs rose by 10 percent, our prices remained stable. [10 words]

WORDY: His partner, who is an engineer, . . . [6 words]
CONCISE: His partner, an engineer, . . . [4 words]

Simplicity

Another way to make your writing concise is to write as simply as possible. Sometimes writers get into the habit of using big words and long, complicated sentences. Such writing is hard to read. Look at the following sentence:

> An increase in an employee's rate of pay will not become effective prior to the date on which the employee has completed a minimum of 13 weeks' actual work at his regular occupational classification.

If we simplify this sentence, it becomes easier to understand:

> An employee must work at least 13 weeks at his regular job before he can receive an increase in pay.[1]

Sometimes words and sentences get so complicated that their meaning is completely lost:

> Ultimate consumer means a person or group of persons, generally constituting a domestic household, who purchase eggs generally at the individual stores of retailers or purchase and receive deliveries of eggs at the place of abode of the individual or domestic household from producers or retail route sellers and who use such eggs for their consumption as food.

Translation:

> Ultimate consumers are people who buy eggs to eat them.[2]

Therefore, another technique for effective writing style is simplicity.

Keep it simple—simple vocabulary and short sentences.

Good writers use short, everyday words as much as possible. For example, they usually write *use* instead of *utilize*, *help* instead of *assistance*. Shorter, familiar words are easier to read and make writing more forceful.

Table 4–1 shows two columns of words. Column B lists short, familiar words; Column A lists longer, more difficult words that are often substituted for the everyday words in Column B. The table also shows how single words (*because*) can often replace phrases (*for the reason that*). As a general rule, use the words and phrases in Column B rather than those in Column A. Some of the terms in Column A can be omitted (such as *it should be noted that*).

Another way to achieve a simple, readable style is to use short sentences. Short sentences are particularly important when you are explaining complicated ideas.

The average sentence should be about 15 words long.

TABLE 4–1 Simplifying Word Choices

As a rule, use the words and phrases in column B rather than those in column A.

COLUMN A	COLUMN B
above-mentioned firms	these firms
absolutely essential	essential
activate	begin
advise	tell
aggregate	total
anticipate	expect
along the lines of	like
as per your request	as you requested
assist	help
at all times	always
at this point in time	now
at this time	now
attempt	try
communicate	write, tell
commence	begin
completely eliminated	eliminated
comprise	include
consider	think
constitute	are, is
discontinue	stop
disutility	uselessness
due to the fact that	because
during the time that	while
earliest convenience	promptly, soon
effort	work
enclosed herewith	enclosed
enclosed please find	enclosed is
endeavor	try
exercise care	be careful
facilitate	ease, simplify
failed to	didn't
few in number	few
for the purpose of	for
for the reason that	since, because
from the point of view that	for
furnish	send, give
i.e.	that is
implement	carry out
in advance of	before
in all cases	always
in many cases	often

TABLE 4–1 Simplifying Word Choices (*cont.*)

COLUMN A	COLUMN B
in most cases	usually
in behalf of	for
in connection with	about
in terms of	in
in the amount of	of, for
in the case of	if
in the event that (of)	if
in the nature of	like
in the neighborhood of	about
in this case	here
inasmuch as	since
in view of the fact that	because
indicate	show, point out
initiate	begin
investigate	study
it has come to my attention	Ms. Jones has just told me; I have just learned
it is felt	I feel; we feel
it is our understanding that	we understand that
it should be noted that	(omit)
maintain	keep
maintain cost control	control cost
make a purchase	buy
make application to	apply
make contact with	see, meet
maximum	most, largest
minimum	least, smallest
modification	change
obtain	get
on the order of	about
on the part of	by
optimum	best
past history	history
per annum	annually, per year
period of time	time, period
pertaining to	about, for
philosophy	plan, idea
please be advised that	(omit)
prepare an analysis	analyze
presently	now
prior to	before
procure	get, buy
provide	give

TABLE 4–1 Simplifying Word Choices (*cont.*)

COLUMN A	COLUMN B
provide continuous indication	indicate continuously
pursuant to your inquiry	as you requested
range all the way from	range from
regarding	about
relative to	about
represent	be, is, are
require	need
so as to	to
subsequent to	after, later
substantial	large, big
sufficient	enough
terminate	end, stop
the major part of	most of
the manner in which	how
the undersigned; the writer	I, me
thereon, thereof, thereto, therefrom	(omit)
this is to acknowledge	thank you for, I have received
this is to inform you that we shall send	we'll send
through the use of	by, with
transpire	happen
true facts	facts
under separate cover	by June 1, tomorrow, separately, by parcel post
until such time as	until
utilize	use
vital	important
with a view to	to
with reference to	about
with regard to	about
with respect to	on, for, of, about
with the object to	to
with the result that	so that

Note that 15 words is an *average*. Some sentences are longer, some shorter. In fact, it's a good idea to vary sentence lengths so that the writing doesn't become monotonous. Sentence variation will be discussed again later in this chapter.

Verbs and Nouns

Another technique to make writing more concise is to use active verbs and descriptive nouns, rather than lots of adverbs and adjectives.

Write with active verbs and descriptive nouns.

See how this sentence can be improved:

WORDY: There are some serious, unfortunate results of accounting based on historical cost during times of decreasing purchasing power of the monetary unit. [22 words]

CONCISE: Historical cost accounting creates problems during periods of inflation. [9 words]

One common cause of wordy writing is hidden verbs. For example,

came to a conclusion that instead of *concluded*

causes a misstatement of instead of *misstates*

makes an analysis of instead of *analyzes*

will serve as an explanation of instead of *will explain*

What are the hidden verbs in the following sentences?

Johnson made reference to the new tax laws to support his recommendation.

The company's history of marginal performance over the past several years may be an indication of future solvency problems.

In the first sentence, the hidden verb is *refer;* in the second sentence, it is *indicate*. The revised sentences are a little less wordy, a little more forceful:

Johnson referred to the new tax laws to support his recommendation.

The company's history of marginal performance over the past several years may indicate future solvency problems.

Here are some other sentences with hidden verbs, followed by revisions to make them more concise:

HIDDEN VERB: We made an analysis of ways to cut costs. [9 words]
REVISED: We analyzed ways to cut costs. [6 words]

HIDDEN VERB: I will make a recommendation concerning the best way to record this transaction. [13 words]
REVISED: I will recommend the best way to record this transaction. [10 words]

HIDDEN VERB: I have come to the conclusion that we should update our equipment. [12 words]
REVISED: I have concluded that we should update our equipment. [9 words]

HIDDEN VERB: This method will result in a distribution of the costs between the balance sheet and the income statement. [18 words]
REVISED: This method will distribute the costs between the balance sheet and the income statement. [14 words]

HIDDEN VERB: We are able to make the determination of the historical cost of an asset due to the fact that we have records of its purchase. [25 words]

REVISED: We can determine an asset's historical cost because we have records of its purchase. [14 words]

Finally, avoid sentence introductions that weaken the sentence idea. Don't apologize for or hedge about what you're saying:

WORDY: Enclosed please find our invoice for $400. [7 words]

CONCISE: Our invoice for $400 is enclosed. [6 words]

WORDY: It has come to my attention that our department has overrun its budget for supplies. [15 words]

CONCISE: Our department has overrun its budget for supplies. [8 words]

WORDY: This report is an attempt to explain the proper accounting treatment for loss contingencies. [14 words]

CONCISE: This report explains accounting for loss contingencies. [7 words]

WORDY: This is to acknowledge receipt of your letter of June 1. [11 words]

CONCISE: Thank you for your letter of June 1. [8 words]

WORDY: This is to inform you that we are sending a check in the amount of $798.14. [16 words]

CONCISE: We're sending a check for $798.14. [6 words]

In summary, clear, readable writing contains no unnecessary or dead words. Be concise—your writing will be more forceful.

CLARITY

Clarity is important because unless writing is clear, the reader may find it difficult to understand. Concise writing is clearer because important ideas are not buried in unnecessary words and details. Writing as simply as possible will also help you achieve clarity because you'll be using words the reader knows and feels comfortable with.

Other techniques for improving the clarity of your writing include the careful use of jargon and precise, concrete word choices.

Jargon

Jargon is the "technical terminology . . . of a special activity."[3] We all know what accounting jargon is. It's words and phrases such as *amortization, accrual, debit, GAAP,* and *deferred income taxes.*

One kind of jargon is acronyms: words composed of the first letter of a group of words, such as *FASB, GAAP,* and *LIFO.* To introduce an acronym, write out the words of the acronym, with the acronym in parentheses:

One of the earliest groups to set accounting standards was the Committee on Accounting Procedure (CAP).

After you have identified the acronym fully, you can use the acronym alone throughout the rest of the document. If you're sure that the readers will be familiar with an acronym, and if you're writing an informal document, it's usually acceptable to use the acronym without writing it out.

Unless you use acronyms and other forms of jargon carefully, they will detract from the clarity of your writing. Two guidelines can help you decide when to use jargon and when to look for other words. The first is to remember the readers' needs and to use language they will understand. Another accountant will probably understand what you mean by *straight-line depreciation*, but managers or clients who have not studied accounting may be unfamiliar with the term. Be careful when using jargon even with your accounting colleagues. Would everyone with a degree in accounting know what you mean by a *derivative*?

The second guideline for the use of jargon is to keep your word choices as simple as possible. Avoid jargon when ordinary language will say what you mean. For example, why say "the bottom line" if you mean net income or loss?

Of course, jargon is often unavoidable when you need to communicate technical information as efficiently as possible, but remember the needs of your readers. Define or explain technical terminology with which they may not be familiar.

Use jargon only when your readers understand it.
Define technical terms when necessary.

Precise Meaning

One of the most important elements of clear writing is precision. Word choices must be accurate and sentences constructed so that their meaning is clear. Precision is particularly important in accountants' writing because accountants are often legally responsible for the accuracy of what they write. Moreover, the technical nature of accounting makes precise writing a necessity. Thus, one rule for an effective writing style is precision.

Be precise—avoid ambiguous and unclear writing.

Word Choices Imprecise writing can result from several causes. One culprit is poor diction, or the inaccurate use of words:

The major *setback* of the current method is that it is inefficient. [Poor diction. The writer meant *drawback*.]

The advantage of measurements in terms of market values is that the values reflect *what the item is worth*. [What is the precise meaning of the italicized phrase? *Worth* is vague.]

In these examples, the diction problems are italicized:

POOR DICTION:	The users of our financial statements may see the decline in our revenues and become *worrisome*.
REVISED:	The users of our financial statements may see the decline in our revenues and become worried.
POOR DICTION:	Our advertising expense, which is 1 percent of total sales, is a *negligent* amount.
REVISED:	Our advertising expense, which is 1 percent of total sales, is a negligible amount.
POOR DICTION:	The reason for this purchase was to *help from* liquidating LIFO layers.
REVISED:	The reason for this purchase was to prevent the liquidation of LIFO layers.
POOR DICTION:	This memo will discuss how to account for the *theft* of the filling station. [This sentence says that the filling station itself was carried off.]
REVISED:	This memo will discuss how to account for the robbery at the filling station.

Unclear, awkward writing can also result from the misuse of words ending in *-ing:*

AWKWARD AND UNCLEAR:	The lease does not meet the 90 percent test, therefore classifying the lease as an operating lease.
REVISED:	The lease does not meet the 90 percent test, so it must be classified as an operating lease.
AWKWARD AND UNCLEAR:	By forming larger inventory groups, the chances of liquidating an early LIFO layer are reduced.
REVISED:	Larger inventory groups reduce the chances of liquidating an early LIFO layer. [Note: This revision also changes the sentence from passive to active voice—see pages 65–67].
AWKWARD AND UNCLEAR:	In finding out this information, we will have to be thorough in our asking of questions of the concerned parties.
REVISED:	To find out this information, we must thoroughly question the concerned parties.

Faulty Modifiers Another type of imprecise writing is misplaced and dangling modifiers. With a misplaced modifier, the modifying word or phrase is not placed next to the sentence element it modifies. The result is a confusing sentence:

Process cost systems are often used by businesses that manufacture products for general distribution *such as oil refineries and dairies.* [The italicized phrase appears to modify *products,* but it really modifies *businesses.*]

Process cost systems are often used by such businesses as oil refineries and dairies, which manufacture products for general distribution.

Consider another sentence with a misplaced modifier:

This technique identifies tax returns for audits with a high probability of error.

Revised:

To identify tax returns for audit, this technique flags returns that have a high probability of error.

Dangling modifiers, which usually come at the beginning of a sentence, do not actually modify any word in the sentence. Usually the word modified is implied rather than stated directly. Look at this sentence:

After buying the bonds, the market price will fluctuate.

The writer probably meant something like this:

After we buy the bonds, the market price will fluctuate.

Here's another example:

As a successful company, disclosure of quarterly profits will attract investors.

One possible revision:

Because we are a successful company, disclosure of our quarterly profits will attract investors.

Pronoun Reference Faulty pronoun reference can also cause writing to be ambiguous and confusing:

Capitalization of interest is adding interest to the cost of an asset under construction which increases its book value.

The meaning of this sentence is unclear. What increases book value? *Which* and *its* are confusing; their references are vague. Here is one possible revision:

Capitalization of interest is adding interest to the cost of an asset under construction. The added interest increases the asset's book value.

Faulty pronoun reference can be labeled *vague, ambiguous,* or *broad.* These terms all mean that the writer doesn't make clear what the pronoun refers to. The pronoun *this* is particularly troublesome:

FAULTY REFERENCE: Last year Excelsor Company modified its products to one-size-fits-all and built a central distributing facility. Because of *this*, the company decided to reduce inventories.

REVISED: Last year Excelsor Company modified its products to one-size-fits-all and built a central distributing facility. Because of these changes, the company decided to reduce inventories.

FAULTY REFERENCE: The use of generally accepted accounting principles does not always produce the true financial position of a company. *This* is a problem for the FASB.

REVISED: The use of generally accepted accounting principles does not always produce the true financial position of a company. This weakness in the principles is a problem for the FASB.

A good rule is never to use *this* by itself. Add a noun or phrase to define what *this* is.

Another pronoun that can cause reference problems is *it*:

FAULTY REFERENCE: Many people prefer to itemize deductions for their income tax to decrease their tax liability, but *it* is not always done.

REVISED: Many people prefer to itemize deductions for their income tax, but not everyone chooses to itemize.

Misplaced and dangling modifiers and faulty pronoun reference are grammatical errors, which are discussed further in chapter 5. However, writing can be grammatically correct and still be imprecise. Consider this sentence:

> The major drawback of the current value method is verifiability.

Revised:

> The major drawback of the current value method is the lack of verifiability.

The revision makes quite a difference in meaning!

Often, the ability to write precisely is a function of precise reading and thinking. An accounting professor assigned his Accounting Theory students two papers for the quarter. He then wrote the following statement on the board:

> An Accounting Theory student who completes the course requirements will write a total of two papers this semester. True or false?

The precise thinkers in the class realized that the statement might not be true. The students could write papers for other classes as well. Therefore, some students could write more than two papers for the semester.

Learn to analyze carefully what you read. Then you will be able to perfect your own writing so that your meanings are clear and precise.

Here are some other examples of sentences revised to improve their clarity:

UNCLEAR: This bond is not considered risky because it sells at only 70 percent of its maturity.

REVISED: The selling price of this bond, which is 70 percent of its maturity value, does not necessarily indicate that the bond is risky.

UNCLEAR: When purchasing bonds at a discount, the investment cost is less than the face value of the investment.

REVISED: When bonds sell at a discount, the investment cost is less than the face value of the investment.

UNCLEAR: When reviewing the prior auditor's workpapers, no recognition of a possible obsolescence problem was found.

REVISED: When we reviewed the prior auditor's workpapers, we found no recognition of a possible obsolescence problem.

UNCLEAR: Historical cost accounting has several problems that do not consider inflation and changing prices.

REVISED: Historical cost accounting causes several problems because it does not take into account inflation and changing prices.

Concrete, Specific Wording

Chapter 3 discussed the use of concrete facts, details, and examples as a way to develop paragraphs. Concrete, specific writing adds clarity to your documents and makes them much more interesting.

We can explain concrete writing by defining its opposite, abstract writing. Abstract writing is vague, general, or theoretical. It's hard to understand because it's not illustrated by particular, material objects. Concrete writing, on the other hand, is vivid and specific; it brings a picture into the mind of the reader.

Illustrations of abstract and concrete writing styles make them easier to understand.

ABSTRACT

Historical cost is important in accounting. It is easy for accountants to use, and it is often seen in the financial statements. Historical cost has some disadvantages, but it has its good points, too.

CONCRETE

Historical cost is the amount of money paid for an object when it was purchased. For example, if a truck was purchased in 1994 for $30,000, then $30,000 is the truck's historical cost. Many accountants favor historical cost accounting because the values of assets are easy to determine from invoices and other records of the original purchase.

However, in times of inflation the historical cost of an asset may not indicate its true value. For example, an acre of land bought in 1950 for $5,000 might be worth several times that amount today, but it would still be recorded in the owner's books and on the balance sheet at its historical cost. Thus, one disadvantage of historical cost accounting is that it often undervalues assets.

By giving more detailed information and specific, concrete examples of historical cost, the second example makes this concept easier to understand and more interesting to read.

In the following examples, vague, abstract sentences are replaced by more concrete writing:

VAGUE: Accountants should write well.

REVISED: Accountants need to write clear, concise letters to their clients and other business associates. [This sentence replaces the vague *well* with two characteristics of effective writing: *clear* and *concise*. The revision also gives an example of one type of accountants' writing: letters to clients and associates.]

VAGUE: Action on today's stock market was interesting.

REVISED: The Dow Jones Industrial Average dropped 200 points today.

The example just given illustrates a particularly effective technique you can use to make your writing concrete: Illustrate your ideas with specific details about the situation you're discussing. That is, if you're writing about action on the stock market, as in the above example, add relevant details about what happened to clarify what you mean.

By adding specific, concrete detail, you will avoid vague sentences like this one:

I believe we should disclose this expense because of comparability.

If we revise the sentence to be more specific and concrete, the meaning becomes much clearer:

I believe we should disclose the advertising expense so that this year's statements will be comparable to those of prior years.

See how specific wording improves the clarity of this sentence:

VAGUE: This liability should appear on the income statement because of materiality.

CLEAR: This liability should appear on the income statement because the amount is material.

Finally, remember the readers' interests when you select the details to include in your writing; choose the details they will find meaningful and relevant. Which of the following two sentences would you prefer to read in a letter from your tax accountant?

Your tax situation this year poses some interesting possibilities.

If you can document your business expenses this year with the necessary receipts, you may be eligible for a refund of at least $5,500.

Be concrete and specific—use facts, details, and examples.

READABLE WRITING

If your writing is interesting to read, it will almost always be clear. Lively, natural sentences hold readers' attention and keep them involved in what you are saying, so they have an easier time understanding your ideas.

This section of the chapter is devoted to several techniques that will make your sentences readable and clear: using the active voice, writing with variety and rhythm, and using the appropriate tone.

Passive and Active Voice

This technique for achieving a good writing style may seem technical, but it will become clear after a few definitions and examples.

Use active voice for most sentences.

In the active voice, the subject of the sentence performs the action described by the verb.

ACTIVE: Most corporations issue financial statements at least once a year.

Passive voice, on the other hand, describes action done to somebody or something by another agent. The agent is not always named in the sentence.

PASSIVE: Financial statements are issued (by most corporations) at least once a year.

This formula will help you identify passive voice verbs:

Passive voice =	a form of the verb *to be*	+	the past participle of another verb (usually ending in - *ed*

forms of the verb *to be:*
is, are, were, was, been,
being, be, am

typical past participles:
accrued, received, used,
computed, given, kept

Sometimes passive verb phrases also contain a form of *to have* (has, have, had, having) or an auxiliary (will, should, would, must, etc.), but passive voice always contains a *to be* form plus a past participle.

Active voice sentences are often clearer than passive voice sentences. Consider these examples:

PASSIVE:	Taxes were increased by 50 percent. [In this example, most readers would want to know who raised taxes.]
ACTIVE:	The Labor Party increased taxes by 50 percent.
PASSIVE:	It was decided that employees would be required to work on Saturday.
ACTIVE:	The company president decided to require employees to work on Saturday.
PASSIVE:	Deliberate understatement of assets and stockholders' equity with the intention of misleading interested parties is prohibited.
ACTIVE:	SEC regulations prohibit deliberate misstatement of assets and stockholders' equity if the intention is to mislead interested parties.

Unfortunately, writers of "officialese," especially in government, business, and research, have so badly overused passive voice that we tend to accept it as standard style. Passive voice is seldom effective—it lacks the forcefulness and clarity of active voice. Compare the following pairs of sentences:

PASSIVE:	This letter hasn't been signed.
ACTIVE:	You haven't signed the letter.
PASSIVE:	A determination has been made that the statements are in violation of GAAP.
ACTIVE:	The auditors have determined that the statements are in violation of GAAP.
PASSIVE:	Further research should be conducted before an opinion can be issued.
ACTIVE:	The auditors should conduct further research before they issue an opinion.
PASSIVE:	In many college accounting courses, effective writing skills are emphasized.
ACTIVE:	Many college accounting courses emphasize effective writing skills.
PASSIVE:	In SAS No. 1 it is required that items such as these be disclosed in the financial statements.
ACTIVE:	SAS No. 1 requires that the financial statements disclose items such as these.

Good writers avoid using passive voice in most situations. They ask themselves two questions. What is the action (verb)? Who or what is doing it (subject)?

One word of warning: Avoid substituting a weak active verb for passive voice. Be particularly careful of colorless verbs such as *to exist* and *to occur*. The following sentences are written in active voice, but the sentences are weak:

Capitalization of option costs on land subsequently purchased should occur.

FIFO bases itself on the assumption that the first inventory acquired is the first inventory sold.

Use descriptive, vigorous verbs to substitute for weak verbs, or reword the sentence.

We must capitalize option costs on land subsequently purchased.
The assumption that underlies FIFO is that the first inventory acquired is the first inventory sold.

When to Use Passive Voice Although it is usually better to write in active voice, passive voice is sometimes preferable. For example, the two sentences in the preceding example could be effectively written in passive voice:

Option costs on land subsequently purchased should be capitalized.
FIFO is based on the assumption that the first inventory acquired is the first inventory sold.

Passive voice may also be necessary to avoid an awkward repetition of sentence subjects, especially in paragraphs where the same agent is performing all the action or the agent is obvious or irrelevant:

The property was appraised in 1998 at $200,000.

In this sentence, it would probably not be necessary to identify who did the appraisal.

Another consideration about active and passive voice is that sometimes you may want to emphasize the passive subject. For example, you would say

The Corner Grocery Store was robbed.

rather than

Some person or persons unknown robbed the Corner Grocery Store.

Finally, passive voice may enable you to be tactful when you must write bad news or some sort of criticism:

These figures were not calculated correctly.

This sentence doesn't say who is at fault for the erroneous calculation; here passive voice may be the most diplomatic way to identify the problem without assigning blame.

We talk more about writing tactfully later in the chapter.

Variety and Rhythm

Another way to make your writing natural and more readable is to add variety.

Vary vocabulary, sentence lengths, and sentence structures. Read the writing aloud to hear how it sounds.

The purpose of sentence variety is to avoid monotony—a sing-song, awkward repetition of the same sentence rhythms or overuse of a word or phrase. Read the following paragraph aloud:

> Financial analysts use ratios to analyze financial statements. Ratios show a company's liquidity. The current ratio shows the ratio of current assets to current liabilities. Ratios also show a company's solvency. The equity ratio is an example of a solvency ratio. It shows the ratio of owners' equity to total assets. Ratios also show profitability. The return-on-investment ratio is an example. It shows the ratio of net earnings to owners' equity.

This paragraph does not sound pleasing. In fact, it could easily lull the reader to sleep. The sentences are too similar in length and structure and the word *ratio* is repeated too often. Let's try again:

> Ratios based on financial statements can reveal valuable information about a company to investors, creditors, and other interested parties. Liquidity ratios show whether a company can pay its debts. The quick ratio, for example, is a good indication of debt-paying ability for companies with slow inventory turnover. Ratios can also indicate a company's solvency; the equity ratio, for instance, shows the percentage of owners' equity to total assets. Investors in bonds use this figure to evaluate the safety of a potential investment. Finally, ratios can give a measure of a company's profitability, which is of special interest to potential investors. The earnings-per-share ratio is probably the most popular of the profitability ratios.

Another cause of monotonous sentences is too many prepositional phrases, particularly when they are linked together to form a chain. Look again at the following sentence. Prepositions are in bold type; the rest of the phrase is underlined:

> There are some serious, unfortunate results **of** <u>accounting</u> based **on** <u>historical cost</u> **during** <u>times</u> **of** <u>decreasing purchasing power</u> **of** <u>the monetary unit</u>.

This sentence contains a chain of prepositional phrases five links (phrases) long. A good rule is to avoid more than two prepositional phrases in a row.

If you are not sure what prepositions are, here is a partial list:

> across, after, as, at, because of, before, between, by, during, for, from, in, in front of, in regard to, like, near, of, on, over, through, to, together with, under, until, up, with

Variety is an important element of readable writing because it gives sentences and paragraphs a pleasing rhythm. Read your paragraphs aloud. If you notice a word or phrase repeated too often, look for a synonym. If the sentences sound choppy and monotonous, vary their structures and lengths. Often a change in the way sentences begin will improve the rhythm of the paragraph. Add an occasional short sentence and an occasional longer one (but be sure longer sentences are still easy to understand). Avoid using too many prepositional phrases. You don't want to bore your readers, and varied sentences are one way to keep your writing lively.

Tone

The tone of a document is the way it makes the reader feel, or the impression it makes. A letter can have a formal or informal tone, be personal or impersonal. It can be apologetic, cold, humorous, threatening, arrogant, respectful, or friendly.

Vary your tone according to the reader. If you are writing to a colleague who is also a good friend, you can be much more informal than if you are writing to someone you know only slightly. Be particularly careful to show respect to those who are much older than you or in higher positions of authority.

One way to decide on the proper tone of a document you are writing is to imagine that you are in a conversation with your reader. How formal would you be? How would you show that you were interested in your reader's point of view and concerns? No matter how formal (or casual) you decide to make your tone, always be courteous. Treat your correspondent with tact, politeness, and respect. Avoid abruptness, condescension, and stuffiness, or any other form of rudeness. Here are some examples of poor tone:

> Tax planning is a complicated subject, so I have tried to simplify it for you. [This sentence is condescending; it implies that the reader is not very bright.]

> I acknowledge receipt of your letter and beg to thank you. [Too formal and artificial—stuffy, in fact.]

> Send me that report immediately. I can't understand why it has taken you so long to prepare it. [In certain situations you might *think* this way, but you'll get better results if you write with tact and courtesy.]

For all but the most formal documents, such as some contracts, the use of personal pronouns (*you, I, we*) can contribute to a warm, personal tone. Keep the first person singular pronouns (*I, me, my*) to a minimum; focus instead on the reader with second person (*you, your*) or, in some cases, first person plural (*we, us, our*).

A personal tone, including personal pronouns, is especially effective when the message you are conveying is good news or neutral information. When you must write bad news or criticize someone, it's better to be impersonal in order to be tactful. Passive voice can also make a sentence more tactful:

TACTLESS: You failed to sign your income tax return.
BETTER: Your return wasn't signed.

Another guideline for an effective tone is to stress the positive. Emphasize what can be done rather than what cannot:

NEGATIVE Because you were late in sending us your tax information, we cannot complete your tax return by April 15.
POSITIVE: Now that we have the information on your taxes, we can complete your tax return. We will request an extension of the deadline so that you will not be fined for a late filing.

Finally, be honest and sincere; avoid exaggeration and flattery.

In the final analysis, the guidelines for an effective writing tone are the same as those for good relationships. Learn to view a situation from the other person's point of view and communicate in a way that shows empathy and respect.

Here, then, is another guideline for an effective writing style.

Write from the reader's point of view.
Use tone to show courtesy and respect.

EDITING FOR STYLE AT THE COMPUTER

The section on revision in chapter 2 mentioned software programs that some writers use to help them edit for style. These programs analyze text and give such information as the average sentence and word length. They may also identify passive voice constructions, clichés, and pretentious word choices. Some programs also tell you how difficult your writing is to read—that is, they use a formula to determine the readability level.

Keep in mind that these programs are not completely reliable. They don't identify all the weaknesses in your writing, and some of the passages they flag are not really errors. For example, we've seen in this chapter that passive voice is sometimes preferable to active voice, yet a style analyzer may identify all passive verbs as potential problems. It takes the writer's own judgment to decide when to change the passive voice and when to let it stand.

On the other hand, some of the information given by a style analyzer can truly be helpful. For example, if the analyzer tells you that your average sentence length is twenty-five words long, you know you have a problem.

In sum, style analyzers do not automatically ensure that you write effectively, but they may point out potential problems that you should consider.

Whatever techniques you use to revise your text, take time to ensure that your prose is readable, clear, and concise. Your readers will be grateful.

This chapter on style has added nine guidelines for effective writing, making a total of sixteen.

1. **Analyze the purpose of the writing and the needs and expectations of the readers.**
2. **Organize your ideas so that readers will find them easy to follow.**
3. **Write the draft and then revise it to make the writing polished and correct.**
4. **Make the writing unified. All sentences should relate to the main idea, either directly or indirectly. Eliminate digressions and irrelevant detail.**
5. **Use summary sentences and transitions to make your writing coherent.**
6. **Write in short paragraphs that begin with clear topic sentences.**
7. **Develop paragraphs by illustration, definition, detail, and appeals to authority.**
8. **Be concise—make every word count.**
9. **Keep it simple—simple vocabulary and short sentences.**
10. **Write with active verbs and descriptive nouns.**
11. **Use jargon only when your readers understand it. Define technical terms when necessary.**
12. **Be precise—avoid ambiguous and unclear writing.**
13. **Be concrete and specific. Use facts, details, and examples.**
14. **Use active voice for most sentences.**
15. **Vary vocabulary, sentence lengths, and sentence structures. Read the writing aloud to hear how it sounds.**
16. **Write from the reader's point of view. Use tone to show courtesy and respect.**

TEST YOURSELF

Revise the following sentences, using the techniques covered in this chapter. Answers are provided on pages 73–74.

a. Can you revise these sentences so that they are simpler and more concise? Watch for hidden verbs.

1. To determine what information to include in our report for 1998, we will make an analysis of the users' needs.
2. The history of United Teacup's performance, which is marginal at best, may be an indication of solvency problems that will occur in the future.

3. The team of auditors came to the conclusion that Flytrap Food Distributors was likely to incur a loss ranging from anywhere around $10,000 to over $100,000.
4. I have attempted to explain the three proposed alternatives for recording the cost of the machinery.
5. It is our recommendation that Hamilton Corporation choose to value the property at $95,000.

b. The meaning of these sentences is not clear. Revise them so that they are unambiguous and precise.

1. After reading the following discussion, a recommendation will suggest a way we can save on our machinery purchase.
2. Each entry has its rational for use.
3. The SEC has not officially written a policy for this kind of disclosure.
4. The new regulations will exasperate the difficulty of reporting income.
5. The letter discussed the alternative ways to finance the purchase of the new equipment. Its purpose was . . .

c. Identify the passive voice verbs in these sentences and revise them so they are in active voice. If necessary, invent a subject for the verb.

1. Complete information was wanted by management on the new project that had been proposed by the engineers.
2. The accounts receivable aging is distorted by inaccurate journal entries.
3. Inventory should be monitored by a system of internal controls.
4. This recommendation can easily be implemented by our clients.
5. This information was prepared by our research department.

d. Identify the prepositional phrases in these sentences. Where too many are linked together, revise the sentence.

1. Now that the choice of sites has been made and the expiration of options is occurring, this transaction must be recorded in the books of our firm correctly.
2. We have designed an audit program for use in future audits of Hudson's Pest Control Company.
3. An accrual of expenses reports a more accurate picture of the operations of the current business period of the company.
4. The important issue to address in this company's situation is that of the expression of an opinion of the going concern.
5. The main problem of this company is to minimize the amount of taxes for 1998.

TEST YOURSELF: ANSWERS

(Note: Some of the errors in the previous sentences can be corrected in more than one way, but this key will show only one possible correction. If you recognize the error, you probably understand how to correct it.)

a.

1. To determine what to include in our 1998 report, we will analyze the users' needs.
2. United Teacup's history of marginal performance may indicate future solvency problems.
3. The audit team concluded that Flytrap Food Distributors would likely incur a $10,000 to $100,000 loss.
4. I have explained the three proposals for recording the cost of the machinery.
5. We recommend that Hamilton Corporation value the property at $95,000.

b.

1. The following discussion will conclude with a recommendation of how we can save on our machinery purchase.
2. Each entry has its rationale for use.
3. The SEC has not written an official policy for this kind of disclosure.
4. The new regulations will <u>exacerbate</u> the difficulty of reporting income.
5. The letter discussed the alternative ways to finance the purchase of the new equipment. The purpose of the letter was . . .

c.

1. Management wanted complete information on the new project the engineers had proposed.
2. Inaccurate journal entries distort the accounts receivable aging.
3. An internal control system is necessary to monitor inventory. [Note: This sentence as it was originally written would be fine in most situations, even though the original sentence is in passive voice.]
4. Our clients can easily implement this recommendation.
5. Our research department prepared this information.

d.

1. Now that the choice **of** <u>sites</u> has been made and the expirations **of** <u>options</u> is occurring, this transaction must be recorded **in** <u>the books</u> **of** <u>our firm</u> correctly.

   Now that we have chosen the site and the options have expired, we must record the transaction correctly in our books.

2. We have designed an audit program **for** <u>use</u> **in** <u>future audits</u> **of** <u>Hudson's Pest Control Company</u>.

We have designed a program for future audits of Hudson's Pest Control Company.

3. An accrual **of** expenses reports a more accurate picture **of** the operations **of** the current business period **of** the company.

   Accrued expenses report a more accurate picture of the company's current operations.

4. The important issue to address **in** this company's situation is that **of** the expression **of** an opinion **of** the going concern.

   Before we can issue our opinion, we must determine whether this company is indeed a going concern.

   [Note: *to address* is an infinitive (a verb), not a prepositional phrase. However, too many infinitive phrases can also make a sentence awkward.]

5. The main problem **of** this company is to minimize the amount **of** taxes **for** 1998.

   This company's main problem is to minimize taxes for 1998.

EXERCISES

Exercise 4–1

Revise the following sentences so that they are written as simply and concisely as possible. Be alert for hidden verbs.

1. We should make reference to the work done by the auditors during the previous year's audit.
2. The benefits of this communications seminar will avail themselves to Zeke's Boutique via language and letters that are fresh, accurate, and clear.
3. I hope this letter will provide for an increased understanding of the best way to reduce your income taxes to a minimum.
4. Wordiness is the problem that makes my writing ineffective.
5. As you are no doubt aware, in the economic environment of today, having these services available from a firm with experience is indispensable and quite valuable.
6. I am in need of improved writing skills.
7. In conclusion, I would like to state that I feel our relationship will provide all of us, both you and us, with many opportunities to work together for our mutual benefit.
8. There are several benefits that can come from attending the seminar.
9. Enclosed please find our analysis of the best way to reduce costs in the departments under your supervision.
10. This method provides proper matching of expenses to revenues.

Exercise 4–2

Review the lists of simplified word choices in Table 4–1 of this chapter (pages 54–56). Then write a shorter or simpler version of the following words and phrases.

1. advise
2. enclosed please find
3. for the purpose of
4. indicate
5. pertaining to
6. terminate
7. true facts
8. this is to acknowledge
9. make a decision
10. earliest convenience
11. in the amount of
12. due to the fact that
13. at all times
14. the writer
15. with regard to
16. vital
17. with the result that
18. this is to inform you that we shall send
19. failed to
20. anticipate
21. commence
22. above-mentioned firms
23. aggregate
24. pursuant to your inquiry
25. transpire
26. at this point in time
27. in advance of
28. optimum
29. exercise care
30. pertaining to

Exercise 4–3

Identify the jargon in the following sentences.

1. We must prepare the financials in accordance with GAAP.
2. The CPA's recommendation is based on thorough research into the regs and the rules.
3. The FASB and the SEC, as well as the AICPA, are organizations that concern the profession of accounting.

4. Negative cash flows may affect our position with our creditors.
5. The project's NPV was negative, so it was rejected.
6. The historical cost of the crane will be easy to determine.
7. My CPA advised me to file a Schedule C with my return.
8. Because of her income this year, she will be able to recapture.
9. Our auditors must follow all SASs.
10. According to SFAS 13, the lease of the warehouse qualifies as an operating lease.

Exercise 4–4

The meaning of the following sentences is not clear. Revise the sentences so that they are unambiguous and precise.

1. The warehouse will be located at a new cite.
2. The return of an investment in bonds is based on the number of years to maturity and the current market rate of interest.
3. Abigail's Energy Company has a unique way of doing business; very few other companies operate in the same way.
4. The HB Transportation Company's improved position is due to decreasing fuel prices and the company's response in increasing prices.
5. All companies incur expenses that do not provide future benefits to keep their business going to produce revenue.
6. Expense recognition states that once a cost expires, we should recognize expense.
7. Calculating the present value of the bonds' principal and future cash flows will determine our risk.
8. The riskiness of these bonds does not depend on their selling price.
9. Under LIFO the lower costs are assigned to inventory which causes the cost of inventory to increase.
10. These financial statements upset two accounting standards.

Exercise 4–5

The following sentences are abstract or vague. Revise them, using facts, details, or examples to make them more concrete. You may need to replace one vague sentence with several concrete sentences, or even a short paragraph. Alternatively, you could introduce a short paragraph with an abstraction and then develop the idea with more concrete, specific sentences. Feel free to invent details that will make the ideas more specific.

1. This is a tricky problem.
2. Sometimes firms keep two sets of records.
3. We must record this asset at its true value. [Hint: what is "true value"?]
4. The financial statements disturbed the investors.
5. The firm sold the asset for its cost. [Hint: what cost?]

6. Accounting for leases is tricky.
7. The nature of this asset requires us to capitalize it.
8. The manager in the service department is not doing his job.
9. These mutual funds look like a good buy.
10. Accountants must use good judgment.

Exercise 4–6

Identify the passive constructions in the following sentences and revise them to active voice. Be careful not to substitute weak active verbs for passive voice. For some sentences, you may need to invent a subject for the active verb. For other sentences, you may decide that passive voice is acceptable.

EXAMPLE

PASSIVE: That alternative could have been followed.

ACTIVE: We [or the firm, our client, McDonough Corporation, etc.] could have followed that alternative.

1. Our earnings statement was distorted by these incorrect figures.
2. All our files were destroyed in the flood.
3. No follow-up work was performed on receivables by our firm.
4. Most letters sent to clients are reviewed by a manager.
5. The opinion to be issued on the 1998 financial statements must be qualified by our firm.
6. Although our computer was purchased last April, it is already obsolete.
7. Each month our company's net income is reduced by accrued expenses.
8. At the seminar the new provisions of the tax code will be explained.
9. The structure of the 1998 financial statements must be changed.
10. The bonds will be recalled as stock is issued during the restructuring.

Exercise 4-7

Identify the prepositional phrases in the following sentences. Where too many phrases are linked together, revise the sentence.

EXAMPLE

The problem of Sam's Enterprises will be solved through the selection of one of the accounting information systems presented.

Prepositional phrases identified

The problem **of** Sam's Enterprises will be solved **through** the selection **of** one **of** the accounting information systems presented.

REVISED

One of these accounting information systems should solve Sam's Enterprises' problem.

1. The effect on the balance sheet of the sale of the division is twofold.
2. The calculation of the present values of the principal of the bonds and their cash flows will reveal our risk.
3. The amortization of the discount of the bond results in the recognition of cash flows of the bond at an even rate throughout the life of the bond.
4. The determination of the accounts receivable aging will pose no problem for the accountants in our department.
5. An increase in advertising will make potential customers more aware of the products of the company.
6. The controller of the company called a meeting at 3:00 p.m. to discuss the annual report for this year.
7. The income tax return for Cindy Baer was filed on Friday.
8. Personnel of the corporation were pleased to learn of the increase in their salaries this year.
9. Representatives from the division in North Georgia met for a meeting in the morning.
10. Clients of our firm are concerned about the proposed flat tax.

Exercise 4–8

Read this paragraph aloud and notice how monotonous it sounds. Then revise it so that sentence lengths and structures are more varied. Note also when a word or phrase is repeated too often.

> Howard's Air Taxi runs scheduled flights between several local communities. Howard also provides charter service for several local businesses. Howard's financial statements reveal marginal profits for the past several years. Last year Howard was forced to raise prices to compensate for increased maintenance expenses. These price increases and several economic downturns caused passenger volume to decline drastically. Thus, 1998 was a disastrous year for Howard's Air Taxi. The preliminary information showed that 1998 losses were in excess of $2,000,000. This will force Howard into a deficit position. The 1997 balance sheet showed a net worth of $2,000,000 with total assets of $10,000,000.[4]

NOTES

1. George deMare, *How to Write and Speak Effectively* (New York: Price Waterhouse, 1958), 9.
2. Ibid., p. 11.
3. *Merriam Webster's Collegiate Dictionary,* 10th ed. (Springfield, Mass.: Merriam-Webster, Incorporated, 1993), 627.
4. The revised paragraph is adapted from Doug Hertha, "Audit Report of Charter Air" (unpublished student paper, University of Georgia, 1982).

5

Standard English: Grammar, Punctuation, and Spelling

One way to improve the clarity of your writing is to use standard English. Standard English has been described as follows:

> There are two broad varieties of written English: standard and nonstandard. These varieties are determined through usage by those who write in the English language. Standard English . . . is used to carry on the daily business of the nation. It is the language of business, industry, government, education, and the professions. Standard English is characterized by exacting standards of punctuation and capitalization, by accurate spelling, by exact diction, by an expressive vocabulary, and by knowledgeable usage choices.[1]

In addition to improving the clarity of what you write, the use of standard English will help you produce professional and polished documents, which is the final tip for writers given in Figure 1–1 on page 5. A mastery of standard English tells the reader much about you as a person and as a professional. Your use of correct grammar says that you are an educated person who understands and appreciates the proper use of language.

A grammatically correct document, free of mechanical and typographical errors, also shows that you know the importance of detail and are willing to spend the time necessary to prepare an accurate, precise document. Careful attention to detail is an important quality of an accountant, whether the detail is verbal or quantitative.

This chapter presents some of the most common errors in grammar, punctuation, and spelling. Because only a few principles can be covered in this short space, you should consult an English handbook for more complete coverage. The discussion here focuses on areas that give accountants the most trouble.

MAJOR SENTENCE ERRORS

Major sentence errors include three kinds of problems: fragments, comma splices, and fused sentences. These errors are very distracting to readers and often interfere seriously with their ability to understand the meaning of the sentence.

Fragments

A sentence fragment is just what its name suggests: part of a sentence. Recall that every sentence needs two essential elements, a subject and a verb. In sentence fragments, one of these elements is left out. Here are some examples:

To record the purchase correctly.

For example, all the employees who are eligible for retirement.

The reason being that we must find ways to cut overhead. [*Being* is a present participle;* it cannot be substituted for a complete verb such as *is* or *was*.]

Although our new computer system makes billing much faster. [This dependent clause has a subject and verb, but it cannot stand alone as a sentence because it is introduced by a subordinate conjunction, *although*.]

Comma Splices

The second major sentence error is comma splices, which occur when independent clauses are linked by a comma alone.

An independent clause is a group of words with a subject and a verb; it can stand alone as a sentence. Here are two independent clauses punctuated as separate sentences:

Increases in expenses decrease net income. Decreases increase net income.

Sometimes writers want to combine two independent clauses into one sentence. This can be done correctly in several ways:

1. Put a semicolon (;) between the clauses.

Increases in expenses decrease net income; decreases increase net income.

*Consult a grammar handbook for explanations of technical grammatical terms such as this.

2. Combine the clauses with a coordinating conjunction (*and, but, for, or, nor, yet, so*).

Increases in expenses decrease net income, and decreases increase net income.

3. Combine the clauses with a semicolon, a conjunctive adverb, and a comma. (Conjunction adverbs include *however, therefore, thus, consequently, that is, for example, nevertheless, also, furthermore, indeed, instead, still.*)

Increases in expenses decrease net income; however, decreases increase net income.

Study the following comma splices. The independent clauses are joined by a comma alone:

COMMA SPLICE:	We found a cheaper source of materials, therefore we can lower our prices.
REVISED:	We have been able to reduce the costs of manufacturing these machines; therefore, we can lower our prices.
COMMA SPLICE:	Accountants write many letters as part of their professional responsibilities, for example, they may write letters to the IRS.
REVISED:	Accountants write many letters as part of their professional responsibilities. For example, they may write letters to the IRS.
COMMA SPLICE:	These transactions were not recorded correctly, they were not recorded in the proper accounts.
REVISED:	These transactions were not recorded correctly; they were not recorded in the proper accounts.
or	
(to make the sentence more concise)	These transactions were not recorded in the proper accounts.

Fused Sentences

Fused sentences, which are also called run-on sentences, occur when two independent clauses are joined without any punctuation at all:

FUSED SENTENCE:	Generally accepted accounting principles are not laws passed by Congress however, the code of professional ethics requires accountants to follow GAAP.
REVISED:	Generally accepted accounting principles are not laws passed by Congress. However, the code of professional ethics requires accountants to follow GAAP.
FUSED SENTENCE:	The controller sent a memo to all the new employees she wanted them to have complete information about their pension benefits.

REVISED: The controller sent a memo to all the new employees; she wanted them to have complete information about their pension benefits.

or

The controller sent a memo to the new employees about their pension benefits.

PROBLEMS WITH VERBS

The correct use of verbs is a complicated matter in any language, as you will appreciate if you have ever studied a foreign language. Fortunately, because English is the native language for most of us, we usually use verbs correctly without having to think about them. We just know what sounds right.

A few kinds of verb problems do occur, however, even in the writing of educated people. We will now look briefly at some of those problems.

Tense and Mood

The *tense* of a verb reflects the time of the action described by the verb:

PAST TENSE: Mr. Roberts *signed* the contract.

PRESENT TENSE: Mr. Roberts *is signing* the contract.

or

Should Mr. Roberts sign the contract now?

or

Everyone *signs* the contract.

FUTURE TENSE: Ms. Jameson *will sign* after she has consulted her attorney.

Usually the choice of tense is logical and gives writers few problems.

The *mood* of a verb, however, is a little more confusing than its tense. Three moods are possible: indicative (states a fact or asks a question), imperative (a command or request), and subjunctive (a condition contrary to fact). The subjunctive mood causes the most trouble, although we often use it without realizing it:

If I *were* you, I would double-check those vouchers. [condition contrary to fact]

The most common use of the subjunctive is to follow certain verbs such *as recommend, suggest*, and *require*:

I recommend that the company *depreciate* the dump truck over five years.

I suggest that he *meet* with the sales representative next week to discuss the lost orders.

The IRS requires that our client *include* that income in this year's return.

One common problem is an unnecessary shift in tense or mood:

TENSE SHIFT:	Sales *dropp*ed by 20 percent last year. That drop *is* the result of increased competition. [Shift from past to present tense.]
REVISED:	Sales dropped by 20 percent last year. That drop was the result of increased competition.
MOOD SHIFT:	We *must credit* Cash to account for the purchase of the computer paper. Then *debit* Office Supplies. [Shift from indicative to imperative mood.]
REVISED:	We must credit Cash to account for the computer paper purchase and then debit Office Supplies.
MOOD SHIFT:	If we *increase* inventory, we *would service* orders more quickly. [Shift from indicative to subjunctive.]
REVISED:	If we increase inventory, we will service orders more quickly.
or	
	If we increased inventory, we would service orders more quickly.
MOOD SHIFT:	If we *changed* our credit policy, we *will attract* more customers. (Shift from subjunctive to indicative.)
REVISED:	If we changed our credit policy, we would attract more customers.
or	
	If we change our credit policy, we will attract more customers.

Subject-Verb Agreement

Another major problem with verbs is subject-verb agreement. A verb should agree with its subject in number. That is, singular subjects take singular verbs; plural subjects take plural verbs. Note that singular verbs in the present tense usually end in *s*:

That [one] *sales prospect* looks promising.
Those [two or more] *sales prospects* look promising.

Some irregular verbs (*to be, to have*, etc.) look different, but you will probably recognize singular and plural forms:

Ms. Jones's investment *is profitable*.
Ms. Jones's investments *are profitable*.
The Drastic Measures *Corporation has* five frantic accountants on its staff.
Some *corporations have* enough accountants to handle the work load efficiently.

There are a few difficulties with this rule. First, some singular subjects are often thought of as plural. *Each, every, either, neither, one, everybody*, and *anyone* take singular verbs:

Each of the divisions *is* responsible for maintaining accounting records.

Second, sometimes phrases coming between the subject and the verb make agreement tricky:

The *procedure* used today by most large companies breaking into international markets *is explained* in this article.

Finally, two or more subjects joined by *and* take a plural verb. When subjects are joined by *or*, the verb agrees with the subject closest to it:

Either *Company A or Company B is planning* to issue new stocks.
Either the *controller or the managers have called* this meeting.

PROBLEMS WITH PRONOUNS

Two common problems with pronouns are agreement and reference. Understanding agreement is easy: A pronoun must agree with its antecedent (the word it stands for). Thus, singular antecedents take singular pronouns and plural antecedents take plural pronouns:

Eric dropped *his* computer on the floor.
Each *department* is responsible for the maintenance on *its* equipment.

This rule usually gives trouble only with particular words. Note that *company, corporation, firm, management*, and *board* are singular; therefore, they take singular pronouns.

The *company* increased *its* net income by 20 percent. [Not *company . . . their.*]

The Financial Accounting Standards *Board* discussed accounting for leases in *its* Statement No. 13. [Not *Board . . . their.*]

Management issued *its* quarterly report. [But: The *managers* issued *their* report.]

The second problem with pronouns is vague, ambiguous, or broad reference. The pronouns that give the most trouble are *that, which*, and *it*. This problem was discussed in chapter 4, but here are some additional examples:

FAULTY REFERENCE: Although our bottling machines were purchased last year, this year's revenue depends on them. *This* associates the true cost with this year's revenues.

REVISED (one possibility): Although our bottling machines were purchased last year, this year's revenue depends on them. To associate the true cost with this year's revenue, we must apply the matching principle.

FAULTY REFERENCE: Adjusting entries are needed to show that expenses have been incurred, but that they have not been paid. *This* is a very important step.

REVISED: Adjusting entries are needed to show that expenses have been incurred but have not been paid. Making these adjusting entries is a very important step.

Although agreement and reference cause writers the most problems with pronouns, occasionally other questions arise.

One of these questions is the use of first and second person, which some people have been taught to avoid. In the discussion of tone in chapter 4 we saw how the use of these personal pronouns can often contribute to an effective writing style for many documents. Personal pronouns are not usually appropriate, however, in formal documents, such as some reports and contracts.

There are a few other cautions about the use of personal pronouns. First, use first person singular pronouns (*I, me, my,* and *mine*) sparingly to avoid writing that sounds self-centered. The second problem to avoid is using *you* in a broad sense to mean people in general, or as a substitute for another pronoun:

INCORRECT: I don't want to file my income tax return late because the IRS will fine *you*.

REVISED: I don't want to file my income tax return late because the IRS will fine me.

Pronouns and Gender

In English, there are no singular personal pronouns that refer to an antecedent that could be either masculine or feminine. Until about a generation ago, the masculine pronouns (*he, him, his*) were understood to stand for either gender:

Each *taxpayer* must file *his* tax forms by April 15.

Sentences like this one were common even though the pronoun's antecedent (in this case, *taxpayer*) could be either male or female.

Most people today believe that this older pronoun usage is no longer appropriate. They prefer the use of language that doesn't indicate gender, including pronouns that are gender neutral, unless, of course, the antecedent is clearly male or female:

The *controller* of Marvelous Corporation was pleased with *his* company's financial statements. [The controller is a man.]

or

The *controller* of Marvelous Corporation was pleased with *her* company's financial statements. [The controller is a woman.]

When the pronoun's antecedent is not clearly male or female, many people write sentences like these:

Each *taxpayer* must file *his or her* tax forms by April 15.
Each *taxpayer* must file *his/her* tax forms by April 15.

Unfortunately, the *he or she* and *he/she* constructions can be awkward, especially if several occur in the same sentence:

Each *taxpayer* must file *his or her* tax forms by April 15 unless *he or she* has filed for an extension.

What is the solution? The best approach for most sentences is to use plural nouns and pronouns:

Taxpayers must file *their* tax forms by April 15 unless *they* have filed for a extension.

For some sentences, though, you won't be able to use plurals. In these situations, some writers use gendered pronouns arbitrarily and switch often; sometimes they use a feminine pronoun and sometimes a masculine one. Whatever approach you use to avoid gender bias in your use of pronouns, keep these guidelines in mind:

- Most of today's business publications use language that avoids a gender bias, including a careful use of pronouns. If you use the older style, your writing will seem outdated.
- Some of your readers will be annoyed by a choice of pronouns that seems to be gender-biased.
- Perhaps the most important guideline is to write what your readers expect.

PROBLEMS WITH MODIFIERS

Chapter 4 discussed the two main problems that can occur with modifiers: misplaced modifiers, which occur when the modifier is not placed next to the word it describes, and dangling modifiers, which do not modify any word in the sentence:

MISPLACED MODIFIER:	We only shipped five orders last week. [*Only* is misplaced. It should be next to the word or phrase it modifies.]
REVISED:	We shipped only five orders last week.

DANGLING MODIFIER: When preparing financial statements, GAAP must be adhered to.

REVISED: When preparing financial statements, we must adhere to GAAP.

The best guideline for using modifiers correctly is to place them next to the word or phrase they describe. For a further discussion of problems with modifiers and additional examples, see chapter 4.

PARALLEL STRUCTURE

Parallel sentence elements are those that are grammatically equal (nouns, phrases, clauses, etc.). When these items appear in a list or a compound structure, they should be balanced, or parallel. Nouns should not be matched with clauses, for example, nor should sentences be matched with phrases:

STRUCTURE NOT PARALLEL: This report will discuss the computer's features, how much it costs, and its disadvantages. [This sentence combines a noun, a dependent clause, and another noun.]

REVISED: This report will discuss the computer's features, cost, and disadvantages.

STRUCTURE NOT PARALLEL: We recommend the following procedures:

- Hire a consultant to help us determine our needs. [verb phrase]
- Investigate alternative makes and models of equipment. [verb phrase]
- We should then set up a pilot program to assess retraining needs for employees who will use the new equipment. [sentence]

REVISED: We recommend the following procedures:

- Hire a consultant to help us determine our needs. [verb phrase]
- Investigate alternative makes and models of equipment. [verb phrase]
- Set up a pilot program to assess retraining needs for employees who will use the new equipment. [verb phrase]

APOSTROPHES AND PLURALS

The rules for apostrophes and plurals are quite simple, but many people get them confused.

Most plurals are formed by adding either *s* or *es* to the end of the word. If you are unsure of a plural spelling, consult a dictionary.

With one exception, apostrophes are never used to form plurals. Apostrophes are used to show possession. For singular words the form is *'s*. For plural words the apostrophe comes after the *s*:

singular	**plural**
client's file	clients' files
statement's format	users' needs
business's budget	businesses' budgets

A common mistake is *stockholder's equity*. When stockholder(s) is plural (it usually is), the apostrophe comes after the *s*: *stockholders' equity*.

There is one exception to the plural-apostrophe rule. The plurals of letters can be formed with *'s*:

Cross your *t*'s and dot your *i*'s.

Often a phrase requiring an apostrophe can be rewritten using *of* or its equivalent:

the company's statements [the statements of the company]
the month's income [the income of the month]
a week's work [the work of a week]
the year's total [the total for the year]

Either of these possessive forms is correct, but remember the caution given in chapter 4 about using too many prepositional phrases in a sentence. The result can be awkward or wordy.

Finally, note these possessive plurals:

two companies' statements
five months' income
three weeks' work
prior years' statements
ten years' total

Ten years' total might also be written *ten-year total*, but analyze the difference in meaning between *ten-year total* and *ten years' totals*.

Finally, some writers confuse *it's* with *its*. *It's* is a contraction of *it is*; *its* is the possessive pronoun:

It's important to make careful estimates of warranty obligations.
The company issued its statements.

COMMAS

Commas are important because they can make sentences easier to understand. Lack of a comma makes the meaning of this sentence ambiguous:

I wouldn't worry because you appear to have a thriving business.

Adding a comma clears up the confusion:

I wouldn't worry, because you appear to have a thriving business.

Comma Guidesheet

USE COMMAS:

1. before *and, but, or, not, for, so,* and *yet* when these words come between independent clauses.

We sent our client an invoice for our services, and they mailed a check the next day.

Our competitors increased their advertising, but our customers remained loyal.

2. following an introductory adverbial clause.

When investors consider buying stock in a corporation, they are especially interested in the company's cash flows.

Because we sold the property, we must pay a capital gains tax.

Although we worked all night, we didn't finish the report.

3. following transitional expressions and long introductory phrases.

In *Statement of Financial Accounting Standards No. 2* (SFAS No. 2), the FASB defined its position on research and development costs.

To improve the service to our Atlanta customers, we are adding three new sales representatives. However, we still need four more representatives.

4. to separate items in a series (including coordinate adjectives).

Accounting students must be intelligent, dedicated, and conscientious.

The controller, the senior bookkeeper, and the manager of the parts department formulated a new policy.

5. to set off nonrestrictive clauses and phrases (compare rule 4, under *DO NOT USE COMMAS*).

The SEC, which is an agency of the federal government, is concerned with the independence of auditors.

The annual report, which was issued in March, contained shocking news for investors.

The main office, located in Boston, employs 350 people.

6. to set off contrasted elements.

Treasury stock is a capital account, not an asset.

We want to lower our prices, not raise them.

7. to set off parenthetical elements.

Changes in accounting methods, however, must be disclosed in financial statements.

"Our goal," he said, "is to dominate the market."

DO NOT USE COMMAS:

1. to separate the subject from the verb or the verb from its complement.

Incorrect:

Some emerging growth companies, have impressive net income.

Correct:

Some emerging growth companies have impressive net income.

2. to separate compound verbs or objects.

Incorrect:

She wrote angry letters to her CPA, and to her attorney.

Correct:

She wrote angry letters to her CPA and to her attorney.

3. to set off words and short phrases that are not parenthetical.

Incorrect:

Financial transactions are recorded, in journals, in chronological order.

Correct:

Financial transactions are recorded in journals in chronological order.

4. to set off restrictive clauses, phrases, or appositives (compare to rule 5, under *USE COMMAS*)

Incorrect:

An advantage, of computerized tax programs, is the accuracy of the returns.

Correct:

An advantage of computerized tax programs is the accuracy of the returns.

5. before the first item or after the last item of a series (including coordinate adjectives).

Incorrect:

Some asset accounts are noncurrent, such as, land, buildings, and equipment.

[The faulty comma is the one before *land.*]

Correct:

Some asset accounts are noncurrent, such as land, buildings, and equipment.

COLONS AND SEMICOLONS

The rules for colons (:) are few and easy to master, although sometimes writers use them incorrectly. Used correctly—and sparingly—colons can be effective because they draw the readers' attention to the material that follows.

Colons can be used in the following situations:

1. to introduce a series.

Three new CPA firms have located in this area recently: Smith and Harrison, CPAs; Thomas R. Becker and Associates; and Johnson & Baker, CPAs.

2. to introduce a direct quotation, especially a long quotation that is set off from the main body of the text.

The senior partner issued the following instruction: "All audit workpapers should include concise, well-organized memos summarizing any problems revealed by the audit."

3. to emphasize a summary or explanation.

Our study of Sebastian Enterprises has revealed one primary problem: unless management hires new researchers to develop technical innovations, Sebastian will lose its position of market dominance.

4. following the salutation in a business letter.

Dear Mr. Evans:

When a colon introduces a series, an explanation, or a summary, the clause that precedes the colon should be a complete statement:

We have sent engagement letters to the following clients: B and B Conglomerates, Abigail's Catnip Boutique, and Sharkey's Aquarium Supplies.

not

We have sent engagement letters to: B and B Conglomerates, Abigail's Catnip Boutique, and Sharkey's Aquarium Supplies.

Semicolons (;) are used for only two situations: between independent clauses (see page 80) and between items in a series, if the items themselves have internal commas:

> The proposal was signed by Joan Underwood, President; Alice Barret, Vice-President; and Sam Barnes, Treasurer.

DIRECT QUOTATIONS

The punctuation of direct quotations depends on their length. Short quotations (fewer than five typed lines) are usually run in with the text and enclosed with quotation marks. Longer quotations are set off from the text—indented five spaces from the left margin—with no quotation marks. Direct quotations should be formally introduced; a colon may separate the introduction from the quoted material. Study the following examples:

> SFAS No. 14 defines an industry segment as a "component of an enterprise engaged in providing a product or service or a group of related products or services primarily to unaffiliated customers . . . for a profit."[2]

> SFAS No. 14 gives the following definition of an industry segment:

> Industry segment. A component of an enterprise engaged in providing a product or service or a group of related products and services primarily to unaffiliated customers (i.e., customers outside the enterprise) for a profit. By defining an industry segment in terms of products and services that are sold primarily to unaffiliated customers, this Statement does not require the disaggregation of the vertically integrated operations of an enterprise.[3]

A direct quotation requires a citation identifying its source. It's also better to identify briefly the source of a quotation within the text itself, as the preceding examples illustrate. If a quotation comes from an individual, use his or her complete name the first time you quote from this person. You may also need to give the title or position of the person you are quoting, or otherwise explain that person's credentials. Study the following examples:

> According to Richard Smith, an executive officer of the Fairways Corporation, "The industry faces an exciting challenge in meeting foreign competition."

> Elaine Howard, who supervised the market research for the new product, provided this assessment of its sales potential: "Within five months from the product's introduction into the market, we expect sales to approach 500,000 units."

Notice the placement of punctuation in relation to quotation marks:

- Inside quotation marks:
  period *quotation.*"
  comma *quotation,*"
- Outside quotation marks:
  colon *quotation*":
  semicolon *quotation*";
- Inside or outside quotation marks:
  question mark ?" or "?
  —depending on whether the question mark is part of the original quotation:

Mr. Misel asked, "Where is the file of our new client?"
Did Mr. Misel say, "I have lost the file of our new client"?

One final remark: Sometimes writers depend too heavily on direct quotation. It's usually better to paraphrase—to express someone else's ideas in your own words—unless precise quotation would be an advantage. As a rule, no more than 10 percent of a paper should be direct quotation. To be most effective, quotations should be used sparingly, and then only for authoritative support or dramatic effect.

Chapter 7, which discusses research papers, gives more information on the use of sources, including direct quotations and paraphrases.

SPELLING

Finished, revised writing should be entirely free of misspelled words. When you work at a word processor, use a spell-check program to catch misspelled words and typographical errors. Note that a spell-check program will not distinguish between homonyms such as *affect* and *effect* or *their* and *there*. If you are writing without a word processor, keep a dictionary on your desk and use it if you have any doubt about a word's spelling.

Spelling: Always check every word!

The following short list contains words commonly misspelled or misused by accountants:

accrual, accrued
advise/advice
affect/effect
cost/costs, consist/consists, risk/risks
led, misled
occurred, occurring, occurrence
principal/principle
receivable, receive
separate, separately

The italicized words in the following sentences are often confused:

Please *advise* us about the status of our account. [*Advise* is a verb.]
We appreciate your *advice*. [*Advice* is a noun.]

This change in accounting policy will not *affect* the financial statements. [*Affect* is usually a verb but in the social and cognitive sciences, it can be used as a noun meaning *emotion* or *mood*.]
This change in accounting policy will have no *effect* on the financial statements. [*Effect* is usually a noun. Rarely, *effect* is a verb meaning to cause to happen.]

The *cost* of the truck fleet is more than we expected. [*Cost* is singular.]
The *costs* to manufacture this part are not recorded correctly. [*Costs* is plural, but when you say the word aloud, you can't hear the final *s*.]

The ambiguous footnote may *mislead* investors. [*Mislead* is present or future tense.]
This ambiguous footnote *misled* investors. [*Misled* is past tense.]

How should we record the *principal* of this bond investment?
This procedure does not follow generally accepted accounting *principles*.

HELP FROM THE COMPUTER

Some writers check their text for grammatical errors by using grammar-check software. These programs can help you identify some problems with grammar, including errors with verbs, pronouns, and punctuation. Like programs that analyze writing style, these computer aids may not catch all your grammatical errors, and they may flag as an error a usage that is indeed correct. Thus, the decision to use grammar checkers to review your text is a matter of personal experience and preference: some excellent writers praise them highly, but others find them of limited use.

A word processor with a good spell-check program is another matter. As we've pointed out many times, it is much easier to make corrections when you use a word processor. Spell-check programs are also a tremendous help in correcting spelling and typographical errors.

A final word: Be sure to proofread the final hard copy of your document for errors you may have missed earlier, whether you or someone else has done the actual keyboarding. Computers aren't foolproof; sometimes what appears on the screen doesn't look the same on a printed page. Any errors, including those caused by the computer or printer, make work look sloppy and the writer seem careless. Effective writing should look professional: correct, neat, and polished.

In summary, standard English—including correct grammar, punctuation, and spelling—is essential for polished, professional writing. Don't just guess about the correct usage. Resolve your uncertainties with a grammar handbook, dictionary, spell checker, or grammar-check computer program. Remember the needs of your readers. The use of standard English is necessary for smooth, clear reading.

This chapter has given us another guideline for effective writing; we now have 17.

1. **Analyze the purpose of the writing and the needs and expectations of the readers.**
2. **Organize your ideas so that readers will find them easy to follow.**
3. **Write the draft and then revise it to make the writing polished and correct.**
4. **Make the writing unified. All sentences should relate to the main idea, either directly or indirectly. Eliminate digressions and irrelevant detail.**
5. **Use summary sentences and transitions to make your writing coherent.**
6. **Write in short paragraphs that begin with clear topic sentences.**
7. **Develop paragraphs by illustration, definition, detail, and appeals to authority.**
8. **Be concise—make every word count.**
9. **Keep it simple—use simple vocabulary and short sentences.**
10. **Write with active verbs and descriptive nouns.**
11. **Use jargon only when your readers understand it. Define technical terms when necessary.**
12. **Be precise—avoid ambiguous and unclear writing.**
13. **Be concrete and specific. Use facts, details, and examples.**
14. **Use active voice for most sentences.**
15. **Vary vocabulary, sentence lengths, and sentence structures. Read the writing aloud to hear how it sounds.**
16. **Write from the reader's point of view. Use tone to show courtesy and respect.**
17. **Proofread for grammar, punctuation, spelling, and typographical errors.**

TEST YOURSELF

Identify and correct the errors in the following exercises, using the guidelines discussed in this chapter. Answers are provided on pages 97–98.

a. Identify and correct fragments, comma splices, or fused sentences. Some sentences are correct.

1. The tax laws for capital gains have changed, therefore, we should reassess our investment plans.
2. Honeybees Honey Supplies Corporation must not only improve its internal control system it must also review its procedures for accounts receivable.

3. Many types of users rely on financial statement information, for example, investors may use the information to decide whether to purchase stock in the company.
4. Physical volume is one factor that affects cost behavior; other factors include efficiency, changes in technology, and unit prices of inputs.
5. In spite of the uncertain outlook for the economy, however, we project that our sales will increase this year by at least 50 percent.

b. Some of these sentences have verb errors (subject-verb agreement or shifts in tense or mood). Identify these errors and correct the sentences.

1. In times of inflation, changes in the general purchasing power of the dollar forces accountants to deal with an unstable monetary unit.
2. If we change our marketing strategy, we would attract more customers.
3. Neither the president nor the supervisors understand the new tax laws.
4. One problem we found in our reviews of the records were that revenues were not always recorded in the proper period.
5. A statement with supplementary disclosures provide additional information to investors.

c. Correct any pronoun errors you find in the following sentences.

1. When an investor or creditor wishes to compare two companies, they cannot always rely on the historical cost statements for the comparison.
2. We should alert the company that they may be required to pay additional taxes.
3. The FASB deals with research and development costs in their Statement of Financial Accounting Standards No. 2.
4. Management is interested in improving the revenue figures for their report to the stockholders.
5. Each auditor is required to keep detailed records of their work on the audit.

d. Revise the following sentence for parallel structure.

We recommend the following improvements in your system of internal controls:

- The controls over cash should be strengthened.
- An accounting manual to ensure that transactions are handled uniformly.
- Improved documentation of accounting procedures.

e. Punctuate the following sentences correctly.

1. When the financial statements were issued in March the company showed a net loss of $5,000,000.
2. To increase the revenues from its new muffin products the Muffet Muffin Company introduced an advertising campaign in New York Chicago and Los Angeles.
3. The biggest problem in our firm however is obsolete inventories.

4. We currently value our inventories according to LIFO not FIFO.
5. We might suggest to the controller that he consider the FASB's *Statement No. 13* which deals with leases.

TEST YOURSELF: ANSWERS

(Note: Some of the errors can be corrected in more than one way. For most sentences, this key will show only one possible correction. If you recognize the error, you probably understand how to correct it.)

a.

1. The tax laws for capital gains have changed; therefore, we should reassess our investment plans.

   or

   The tax laws for capital gains have changed. Therefore, we should reassess our investment plans.
2. Fused sentence. Correction:

   Honeybees Honey Supplies Corporation must not only improve its internal control system; it must also review its procedures for accounts receivable.
3. Comma splice. Correction:

   Many types of users rely on financial statement information; for example, investors may use the information to decide whether to purchase stock in the company.
4. Correct.
5. Correct. [*However* doesn't come between two independent clauses in this sentence.]

b.

1. Subject-verb agreement. Correction:

   In times of inflation, changes in the general purchasing power of the dollar force accountants to deal with an unstable monetary unit. [The verb should agree with the subject *changes*.]
2. Mood shift. Correction:

   If we changed our marketing strategy, we would attract more customers.

   or

   If we change our marketing strategy, we will attract more customers. [The original sentence contained a shift in mood from indicative to subjunctive. Either mood is correct here; the key is to be consistent.]
3. Correct.
4. Subject-verb agreement. Correction:

   One problem we found in our reviews of the records was that revenues were not always recorded in the proper period. (The verb should agree with *problem*.)

5. Subject-verb agreement. Correction:

   A statement with supplementary disclosures provides additional information to investors. [The verb should agree with *statement.*]

c.

1. When investors or creditors wish to compare two companies, they cannot always rely on the historical cost statements for the comparison. [Alternative: *investor or creditor/he or she.*]
2. We should alert the company that it may be required to pay additional taxes.
3. The FASB deals with research and development costs in its *Statement of Financial Accounting Standards No. 2.*
4. Management is interested in improving the revenue figures for its report to the stockholders.
5. The auditors are required to keep detailed records of their work on the audit. [Alternative: *each auditor/his or her.*]

d.

We recommend the following improvements in your system of internal controls:

- stronger controls over cash
- an accounting manual to ensure that transactions are handled uniformly
- improved documentation of accounting procedures

e.

1. When the financial statements were issued in March, the company showed a net loss of $5,000,000.
2. To increase the revenues from its new muffin products, the Muffet Muffin Company introduced an advertising campaign in New York, Chicago, and Los Angeles.
3. The biggest problem in our firm, however, is obsolete inventories.
4. We currently value our inventories according to LIFO, not FIFO.
5. We might suggest to the controller that he consider the FASB's *Statement No. 13*, which deals with leases.

EXERCISES

Exercise 5–1

Join the independent clauses together in three ways.

the CPA profession is undergoing rapid change

changing technology is a major reason

Exercise 5–2

Identify and correct fragments, comma splices, or fused sentences. Some sentences are correct.

1. The accounting department had added several new employees, therefore, we had a training session.
2. To increase employee satisfaction; therefore, we tried a new system of promotion.
3. However, not all committee members agreed with the president.
4. Tax season is our busiest time of the year everyone works long hours.
5. Because everyone worked extra hours, we were able to finish on time.
6. Although, the new equipment has improved our rate of production.
7. The reason for our low inventory turnover being that this is our slow season.
8. My new computer is much faster than the old one, therefore, I will complete the report on time.
9. Historical cost usually results from arms'-length transactions and therefore provides reliable measures of transactions.
10. Although the consultant reviewed the recommendations at some length, five staff members still didn't understand what would be involved.

Exercise 5–3

Some of these sentences have verb errors (subject-verb agreement or shifts in tense or mood). Identify these errors and correct the sentences.

1. If we hired a systems specialist, we will be able to design a new system.
2. Either the auditors or the controller is responsible for this report.
3. One of our biggest successes during recent years are the number of models we offer.
4. Selling some of the stocks results in realized holding gains.
5. Each of these statements is prepared according to GAAP.
6. Neither John nor Elena is participating in this audit.
7. We will depreciate this asset over ten years. First, however, determine its salvage value.
8. The future benefits provided by the bond is partly due to its high interest rate.
9. Restating asset values to market value results in unrealized holding gains and losses.
10. We review the client's system of internal control. Then we will recommend ways to improve it.

Exercise 5–4

Correct any faulty pronouns you find in the following sentences.

1. According to the IRS, each taxpayer must sign his tax form when he files his income tax return.

2. Hamilton Exports increased their revenues last year.
3. Three new procedures were used to improve the internal control system. This was the responsibility of Nancy Copeland.
4. A switch to stocks usually results in a higher return over a long period of time; this would be important to our company.
5. I find the new tax forms confusing because you have so much trouble understanding them.
6. Dell's Delights has greatly increased it's advertising expense.
7. Although accountants may use one method for financial accounting purposes, they may legitimately use a different method for tax purposes.
8. The Board of Directors will hold its next meeting in July.
9. Every corporation coming under SEC regulations must follow certain procedures in preparing their financial statements.
10. Everyone registering for the convention will receive a package of information when they arrive.

Exercise 5–5

Revise the following sentences for parallel structure.

1. Three people attended the July meeting:
   - the internal auditor
   - the manager of the marketing department
   - the president also attended
2. This committee will study the problem, a recommendation for correcting it, and oversee the correction procedures.
3. The hiring decisions will be based on three criteria: experience, training, and whether the applicants have good communication skills.

Exercise 5–6

a. Complete the following chart.

SINGULAR	SINGULAR POSSESSIVE	PLURAL	PLURAL POSSESSIVE
liability			
statement			
corporation			
user			
revenue			
risk			
CPA			
year			
industry			
equity			

b. Use the words from the chart to fill in these sentences. The singular form of the correct word is given in the parentheses.

1. (CPA) ______________ from all over the country will be at the convention.
2. (corporation) Investors examine a ______________ statements to determine its financial condition.
3. (revenue) Record all these ______________ in the proper accounts.
4. (statement) Which of the ______________ is in error?
5. (liability) What will be our estimated ______________ this year under the warranty?
6. (risk) Investors in these bonds must accept certain ______________ .
7. (industry) Research and development are crucial in many ______________ .
8. (user) Financial statements should provide information for different types of __________.
9. (equity) Management is considering investing in several different __________.
10. (statement) We are making changes in the two ______________ totals.

Exercise 5–7

Punctuate the following sentences correctly.

1. Most companies base asset values on their historical cost however there are exceptions to this rule.
2. To provide this important information to the users of our financial statements we should include supplementary disclosures.
3. The report was filed February 12 1998 in Washington D.C.
4. Before we can issue an opinion on these financial statements we must be sure that this transaction was recorded according to the new FASB standard.
5. The report was signed by the controller the internal auditor and the vice president.
6. The audit revealed several problems in Hudson Hat Company's financial records such as its depreciation policy its handling of bad debts and its inventory accounting.
7. The presidents letter contained the following warning "If our revenues don't increase soon the plant may be forced to close"
8. "We're planning a new sales strategy" the manager wrote in reply.
9. We have decided not to invest in new trucks at this time instead we are considering subcontracting our deliveries.
10. Although our revenues increased during June expenses rose at an alarming rate.

Exercise 5–8

Identify and correct any misspelled words in the following list. Look up any words you are unsure of; not all these words were included in the chapter.

1. believe
2. receive
3. occured
4. seperate

5. accural
6. benefitted
7. existance
8. principle (the rule)
9. cost (plural)
10. mislead (past tense)
11. advise (the noun)
12. effect (the noun)
13. thier
14. intrest
15. trail balance

NOTES

1. Charles R. Brusaw, Gerald J. Alred, and Walter E. Oliu, *The Business Writer's Handbook,* 3rd ed. (New York: St. Martin's Press, 1987), 220.
2. *Statement of Financial Accounting Standards No. 14: Financial Reporting for Segments of a Business Enterprise* (Stamford, Conn.: Financial Accounting Standards Board, 1976), para. 10a. Copyright by Financial Accounting Standards Board, High Ridge Park, Stamford, Connecticut, 06905, U.S.A. Reprinted with permission. Copies of the complete document are available from the FASB.
3. Ibid.

6

Format for Clarity: Document Design

How a document looks at first glance can make a big difference in how the reader reacts to it. An attractive document generally gets a positive response, but a paper that is not pleasing to the eye may never be read. A good design does more for the readers than appeal to them visually. A well-planned format also contributes to the clarity of documents by making them easier to read. Good design will also help you create a document that looks polished and professional, which is the sixth tip for effective writing, as shown in Figure 1–1 on page 5.

This chapter looks at techniques of document design that make letters, memos, and reports more attractive.

Later chapters cover the conventions and formats specific to particular kinds of documents, such as the standard parts of letters, memos, and reports. The techniques covered in this chapter are ones you can use for any kind of document. We consider ways to make documents look professional and attractive, such as the choice of paper and print and the use of white space. We also show how techniques of formatting, such as headings, lists, and graphic illustrations, can make your documents clearer and more readable.

GOOD DESIGN: AN ILLUSTRATION

To illustrate the difference good design can make in the readability of a document, study the example in Figures 6–1 through 6–3, which are three versions of the same memo. Figure 6–1 shows straight text, with no divisions for paragraphs, headings, or other features of good document design. Figure 6–2 divides the text into readable paragraphs with a little more white space; and Figure 6–3 uses additional white space, headings, and a set-off list. Which version of the memo do you think is most effective? Does the version in Figure 6–3 suggest formatting techniques you can use in your own writing?

A PROFESSIONAL APPEARANCE

If you already have a job, you may find models of well-designed documents by looking at papers written by people with whom you work. In fact, your employer may expect all documents to be written a certain way—in a standard format, for example, and on the company's letterhead and standard stock paper. You will seem more professional if you learn your employer's expectations for document design and then adhere to them.

Often, however, whether you're on the job or still in school, you will have a fair amount of leeway in how you design your documents. The remainder of this chapter looks at techniques you can use to give your documents a professional appearance. For example, a professional-looking document uses high-quality material—the best paper and the best print. It incorporates an attractive use of margins and white space, and it is perfectly neat.

Paper and Print

If you're already employed, you may not have any choice about the paper; you probably use your company's letterhead stationery and standard stock for all your documents. If you are still a student, however, you need to select a paper that makes a good impression. For the final copy of a paper you submit for a grade, your instructor may prefer you to use 8 1/2 × 11-inch paper of a high-quality bond, about 24-pound weight, in white or off-white. Never submit a paper printed on the large green-and-white striped computer paper (unless you have your instructor's permission), and never use erasable bond paper.

The print of your document is another consideration. After you prepare your final manuscript on a word processor, print it on a good printer (letter-quality or near-letter-quality) using a good ribbon or cartridge that gives a professional appearance.

FIGURE 6–1 ***Memo for Comparison (see Figures 6–2 and 6–3)***

TO:	Paul J. Streer, Partner
FROM:	Billie Sanders
DATE:	April, 17, 1998
SUBJECT:	Tax implications of Robert Burke's prospective joint purchase of rental real estate.

Our client, Robert Burke, has expressed concern about the tax implications of a venture he is considering, a joint purchase of real estate with Anne Simmons. The issue that must be considered is whether Mr. Burke will be subject to a deduction limitation because the property will be used as a residence by Ms. Simmons. The conclusion is that because the rental agreement is a shared equity financing agreement, Mr. Burke will not be subject to a deduction limitation. On January 1, 1999, Ms. Simmons and Mr. Burke plan to purchase rental real estate, which Ms. Simmons will occupy as her residence. They will enter into an agreement whereby Mr. Burke will provide the downpayment and one-half of the monthly mortgage payment. Ms. Simmons will pay the remaining portion of the monthly mortgage, monthly rental payments to Mr. Burke, and the monthly operating costs of the home. They will split the property taxes evenly. Mr. Burke will receive one-half of the appreciation value of the home upon its sale and has the option to demand that his interest in the property be paid to him after five years. The issue to be settled is whether Mr. Burke is subject to the deduction limitation in 280A(c)(5) because the rental property was used as a residence by the taxpayer. The agreement between Ms. Simmons and Mr. Burke qualifies as a shared equity financing agreement under 280A(d)(3)(C). Because the agreement can be classified as such, 280A(c)(5) will not apply and cannot limit the deductions attributable to the rental of Mr. Burke's share of the property to the gross income derived from the rental. This conclusion was also reached by the IRS in Private Letter Ruling 8410038. To override the limitation of 280A(c)(5), the shared equity financing agreement must meet certain requirements: (1) under 280A(d)(3)(D), both Ms. Simmons and Mr. Burke must have a qualified ownership interest in the property (an undivided interest for more than fifty years in the entire property) and (2) the rent Ms. Simmons pays to Mr. Burke must be the fair rental at the time the agreement is entered, taking into account Ms. Simmons's qualified interest. Because Mr. Burke will be allowed the deductions and Ms. Simmons will not (except for expenses allowable even if the dwelling were not rented), payment of expenses should be the responsibility of Mr. Burke. The agreement can contain a provision that compensates Mr. Burke for this additional encumbrance. If those expenses were paid by Ms. Simmons, the deduction would go unused. The joint purchase Mr. Burke proposes to enter into is sound. The agreement will not have unfavorable tax implications for him if he is careful to follow these recommendations.

FIGURE 6–2 ***Memo for Comparison (see Figures 6–1 and 6–3)***

TO: Paul J. Streer, Partner
FROM: Billie Sanders
DATE: April, 17, 1998
SUBJECT: Tax implications of Robert Burke's prospective joint purchase of rental real estate.

Our client, Robert Burke, has expressed concern about the tax implications of a venture he is considering, a joint purchase of real estate with Anne Simmons. The issue that must be considered is whether Mr. Burke will be subject to a deduction limitation because the property will be used as a residence by Ms. Simmons. The conclusion is that because the rental agreement is a shared equity financing agreement, Mr. Burke will not be subject to a deduction limitation.

On January 1, 1999, Ms. Simmons and Mr. Burke plan to purchase rental real estate, which Ms. Simmons will occupy as her residence. They will enter into an agreement whereby Mr. Burke will provide the downpayment and one-half of the monthly mortgage payment. Ms. Simmons will pay the remaining portion of the monthly mortgage, monthly rental payments to Mr. Burke, and the monthly operating costs of the home. They will split the property taxes evenly. Mr. Burke will receive one-half of the appreciation value of the home upon its sale and has the option to demand that his interest in the property be paid to him after five years.

The issue to be settled is whether Mr. Burke is subject to the deduction limitation in 280A(c)(5) because the rental property was used as a residence by the taxpayer.

The agreement between Ms. Simmons and Mr. Burke qualifies as a shared equity financing agreement under 280A(d)(3)(C). Because the agreement can be classified as such, 280A(c)(5) will not apply and cannot limit the deductions attributable to the rental of Mr. Burke's share of the property to the gross income derived from the rental. This conclusion was also reached by the IRS in Private Letter Ruling 8410038.

To override the limitation of 280A(c)(5), the shared equity financing agreement must meet certain requirements: (1) under

FIGURE 6–2 ***Memo for Comparison (see Figures 6–1 and 6–3) (cont.)***

280A(d)(3)(D), both Ms. Simmons and Mr. Burke must have a qualified ownership interest in the property (an undivided interest for more than fifty years in the entire property) and (2) the rent Ms. Simmons pays to Mr. Burke must be the fair rental at the time the agreement is entered, taking into account Ms. Simmons's qualified interest.

Because Mr. Burke will be allowed the deductions and Ms. Simmons will not (except for expenses allowable even if the dwelling were not rented), payment of expenses should be the responsibility of Mr. Burke. The agreement can contain a provision that compensates Mr. Burke for this additional encumbrance. If those expenses were paid by Ms. Simmons, the deduction would go unused.

The joint purchase Mr. Burke proposes to enter into is sound. The agreement will not have unfavorable tax implications for him if he is careful to follow these recommendations.

Whatever word processor program and printer you use, you will probably have a choice of type sizes and font styles. Choose a 10- or 12-point type size and a standard font such as New Times Roman throughout your document. Your type sizes, fonts, and bullets should be simple and easy to read, but they should not draw attention to themselves, so be conservative in your choices. Never use unusual fonts for business documents.

White Space and Margins

White space is the part of a page that does not have any print. White space includes margins, the space between sections, and the space around graphic illustrations.

A document with visual appeal will have a good balance between print and white space. White space also makes a document easier to read. The space between sections, for example, helps the reader to see the paper's structure.

There are no hard-and-fast rules for margin widths or the number of lines between sections. As a general guideline, plan about a one-inch margin for the sides and bottoms of your papers. The top of the first page should have about a two-inch margin; subsequent pages should have a one-inch margin at the top.

FIGURE 6–3 ***Memo for Comparison (see Figures 6–1 and 6–2)***

TO:	Paul J. Streer, Partner
FROM:	Billie Sanders
DATE:	April, 17, 1998
SUBJECT:	Tax implications of Robert Burke's prospective joint purchase of rental real estate.

Our client, Robert Burke, has expressed concern about the tax implications of a venture he is considering, a joint purchase of real estate with Anne Simmons. The issue that must be considered is whether Mr. Burke will be subject to a deduction limitation because the property will be used as a residence by Ms. Simmons. The conclusion is that because the rental agreement is a shared equity financing agreement, Mr. Burke will not be subject to a deduction limitation.

Client's Situation

On January 1, 1999, Ms. Simmons and Mr. Burke plan to purchase rental real estate, which Ms. Simmons will occupy as her residence. They will enter into an agreement whereby Mr. Burke will provide the downpayment and one-half of the monthly mortgage payment. Ms. Simmons will pay the remaining portion of the monthly mortgage, monthly rental payments to Mr. Burke, and the monthly operating costs of the home. They will split the property taxes evenly. Mr. Burke will receive one-half of the appreciation value of the home upon its sale and has the option to demand that his interest in the property be paid to him after five years.

Tax Issue

The issue to be settled is whether Mr. Burke is subject to the deduction limitation in 280A(c)(5) because the rental property was used as a residence by the taxpayer.

Tax Implications

The agreement between Ms. Simmons and Mr. Burke qualifies as a shared equity financing agreement under 280A(d)(3)(C). Because the agreement can be classified as such, 280A(c)(5) will not apply and cannot limit the deductions

FIGURE 6–3 *Memo for Comparison (see Figures 6–1 and 6–2) (cont.)*

attributable to the rental of Mr. Burke's share of the property to the gross income derived from the rental. This conclusion was also reached by the IRS in Private Letter Ruling 8410038.

Recommendations

To override the limitation of 280A(c)(5), the shared equity financing agreement must meet certain requirements: (1) under 280A(d)(3)(D), both Ms. Simmons and Mr. Burke must have a qualified ownership interest in the property (an undivided interest for more than fifty years in the entire property) and (2) the rent Ms. Simmons pays to Mr. Burke must be the fair rental at the time the agreement is entered, taking into account Ms. Simmons's qualified interest.

Because Mr. Burke will be allowed the deductions and Ms. Simmons will not (except for expenses allowable even if the dwelling were not rented), payment of expenses should be the responsibility of Mr. Burke. The agreement can contain a provision that compensates Mr. Burke for this additional encumbrance. If those expenses were paid by Ms. Simmons, the deduction would go unused.

The joint purchase Mr. Burke proposes to enter into is sound. The agreement will not have unfavorable tax implications for him if he is careful to follow these recommendations.

Leave an extra line space between the sections of your document. A double-spaced page, for example, would have three lines between sections.

For any document that is single-spaced, be sure to double-space between paragraphs.

Neatness Counts!

Sloppy writing suggests sloppy content. Managers do not want to sift through sloppy writing to find the excellent content. Whatever you write, the final copy should be error-free and extremely neat. A word processor, especially one with a spell checker, enables you to find errors and make corrections with ease. Sloppiness in a document is unprofessional and careless.

FORMATTING

Some writers think of the format of their document only in terms of straight text: page after page of print unbroken by headings or other divisions. If you look at almost any professional publication, including this handbook, you will see how various formatting devices, such as headings, lists, and set-off material, make pages more attractive and easier to read.

Headings

For any document longer than about half a page, headings can be used to divide the paper into sections. Headings make a paper less intimidating to readers because the divisions break up the text into smaller chunks. In a sense, headings give readers a chance to pause and catch their breath.

Headings also help the readers by showing them the structure of the paper and what topics it covers. In fact, many readers preview the contents of a document by skimming through it to read the headings. For this reason, headings should be worded so that they indicate the contents of the section to follow. Sometimes headings suggest the main idea of the section, but they should clearly identify the topic discussed. If you look through this book, you will see how headings suggest the content of the chapters. Chapter 1 uses questions for headings, which is a good technique if not overused.

Headings can be broken down into several levels of division. Some headings indicate major sections of a paper and others indicate minor divisions. In other words, a paper may have both headings and subheadings. In this chapter, for example, "A Professional Appearance" indicates a major section of the chapter; "Paper and Print" marks the beginning of a subtopic, because it is just one aspect of a document's appearance. Generally, a short document needs only one heading level, but this rule can vary depending on what you are writing.

The style of the heading (how the heading is placed and printed on the page) varies with the levels of division. Some styles indicate major headings; other styles indicate subheadings. As an example, the major headings may be printed in a boldface font in all capital letters at the left margin, and subheadings may be indented, boldfaced, with only the initial letter of each main word capitalized as follows:

FIRST LEVEL: BOLD FONT, LEFT MARGIN, ALL CAPS

Second Level: Bold Font, Initial Letters Capitalized, Indented

THIRD LEVEL: INDENTED, ITALICIZED

Here is another example of heading styles and the corresponding levels of division:

FIRST LEVEL: CENTERED, ALL CAPS, BOLDFACED

Second Level: Left Margin, Boldfaced

Third Level: Indented, Italicized

Fourth Level: Left Margin, Underlined

If you use fewer than four levels, you may follow this last system of headings, using any of the three styles, as long as they are in descending order. For example, you might use second-level headings for main topics and third-level headings for subtopics. If you are using only one level of headings, any style is acceptable.

It's possible to overuse headings. You would not, for example, put a heading for every paragraph.

Lists and Set-Off Material

Another formatting technique that can make a document easier to read is set-off material, especially lists. Mark each item on the list with a number, a bullet, or some other marker. Double-space before and after the list and between each item. The items may be single- or double-spaced.

Here is an example using bullets:

Your firm should update its systems in these areas:

- Budgets
- Payrolls
- Fixed assets
- Accounts payable
- Accounts receivable

Set-off lists not only improve the appearance of the paper by providing more white space, but they may also be more readable. The following example presents the same information as straight text and in a list format. Which arrangement do you prefer?

Special journals increase our efficiency. They do this by providing a greater division of labor. Also, they cut down on the time needed to post transactions. Finally, they give us quick and easy access to important financial information.

Special journals increase our efficiency because they

- Provide a greater division of labor
- Reduce the time needed to post transactions
- Give us easy access to important financial information

Remember that set-off lists should be written with parallel grammatical structure (see page 87).

Occasionally you will use set-off material for other purposes besides lists. Long direct quotations are set off, and rarely you may set off a sentence or two for emphasis. Chapters 2 through 6 use this technique to emphasize the guidelines for effective writing.

Pagination

The next formatting technique is a simple one, but it's overlooked surprisingly often. For every document longer than one page, be sure to include page numbers. They can be placed at either the top or the bottom of the page, be centered, or be placed in a corner. Begin numbering on page 2.

GRAPHIC ILLUSTRATIONS

Graphic illustrations such as tables, graphs, and flowcharts can make a document more interesting and informative. They may enable you to summarize a great deal of information quickly and help readers identify and remember important ideas.

Tables are an efficient way to summarize numerical data in rows and columns. The consolidated income statement of Pfizer Inc. and subsidiary companies shown in Table 6–1 is an example of a table.

When you use a table, be sure you label the rows and columns, indicate the units of measure you are reporting, and align the figures.

A pie chart shows how a whole is divided into parts, just as a pie is divided into slices. The pie chart in Figure 6–4 shows how the expenses of Gabe's Technologies, Inc., for the fourth quarter of 1998 might be displayed. The circle represents the total expenses, and the slices show the portions for each individual expense.

When you use a pie chart, label the wedges and show what percentages of the whole they represent.

Graphs, which may take several forms, are useful for comparisons. Two of the most common types of graphs are bar graphs and line graphs. Bar graphs compare quantities or amounts. The bar graph in Figure 6–5 shows net sales for the Lands' End company, as presented in Lands' End's 1996 annual report. This graph shows that sales grew at an average compound annual growth rate of 11.4% between 1992 and 1996.

A line graph, which also compares quantities, is helpful for showing trends. A line graph may have a single or multiple lines. The line graph in Figure 6–6 compares the sales performance of Winston's Sports, Inc., as compared with the sales of its two top competitors. This graph shows how sales for the three companies have changed individually over the

TABLE 6–1 Pfizer Inc. and Subsidiary Companies Consolidated Statement of Income

	YEAR ENDED DECEMBER 31		
(MILLIONS, EXCEPT PER SHARE DATA)	**1997**	1996	1995
Net sales	**$12,188**	$11,306	$10,021
Alliance revenue	**316**	—	—
Total revenues	**12,504**	11,306	10,021
Costs and expenses			
Cost of sales	**2,274**	2,176	2,164
Selling, informational and administrative expenses	**4,956**	4,366	3,855
Research and development expenses	**1,928**	1,684	1,442
Other deductions—net	**258**	276	261
Income from continuing operations before provision for taxes on income and minority interests	**3,088**	2,804	2,299
Provision for taxes on income	**865**	869	738
Minority interests	**10**	6	7
Income from continuing operations	**2,213**	1,929	1,554
Discontinued operations—net of taxes on income	—	—	19
Net income	**$ 2,213**	$ 1,929	$ 1,573
Earnings per common share—basic			
Income from continuing operations	**$ 1.76**	$ 1.55	$ 1.26
Discontinued operations—net of taxes on income	—	—	.02
Net income	**$ 1.76**	$ 1.55	$ 1.28
Earnings per common share—diluted			
Income from continuing operations	**$ 1.70**	$ 1.50	$ 1.23
Discontinued operations—net of taxes on income	—	—	.02
Net income	**$ 1.70**	$ 1.50	$ 1.25
Weighted average shares—basic	**1,257**	1,248	1,229
Weighted average shares—diluted	**1,303**	1,288	1,259

See Notes to Consolidated Financial Statements, which are an integral part of these statements.
Source: Pfizer Inc., *1997 Annual Report: Setting the Pace.* New York: Pfizer Inc., p. 41.

FIGURE 6–4 ***Gabe's Technologies, Inc. Expense Distribution, 4th Quarter 1997***

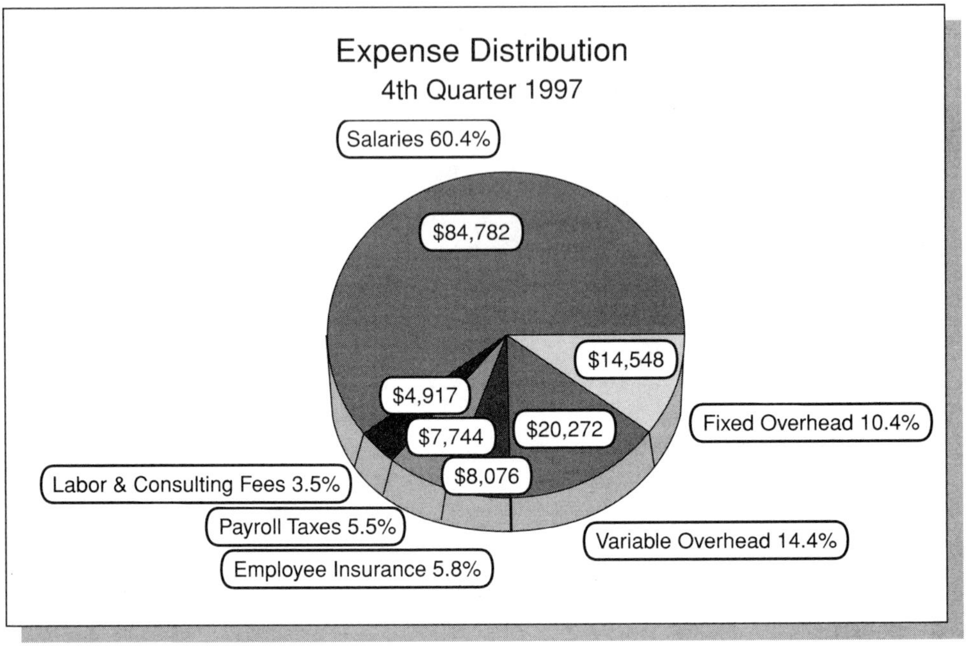

FIGURE 6–5 ***Lands' End's Net Sales***[1]

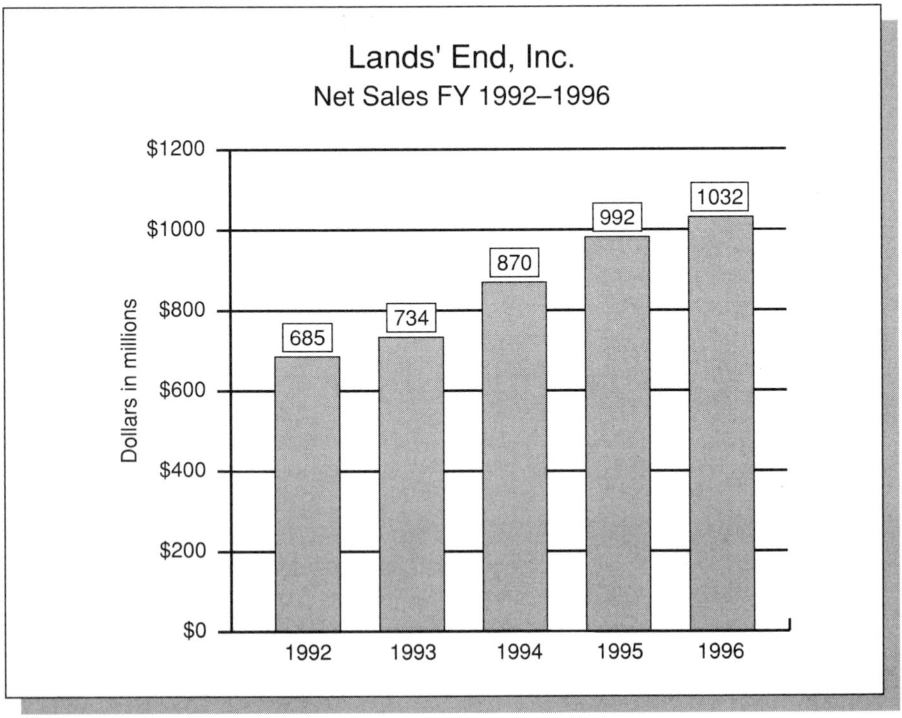

Reprinted with permission of Lands' End, Inc.

FIGURE 6–6 *Winston's Sports, Inc. Sales Comparisons with Competitors, 1993–1998*

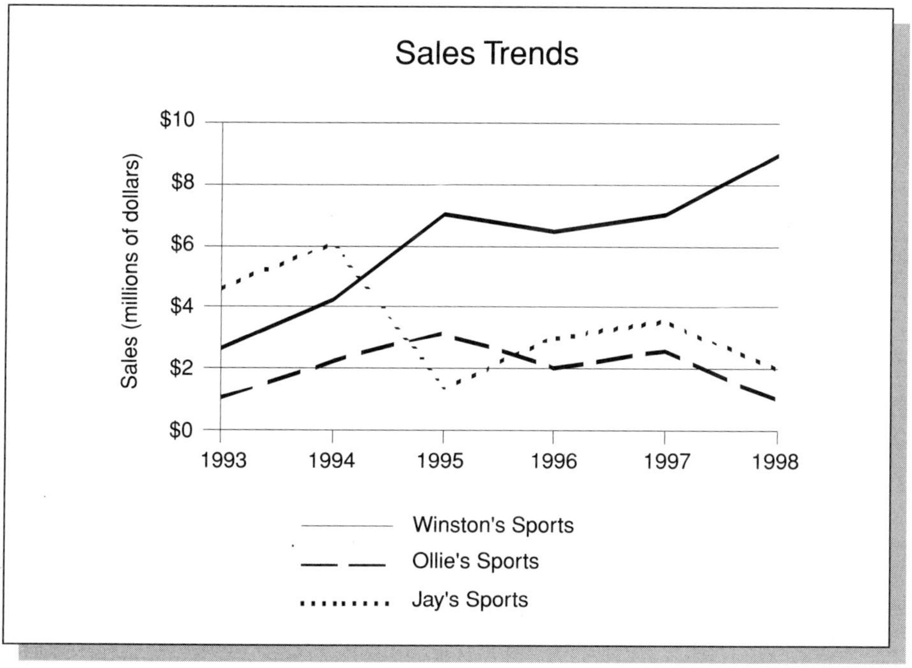

FIGURE 6–7 *The Cash Flow Estimation Process in Capital Budgeting*

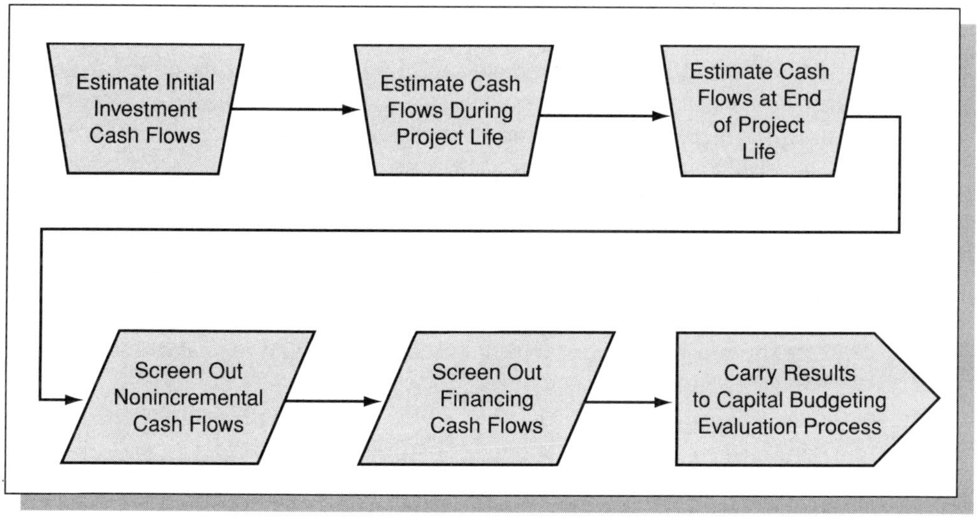

Adapted with permission from Timothy J. Gallagher and Joseph D. Andrew, Jr., *Financial Management: Principles and Practice* (Upper Saddle River, NJ: Prentice-Hall, Inc. © 1996, p. 281).

past five years, and it also makes clear that Winston's sales trend has outstripped that of its competitors.

Another type of graphic illustration is a flowchart, which shows the steps in a process or procedure. Figure 6–7 shows a typical example.

If you use a flowchart in your documents, use boxes or other shapes to show activities or outcomes; label each box or shape and arrange them so that the process flows from left to right and from the top to the bottom of the page. Use arrows to show the direction of the flow.

Systems analyses often include very sophisticated flowcharts to show how a system works, with established symbols and formats to represent different components of the system.

If you include graphic illustrations in the documents you write, whether flowcharts, graphs, or tables, there are certain guidelines to follow. Be sure to number them and give them descriptive titles. Tables should be called Tables (such as *Table 6–1*), and graphs and flowcharts should be called Figures (such as *Figure 6–7*). Graphic illustrations should be labeled sufficiently so that they are self-explanatory, but they should also be discussed in the text of the document. This discussion should refer to the illustration by description, name, and number. The discussion should precede the illustration. The illustrations may be placed either in the body of the document, close to the place in the text where they are discussed, or in an appendix.

Finally, if you use a graphic illustration from another source, identify the source fully at the bottom of the illustration.

DOCUMENT DESIGN AT THE COMPUTER

Many of the formatting techniques we've talked about in this chapter are easily done with a word processor. Word processors make it easy to change margins, arrange set-off materials, add white space, and design headings. In addition, software programs can help you produce graphic illustrations of an excellent quality. Because you can make corrections on the computer to the text just before you print your final draft, you will be able to submit a document that is flawless and professional.

This chapter has completed the guidelines for effective writing.

1. **Analyze the purpose of the writing and the needs and expectations of the readers.**
2. **Organize your ideas so that readers will find them easy to follow.**
3. **Write the draft and then revise it to make the writing polished and correct.**
4. **Make the writing unified. All sentences should relate to the main idea, either directly or indirectly. Eliminate digressions and irrelevant detail.**
5. **Use summary sentences and transitions to make your writing coherent.**

6. **Write in short paragraphs that begin with clear topic sentences.**
7. **Develop paragraphs by illustrations, definition, detail, and appeals to authority.**
8. **Be concise—make every word count.**
9. **Keep it simple—use simple vocabulary and short sentences.**
10. **Write with active verbs and descriptive nouns.**
11. **Use jargon only when your readers understand it. Define technical terms when necessary.**
12. **Be precise—avoid ambiguous and unclear writing.**
13. **Be concrete and specific. Use facts, details, and examples.**
14. **Use active voice for most sentences.**
15. **Vary vocabulary, sentence lengths, and sentence structures. Read the writing aloud to hear how it sounds.**
16. **Write from the reader's point of view. Use tone to show courtesy and respect.**
17. **Proofread for grammar, punctuation, spelling, and typographical errors.**
18. **Use formatting techniques to give your writing clarity and visual appeal.**

EXERCISES

Exercise 6–1

Collect examples of effective and ineffective formatting (personal correspondence as well as professional publications). How could the ineffective documents be improved?

Assume you are the supervisor of your company's accounting department. Write a memo to the staff suggesting ways they might improve the design of the documents they write. Use some of the examples you've found to illustrate your memo.

Exercise 6–2

Choose a paper you've already written on the job or for a class assignment. Revise the paper, using at least two of these techniques:

- Headings
- Set-off lists
- Graphic illustrations
- Improved use of white space

NOTE

1. Lands' End, *1996 Annual Report,* p. 1.

7

Accounting Research

Accountants often engage in research to solve technical accounting or tax problems or to gather information about some more general topic of interest, such as the feasibility of offering a new service to their clients. This chapter discusses how to conduct research and write a research paper or technical memorandum. Much of the material will be review for students or professionals who have written term papers or documented reports. However, the suggestions should be helpful to anyone who must conduct research and write a summary of the results.

The first part of the chapter discusses basic guidelines for all research, including use of electronic and printed sources of information, note taking and use of notes, use of direct quotations and paraphrases, and documentation techniques. The remainder of the chapter focuses on specific steps in the technical accounting research process including determination of relevant facts, identification of issues, researching the literature, identification of alternative solutions, and communication of results.

RESEARCH: BASIC GUIDELINES

If your project requires research, chances are you already know something about the topic. If you don't, or if your memory is vague, you may need to do some initial reading so that you have a basic familiarity with your subject. Once you have a general idea of what your topic involves, you are ready to begin your research in more depth.

One author has had this to say about research:

> Research . . . is the process of obtaining information systematically. That process is deliberate and is conducted carefully and with diligence. Usually, research implies an exhaustive search for and collection of information.[1]

The key here is that good research requires deliberation, care, and diligence. You should look at all possible sources of information so that you won't overlook something important.

Often it's a good idea to write out a research plan before you begin your research. In your research plan you can list known sources of information and references to consult to determine additional resources. For example, let's assume your research topic is "assurance services" and that you are aware that the AICPA has published a report by one of its subcommittees on this topic and, furthermore, that articles have been published in professional journals on assurance services. Initially, your research plan might list the following:

- Check the AICPA Web site to see if the subcommittee report on assurance services is posted. You can also check the Web site for other information on assurance services or links to such information.
- Call the AICPA library to see if it has any additional information.
- Check back issues of the *Journal of Accountancy* for articles.
- Do a keyword search of any electronic literature indexes available at the library for articles or reports during the past two years.
- Do a topical and keyword search of the Web.

As you begin to follow your research plan, you should modify it to include references to other resources you find. Thus, you may add references to specific articles, reports, Web sites, indexes, or searchable databases you find. As you come across specific sources, such as published articles and reports, don't forget to look at the bibliographical, footnote, or endnote references they contain. These will often lead you to useful material you may not otherwise find.

As you conduct your research, you should keep track of what you have done by checking off the steps you listed in your plan. If your research includes a keyword search of an electronic index or database, be sure to keep a log of the keywords and keyword combinations you have used in your search and the results they have obtained. Keeping good records will increase the efficiency of your research because you can avoid duplicating searches; at the same time, you can critique the search process you have followed to determine what you may have missed or how to refine the process.

Electronic Sources of Information

Electronic sources of information include the Internet, on-line databases, and CD-ROM databases. The quantity and availability of these electronic sources, along with the ease and speed with which they may be searched, should place them high on your list of resources for most research.

The Internet One step in your research plan will often be to search the Internet for material related to your topic. You have probably already used a Web browser program such as *Netscape*™ or Microsoft's *Internet Explorer*™ to visit hundreds of popular home pages. Search programs such as Excite™, Infoseek™, Lycos™, Web Crawler™, and Yahoo™, which are accessible with your Web browser, enable you to locate documents ("pages") on the Web. Once you have selected a search program, follow the directions to tailor the search to your needs by using key words or phrases associated with your research topic.

The Internet may lead you to publications available at your library or to documents that you can download to your computer. Read the material you find on the Internet carefully and take accurate notes of your findings, including references to the sources you are using. A later section of this chapter discusses note taking and how to properly indicate references in more detail. It is good practice to print out useful material you may find unless the length of a particular source makes this impractical in which case you should save it on a diskette along with the URL.

Appendix 7–A shows some of the better Web sites available on the Internet that offer information related to accounting and finance, as well as links to other useful sites.

CD-ROM and On-Line Databases Many information databases are available on CD-ROM or on-line. The FASB Accounting Standards and AICPA Professional Standards are both available in this manner. *CCH's Access* and *RIA's OnPoint System* information databases are electronic versions of CCH's *Standard Federal Tax Reports* or RIA's *U.S. Federal Tax Reporter* and *Tax Coordinator*. You can easily search these databases by using keywords and then download and print the results.

Many other databases are available on CD-ROM or on-line. Appendix 7–B contains a list of many of the most useful computerized reference and databases available for accounting and finance research.

Printed Sources of Information

While electronic media can provide excellent sources for your research, it's not a good idea to limit your research to electronic sources, because not everything is available in electronic form as yet. Some research will require conventional library research for printed information sources. When electronic sources are unavailable, you will have to use printed resources.

Even if your library doesn't have specialized electronic databases, it will very likely have the *Infotrac* computer database, which lists articles published in most periodicals, including accounting periodicals. This database may be accessed by keyword search. Be imaginative in looking for articles on your topic; consider the different headings under which articles might be listed.

One step may be to look at official accounting pronouncements, such as those found in *Accounting Standards: Current Text*,[2] or you may need to study government regulations or laws to find out how to handle a client's technical problem. In either case, read the material carefully and take accurate notes of your findings, including references to the sources you use.

Appendix C contains a list of some of the popular printed sources of accounting information. The library will probably have other references you may find helpful. For example, many newspapers, including *The Wall Street Journal*, publish an index. Many of these indices are available both as reference books and as computerized reference services.

A librarian can help you find references that will help you to prepare your paper.

Note Taking

Once you have located a useful source, take notes on what you read. You may decide to do this on a computer, particularly if you have a laptop computer that you can take to the library or keep next to the terminal at which you are conducting an electronic search. Using a computer makes it easy to organize your notes while you make them and then search them later. Any good word processor can be used to take notes, or you may use a database program.

Some people prefer to take notes by hand instead of using a computer. Most of the techniques discussed below apply in either case.

If you take notes by hand, you will need two sets of cards—3 × 5-inch cards for the bibliography and 4 × 6-inch (or 5 × 8-inch) cards for the notes. Using these cards will save time and trouble in the long run, even though they may seem like a bother while you are reading. They will help you keep track of your sources and notes, and they will be easy to use when you write your draft. (If you take notes on a computer, you can use this same principle by creating one file for your notes and another file for your bibiliography.)

Let's look first at a bibliography card, which is illustrated in Figure 7–1.

Be sure to include on the card all the information you will need for your bibliography (see the section on documentation later in this chapter). It's frustrating to make an extra trip to the library just to check on a date or page number.

FIGURE 7–1 *Bibliography Card*

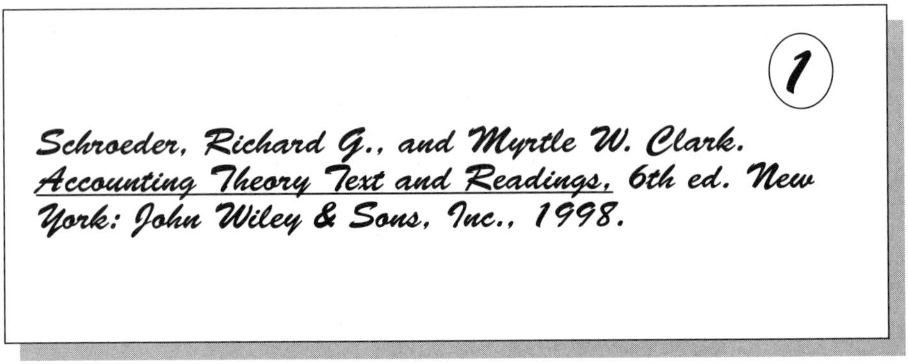
1

Schroeder, Richard G., and Myrtle W. Clark. Accounting Theory Text and Readings, 6th ed. New York: John Wiley & Sons, Inc., 1998.

Note cards contain the information you will actually use in your paper. Notice the parts of the note card in Figure 7–2. The numbers in the upper right-hand corner give the source (from the bibliography card) and the pages or paragraph numbers where this information was found. The heading gives you an idea of what this note card is about. The note itself is taken from the source. It is the material you will use in your paper. The outline code corresponds with the section in your outline where the note fits in.

Direct Quotation and Paraphrase

You can take notes in two ways: as a direct quotation (the exact words from the source) or as a paraphrase (your own words and sentence structures). It may be best to take the notes in your own words if you do not plan to use any direct quotations. If you take the time to paraphrase as you research, you will save time when you write your draft.

Here is a good way to paraphrase. Read a section from your source —perhaps several short paragraphs. Then look away from the page and

FIGURE 7–2 *Note Card*

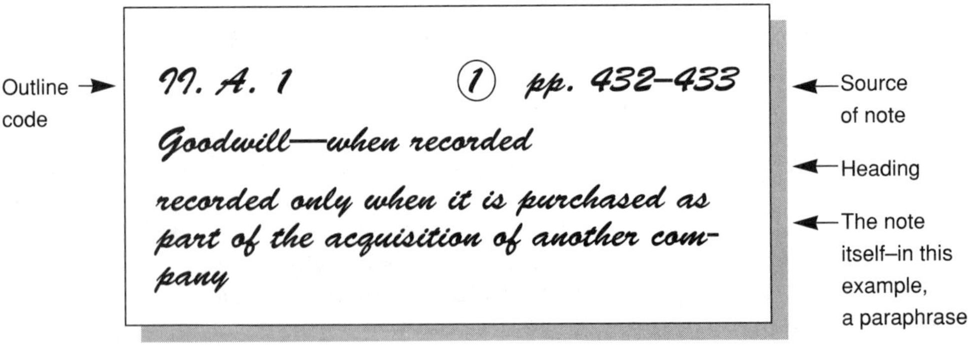

try to remember the important ideas. Write them down. Then your source to check your notes for accuracy.

Occasionally you may want to use a direct quotation. Wh copy a quotation on a note card, use quotation marks so you'll know that these are someone else's words. Copy the quotation exactly, includ ing capitalization and punctuation. It's important that direct quotations be accurate in every way and that paraphrases be your own words and sentence structures, not just a slight variation of your source.

It's also important to give credit for material you borrow from another writer. If you don't, you'll be guilty of plagiarism. The *Prentice Hall Handbook for Writers* contains the following discussion of plagiarism:

> Plagiarism consists of passing off the ideas, opinions, conclusions, facts, words—in short, the intellectual work—of another as our own. . . .
>
> The most obvious kind of plagiarism occurs when you appropriate whole paragraphs or longer passages from another writer for your own paper. . . . No less dishonest is the use of all or most of a single sentence or an apt figure of speech appropriated without acknowledgment from another source.
>
> . . . even though you acknowledge the source in a citation, you are also plagiarizing when you incorporate in your paper faultily paraphrased or summarized passages from another author in which you follow almost exactly the original's sentence patterns and phrasing. Paraphrasing and summarizing require that you fully digest an author's ideas and interpretations and restate them in your own words—and you must reference the source. It is not enough simply to modify the original author's sentences slightly, to change a word here and there.[3]

Plagiarism, therefore, can involve the unacknowledged (undocumented) use of someone else's *idea*—not just the use of the person's exact words.

The key to avoiding plagiarism is to document your sources adequately with either internal documentation or notes (see the section on documentation). In actual practice, however, there may be situations when you will not know whether you should identify the source of information you wish to use in your paper. The difficulty arises because information that is considered common knowledge in a given field need not be documented.

Obviously the problem is to decide what is common knowledge. One guideline says that if you can find the same information in three different sources, that information is considered common knowledge and therefore need not be documented.

There are many gray areas when it comes to issues of plagiarism. Perhaps the safest rule is to document your sources whenever there is any question of possible plagiarism.

Organizing Your Notes and Ideas

As you are taking notes, you will probably form some idea of the major divisions of the paper. That is, you should be getting a rough idea of its outline.

Go ahead and write down your ideas for an outline. The more reading you do, the more complete the outline will become. Stop and evaluate the outline from time to time. Are you covering all the important areas of your topic? Is the outline getting too long? Should you narrow the topic? Are some sections of the outline irrelevant to the topic? Answering these questions will guide you as you continue your research.

Writing Your Research Report or Memo

Once your research is complete, you are ready to begin writing your report or memo. Your first step should be to refine your outline. Be sure that your topic is covered completely and that the ideas are arranged in the most effective order. Think about the introduction and conclusion to your paper, as well as any other relevant parts. For example, do you want to include charts, tables, or graphs?

Next, arrange your notes in the order of the outline and write the appropriate outline code beside each note.

With a completed outline and an orderly arrangement of your notes, you are ready to write the draft of your report or memorandum.

Integrating Notes into Your Writing

The draft of a research paper is written just like that of any other kind of writing, except that you are incorporating notes taken from your sources into your own ideas. If you have already paraphrased the notes, your task is much easier.

Include in your draft an indication of where your notes came from. In other words, you must give credit for words or ideas that are not your own. In the final version of your paper, these references will be footnotes, endnotes, or parenthetical citations. In the draft, you can indicate your sources with a parenthetical notation like this: *([1] p. 403).* The numbers come from your notes and refer to the source and page or paragraph number of each note.

Revising

After you have completed the draft, you will need to revise it to perfect the organization, development, style, grammar, and spelling. It may also be a good idea to have a colleague review your paper and suggest ways in which it can be improved.

Documentation

Any information you get from a source other than your own knowledge must be documented; that is, you must say where you got the information. Styles for documentation vary, but we will look at two of the most common: internal documentation and notes.[4] The format we illustrate for both styles is consistent with *The Chicago Manual of Style*[5] and Kate L. Turabian's *A Manual for Writers of Term Papers, Theses, and Dissertations*.[6] You may want to consult one of these works as you write your paper.

Internal Documentation Many writers prefer to use internal documentation, which places abbreviated information about sources within the text, using parentheses ( ) or brackets [ ], followed by a list of references at the end of the paper. What goes within the parentheses or brackets depends on the kind of source you are using. Appendix 7–D at the end of this chapter gives sample citations and reference list entries for sources typically used by accounting professionals.

It's a good idea to introduce quotations or paraphrases within the text itself:

> According to ARB 43, current assets are "reasonably expected to be realized in cash or sold or consumed during the normal operating cycle of the business" (Ch. 3A, par. 4).

Information you include in the introduction to the quotation or paraphrase need not be repeated within the parentheses. Thus, in this example, *ARB 43* was left out of the parentheses because it was mentioned in the introductory phrase. If readers check the reference list at the end of the paper, they will find

> Committee on Accounting Procedure. 1953. *Accounting research bulletin no. 43* (ARB 43). New York: AICPA.

Note also that the end punctuation for the quotation, in this case the period, comes after the parentheses.

Here's one reminder about the use of technical sources. Consider whether the readers of your paper will be familiar with the literature cited. If they aren't, it's helpful to identify the source more fully and briefly explain its significance.

Endnotes or Footnotes The other style of documentation in wide use is endnotes or footnotes. The difference between these two note forms is that footnotes come at the bottom of the page where the references occur, whereas endnotes come at the end of the paper. Most authorities consider endnotes quite acceptable. If you prefer footnotes, however, your word processor may have the ability to place footnotes on the right pages, in acceptable format. With either endnotes or footnotes, you have the option of adding a bibliography at the end of your paper, listing your sources in alphabetical order.

Appendix 7–E at the end of this chapter gives examples of notes and bibliographical entries for typical accounting sources.

As with internal documentation, you should introduce your paraphrased or quoted material:

> According to an article in *The Wall Street Journal,* many accounting firms find the poor writing skills of their new employees a serious problem.[7]

The introduction to this paraphrase tells generally where the information came from; the note and bibliographical entry give complete information about the source.

Citing Electronic Sources Electronic sources have recently become so important to the research process that the chances are high you will need to cite material that you have found on-line, on CD–ROM, or on the Internet.

An acceptable form of citation for documents available from electronic sources usually resembles the pattern of citations for hard-copy sources, but you will need to provide additional information so that your readers can find the file or document on-line.

It's important to provide the date you accessed the document, because the document may be modified or even removed from on-line availability after you have accessed it. For the same reason, it's also a good idea to print out and keep a hard copy of the document you are citing unless the size of the document makes this impractical.

Electronic sources of information may come from the World Wide Web (www in Web addresses), File Transfer Protocol (FTP) sites, telnet sites, gopher sites, listservs, newsgroups, and e-mail. Examples of citations for sources on the World Wide Web are illustrated in Appendices 7–C and 7–D at the end of this chapter.

TECHNICAL ACCOUNTING RESEARCH

In *An Introduction to Applied Professional Research for Accountants,* Professor David A. Ziebart has this to say about technical accounting research:

> . . . [technical accounting] research . . . is a process, and its result is a defensible solution to the problem or issue at hand. By process we mean a systematic routine of identifying the problem or issue, specifying alternative plausible solutions, conducting an inquiry into the propriety of the alternatives, evaluating the authoritative literature found, making a choice among the alternatives, and communicating the results. Since the solution must be

defensible, the accounting professional must be certain that the search of the professional literature is exhaustive and the reasoning employed in determining the solution is sound.[8]

Technical accounting research is most often done in either financial or tax accounting. The following discussion, which focuses on financial accounting, will give you an idea of the complexity of this kind of research, as well as a strategy you can use when faced with a difficult accounting problem.

Financial Accounting Research

Research in financial accounting is often necessary (particularly in larger accounting firms and industry) because financial transactions may not always be directly covered by generally accepted accounting principles. In other words, you may not always be able to find guidance in published accounting standards that fits a particular transaction or that fairly represents the conditions under which the transaction occurred. When this situation occurs, you must devise an accounting solution that can be defended based on accounting theory and logic found elsewhere in generally accepted accounting principles (GAAP). The following section suggests a procedure you can use for this research.

Steps in the Financial Accounting Research Process

Financial accounting research involves the following steps:

1. Determining the relevant facts.
2. Identifying issues involved.
3. Researching the accounting literature.
4. Identifying alternative solutions and arguments for and against each.
5. Evaluating alternative solutions and choosing the one that can be best defended.
6. Communicating the results of your research to interested parties.

Let's discuss these steps one at a time.

Determining the Relevant Facts Determining the relevant facts is often fairly straightforward. If you realize that research is necessary, you're probably already aware of most of the facts of the transaction. Be sure you have *all* the facts before you begin your research. Do you fully understand the transaction and the conditions under which it was made? If the transaction is supported by a contract or other documents, be sure you have examined them thoroughly. Are there any hidden contingencies, liabilities, or unperformed duties on the part of any of the participants? What was the motivation of the parties to the transaction?

Identifying the Issues Involved It often comes as a surprise to many people that identification of the issues can be one of the more difficult steps in the accounting research process. It's not uncommon for facts (or lack of facts), terminology, and bias of the researcher to obscure some issues rather than to clarify them.

For example, consider the case of a manufacturer of custom machine parts that routinely manufactures more parts than its customers order, expenses the cost of these extra parts as part of cost of goods sold, and physically holds the parts in inventory at a carrying value of zero. If a customer later has an emergency need for another part or two, the parts can be delivered immediately; but this almost never happens, and the additional revenue from sale of these extra parts is of no consequence. The question is whether the manufacturer's method of accounting for this situation is appropriate. What are the issues?

A quick reading of the facts presented may suggest that the issue is whether the cost of manufacturing the extra parts is properly accounted for by expensing it as part of cost of goods sold and carrying the inventory at zero, or whether the cost of the extra parts should be attributed to the inventory. Certainly the questions of inventory valuation and accounting for cost of goods sold will be answered by our research and the conclusions we draw from it. However, the central issue is best stated quite differently.

The basic issue in this case is the nature of the expenditure involved in producing the extra parts. That is, which one of the elements discussed in *Statement of Financial Accounting Concepts No. 6* best describes the expenditure? Does the expenditure result in an asset (not necessarily the physical parts)? Because definitions of the other elements depend on the definition of an asset, this is the question to start with. If an asset has resulted from the expenditure, the type of asset is still in question: Is it inventory, goodwill, or some other intangible asset? If an asset has not been the result, has an expense been incurred? If so, is it appropriate to include it as part of cost of goods sold, or is it some other type of expense? If an expense has not been incurred, it must be accounted for as a loss.

Researching the Accounting Literature Once you have identified the issues, the next step is to research the accounting literature to gather all relevant material. If the issues involve theoretical questions, as probably most will, you should consult relevant parts of the *Statements of Financial Accounting Concepts*. Certainly, Accounting Research Bulletins (ARBs) of the Committee on Accounting Procedure, Opinions of the Accounting Principles Board (APBs), and Statements of Financial Accounting Standards (FASs) should be reviewed to identify Generally Accepted Accounting Principles (GAAP) bearing directly or indirectly on the issues.

Sometimes you may find useful information in GAAP covering an unrelated area. For example, if an issue involves revenue recognition of an entity in the software industry, GAAP covering the music industry or some industry even further removed from the software industry may contain logic or guidance that could serve as a basis for a solution.

It's possible that your research may take you beyond the materials just discussed. Positions of the FASB's Emerging Issues Task Force (EITF) and the AICPA's Accounting Standards Executive Committee (AcSEC) may be useful. Regulations of the Securities and Exchange Commission (SEC), regulations of other federal agencies, accounting books, and articles in accounting journals all may prove useful. SEC regulations may be controlling if the entity involved falls under SEC jurisdiction. On-line and CD-ROM databases such as those listed in Appendix 7–B are good sources for much of this material.

Identify Alternative Solutions and Arguments For and Against Each It's important to realize that if you're engaged in technical accounting research, you're probably dealing with issues for which there are no established solutions. It is up to you to identify all alternative solutions, determine the best solution, and defend that solution against all others.

Evaluate Alternative Solutions and Choose the One That Can Be Best Defended In the end, you must be able to present a well-reasoned defense of your accounting method. Although accounting is not law (except as governed by the SEC), just as a lawyer may prepare a well-reasoned defense of an issue using legal precedent and logic, an accountant doing technical accounting research must use many of the same skills in preparing a defense of a proposed solution to an accounting issue. Indeed, although we all hope it would not occur, it's possible that the solution you choose may have to be defended in a court during some legal proceeding.

Communicate the Results of Your Research to the Interested Parties You will usually communicate the results of your research in a report, letter, or a memo, although occasionally you may report orally as well. However you report your research, incorporate all the elements of effective communication discussed in this book. Audience analysis, precision, clarity, and logical development are particularly important.

EXERCISES

Exercise 7–1

Choose one of the following topics and narrow it if necessary. (For example, you might select "Careers with the Internal Revenue Service" rather than "Careers in Accounting.") Write a documented research paper on your topic, using the steps discussed in this chapter.

- The CPA's future role in assurance services
- The Independence Standards Board
- Harmonization in International Accounting Standards

- Careers in Accounting
- Accounting for Derivatives
- Accounting for Compensatory Stock Options
- The Impact of Technology on the Accounting Profession
- The General Accounting Office (GAO)

Exercise 7–2

Columbia Power Company has entered into several long-term purchase contracts with suppliers of fuel for its power plants. Most of these contracts were for a period of five years. By October 1997, the market price of fuel had plummeted so that contractual price commitments exceeded current market prices and market prices projected through the end of the contracts by $200,000,000. Consequently, Columbia Power booked a $200,000,000 loss in the fourth quarter of 1997 with the following entry:

Estimated Loss on Purchase Commitments	200,000,000	
Estimated Liability for Purchase Commitments		200,000,000

During the first two quarters of 1998, Columbia Power ran into severe cash flow problems unrelated to the purchase commitment problem of the previous year. As a consequence, Columbia found it necessary to file for bankruptcy protection from its creditors.

Columbia's lawyers have determined that in similar situations the bankruptcy court typically will grant relief to the petitioner by reducing its obligations to creditors by 50 percent. There have been many cases in which the court has nullified purchase agreements altogether, arguing that to the extent such contracts are unfulfilled they are executory contracts.

If the court reduced Columbia's obligations to creditors by only 25 percent, the entire $200,000,000 estimated liability for purchase commitments booked the previous year would be eliminated. (None of the originally booked liability has been reduced by payments to suppliers.) In the opinion of Columbia's lawyers, it is highly probable that Columbia will never have to pay any of the estimated liability. Your own CPA firm's legal staff agrees. In fact, in their words "it is inconceivable" that Columbia will have to pay more than current market price for any fuel it has purchased or will purchase after the bankruptcy court has ruled.

Columbia Power wants to eliminate the estimated liability for purchase commitments in its second-quarter financial statements. Should this be permitted? As a member of the CPA firm responsible for auditing Columbia Power's financial statements, you have been asked by your boss, Ms. Susan Chase, to research this technical accounting problem and to prepare a memo recommending what should be done and why.

Exercise 7–3

The President of High Roller Ball Bearing Corporation, a closely held corporation, has directed that the company purchase $1,000 worth of state lottery tickets each week in the company's name. The state holds a lottery every other month. At the fiscal year-end, the company has $6,000 worth of lottery tickets on hand for the lottery to be held the following month. The President wants to show these tickets as a deferred charge.

As High Roller's CPA, would you go along with this? Write a memo to your boss, Mr. John Sampson, recommending what position your firm should take with this client and why.

Exercise 7–4

Your client, Smooth Brew Company, has just purchased a brewery known for the unique taste of its beer. This taste is primarily the result of using sparkling spring water that flows from a particular stream made famous in the brewery's advertisements. The brewery is located on twenty acres at the foot of a large mountain. The famous stream flows down the mountain out of North Carolina and through the brewery's property in Georgia.

Your client paid a high price for these brewing operations—$1 million above the fair market value of the tangible assets acquired. The President of Smooth Brew has made it clear that the main reason he agreed to pay the price is to get access to the special water. Accordingly he has requested that an account entitled "Water" be set up in the balance sheet and valued at $1 million.

As Smooth Brew's CPA, you know your firm will have to take a position on this issue. Should your firm allow the client to account for the $1 million the way it suggests? If not, what will be the position of your firm on how the transaction should be accounted for?

Write a memo to your boss, Ms. Claire Sanders, recommending what position your firm should take with this client and why.

NOTES

1. David A. Ziebart, *An Introduction to Applied Professional Research for Accountants* (Upper Saddle River, N.J.: Prentice Hall, 1998), 2.
2. Financial Accounting Standards Board, *Accounting Standards: Current Text as of June 1, 1994* (Homewood, Ill.: Irwin, 1990), 3.
3. Melinda G. Kramer, Glenn Leggett, and C. David Mead, *Prentice Hall Handbook for Writers,* 12th ed. (Englewood Cliffs, NJ: Prentice Hall, 1995), 503.
4. There are many documentation styles in current use. The sample entries in this chapter illustrate acceptable usage, but you may use another acceptable style as long as you're consistent within each paper.
5. *The Chicago Manual of Style*, 14th ed. Chicago: University of Chicago Press, 1993.

6. Kate L. Turabian, *A Manual for Writers of Term Papers, Theses, and Dissertations*, 6th ed. Chicago: The University of Chicago Press, 1996.
7. Lee Burton, "Take Heart, CPAs: Finally a Story That Doesn't Attack You as Boring," *The Wall Street Journal* (13 May 1987), 33.
8. David. A. Ziebart, *An Introduction to Applied Professional Research for Accountants* (Upper Saddle River, N.J.: Prentice Hall, 1998), 3.

Appendix 7–A

Sources of Accounting and Financial Information on the Internet

Accounting Organizations:	
American Institute of CPAs	http://www.aicpa.org
American Accounting Association	http://www.rutgers.edu/Accounting/raw/aaa
Financial Accounting Standards Board	http://www.fasb.org
Government Accounting Standards Board	http://www.gasb.org
Institute of Management Accountants	http://www. rutgers.edu:80/Accounting/raw/ima/
Business and accounting news network services:	
CNNfn	http://www.cnnfn.com
CNBC	http://www.cnbc.com
Electronicaccountant	http://www.electronicaccountant.com
Business newspapers:	
Barrons	http://www.barrons.com
Financial Times of London	http://www.ft.com
Investors Business Daily	http://www.investors.com
The Wall Street Journal Interactive Edition	http://www.wsj.com

Appendix 7–A: Sources of Accounting and Financial Information on the Internet (cont.)

Business magazines:	
Business Week	http://www.businessweek.com
Fortune Magazine (available at)	http://www.pathfinder.com
Money Magazine (available at)	http://www.pathfinder.com
Worth Magazine	http://www.worth.com
Data on the economy, industries, market indexes, and financial statistics—domestic and foreign:	
Bloomberg Personal Magazine	http://www.bloomberg.com
Briefing.Com	http://www.briefing.com
Data Broadcasting Company	http://www.dbc.com
Dow Jones	http://www.djmarkets.com
International Monetary Fund (IMF)	http://www.imf.org
New York Federal Reserve Bank—exchange rates	http://www.frb.org/pihome/mktrates/forex10.shtml
The World Bank	http://www.worldbank.org
Information about stocks—company performance; corporate financial data, charts, company home pages, etc.:	
AMEX Listed Companies	http://www.amex.com/stocks/stk_txt1.html
Ed Yardeni's Chart Room	http://www.webcom.com/~yardeni/economic.html
EDGAR (available at)	http://www.sec.gov
INVESTools	http://www.investools.com
Morningstar International Stocks On Demand	http://www.investools.com/cgi-bin/Library/msis.pl
NASDAQ Listed Companies	http://www.nasdaq.com/scripts/html3/comlookup.idc?srch=name&contain=0&mkt=nn
NYSE Listed Companies	http://www.nyse.com/public/listings/nglistco.html
Quicken Financial Network	http://www.quicken.com
Quote.com	http://www.quote.com
Stockguide	http://www.stockguide.com/alpha/html
StockMaster	http://www.stockmaster.com
Wall Street Research Net	http://www.wsrn.com
Yahoo Financial Research	http://www.yahoo.com
Information about bonds:	
Bonds Online	http://www.bonds-online.com
Quote.com	http://www.quote.com

Appendix 7–A: Sources of Accounting and Financial Information on the Internet (cont.)

Information about mutual funds:	
Morningstar Mutual Funds On Demand	http://www.investools.com/cgi-bin/Library/msmf.pl
Mutual Fund Cafe	http://www.mfcafe.com
Mutual Funds Interactive	http://www.brill.com
Standard and Poor's Rating Service	http://www.ratings.standard-poor.com/funds
StockMaster	http://www.stockmaster.com
Academic research:	
Financial Economists Network	http://www.SSRN.com
Securities exchanges:	
American Stock Exchange (AMEX)	http://www.amex.com
NASDAQ	http://www.nasdaq.com
New York Stock Exchange (NYSE)	http://www.nyse.com
Government sites:	
Fed World (National Technical Information Service)	http://www.fedworld.gov
General Accounting Office (GAO)	http://www.gao.gov
General Services Administration (GSA)	http://www.info.gov
Internal Revenue Service (IRS)	http://www.irs.ustreas.gov/prod/
Securities and Exchange Commission (SEC)	http://www.sec.gov
Thomas (Legislature)	http://www.thomas.loc.gov
House of Representatives—Tax Laws	http://law.house.gov/109.htm
Links to other organizations, firms, journals, and a wealth of other excellent sites:	
Rutgers Accounting Network	http://www.rutgers.edu/Accounting/raw
International accounting organizations and sites:	
International Accounting Standards Committee	http://www.iasc.org.uk
International Federation of Accountants	http://www.ifac.org
International Organization of Securities Commissions	http://www.iosco.org

Appendix 7–B

Computerized Reference and Database Services

CD-ROM DATABASES

Business Index, by Information Access Co. Contains indexing of more than 800 business and trade journals and selective indexing of 3,000 other magazines and newspapers.

Business Indicators, by Slater Hall Information Products. Includes National Income and Product Accounts from 1929 to present; State Income and Employment data from 1958 to present; and Business Statistics from 1961 to present corresponding to the Survey of Current Business.

Business Source, by EBSCO Information Services. Provides citations and abstracts to articles in about 600 business periodicals and newspapers. Full text is provided from 49 selected periodicals, covering accounting, communications, economics, finance, management, marketing, and other business subjects.

WILSONDISC: Wilson Business Abstracts, by H. W. Wilson Co. Provides CD-ROM "cover-to-cover" abstracting and indexing of over 400 prominent business periodicals. Indexing is from 1982 to present, and abstracting is from 1990 to present.

Appendix 7–B: Computerized Reference and Database Services (cont.)

ON-LINE DATABASES

ABI/INFORM, by UMI/Data Courier. Provides on-line indexing to business-related material occurring in over 900 periodicals from 1971 to the present.

Banking Information Source, by UMI. Provides indexing and abstracting of periodical and other literature from 1982 to date, with weekly updates. Covers the financial services industry, including banks, savings institutions, investment houses, credit unions, insurance companies, and real estate organizations. Emphasis is on marketing and management.

CITIBASE (Citicorp Economic Database), by FAME Software Corp. Presents over 6,000 statistical series relating to business, industry, finance, and economics. Time period is 1947 to date, with daily updates.

Compustat, by Standard and Poor's. Financial data for the most recent 20 years on publicly held U.S. and some foreign corporations.

Disclosure SEC Database, by Disclosure, Inc. Provides information from records filed with the Securities and Exchange Commission by publicly owned corporations, 1977 to present. Updated weekly.

DRI Financial and Credit Statistics, by DRI/McGraw-Hill, Data Products Division. Contains U.S. and international statistical data relating to money markets, interest rates, foreign exchange, banking, and stock and bond indexes.

Economic Literature Index, by the American Economic Association. Covers the worldwide literature of economics as contained in selected monographs and about 400 journals. Subjects include microeconomics, macroeconomics, economic history, inflation, money, credit, finance, accounting theory, trade, natural resource economics, and regional economics.

NAARS, by the American Institute of Certified Public Accountants. National Automated Accounting Research System. Financial statements, authoritative accounting literature, most current five years on-line, 1972 to present off-line.

InvesText, by Thomson Financial Services. Contains full text of investment research reports from more than 300 sources, including leading brokers and investment bankers. Reports from 1982 to date are available on approximately 25,000 U.S. and international corporations. Separate industry reports cover 53 industries.

Source: James Way, ed., *Encyclopedia of Business Information Sources, 1997–98,* 11th ed. (Detroit: Gale Research, 1996), 295–301.

Appendix 7–C

Other Printed Sources of Accounting and Financial Information

Business news, articles, market data; stock, bond, and mutual fund price quotes:

- *Barron's*
- *USA Today*
- *Investor's Business Daily*
- *The Wall Street Journal*

Business news, articles:

- *Business Week*
- *Forbes Magazine*
- *Fortune Magazine*
- *Money Magazine*

Data on the economy and industries; financial and economic statistics:

- *Business Conditions Digest*
- *Economic Report of the President*
- *Federal Reserve Bulletin*
- *Standard & Poor's Industry Surveys*
- *Standard & Poor's Statistical Surveys*
- *Statistical Abstract of the United States*
- *US Industrial Outlook*
- *World Almanac*

Appendix 7–C: Other Printed Sources of Accounting and Financial Information (cont.)

Summary data about industries, companies; advice on industries, stocks; analysis and forecasts:

Standard & Poor's Outlook
Value-Line Investment Survey

Stock information, company performance; corporate financial data:

Annual reports of companies
Moody's Bank & Finance Manual
Moody's Bond Record
Moody's Bond Survey
Moody's Handbook of Common Stocks
Moody's Industrial Manual
Moody's International Manual
Moody's OTC Manual
Moody's Public Utility Manual
Moody's Transportation Manual
Standard & Poor's Corporation Records
Standard & Poor's Stock Reports

Bond information:

Moody's Bond Record
Moody's Bond Survey

Mutual fund information:

Morningstar Mutual Funds
Weisenberger's Management Results
Weisenberger's Current Performance & Dividend Record

Appendix 7–D

Internal Documentation Style

C = Citation within the text
R = Entry in reference list

Book—Single Author
C (Chambers 1966, 12)
R Pacter, P. 1994. *Reporting financial information by segment.* London, UK: International Accounting Standards Committee.

Book—Single Editor
C (Frankel 1994, 64)
R Frankel, J. A., ed. 1994. *The internationalization of equity markets.* Chicago: University of Chicago Press.

Book—Two Authors
C (Gallagher and Andrew 1996, 403)
R Gallagher, Timothy J. and Joseph D. Andrew. 1996. *Financial management: Principles and practice.* Upper Saddle River, N.J.: Prentice Hall.

Book—More than Two Authors
C (Kiger, Loeb, and May 1987, 602)
R Kiger, Jack E., Stephen E. Loeb, and Gordon S. May. 1987. *Principles of accounting,* 2d ed. New York: Random House.

Appendix 7–D: Internal Documentation Style (cont.)

Book—Author is an Association, Institution or Organization

C (AICPA 1993, 2)

R American Institute of Certified Public Accountants (AICPA). 1993. *The information needs of investors and creditors: A report on the AICPA special committee's study of the information needs of today's users of financial reporting, November, 1993.* New York: AICPA.

Article in a Journal—Single Author

C (Schwartz 1996, 20)

R Schwartz, Donald. 1996. The future of financial accounting: Universal standards. *Journal of Accountancy* 181, no. 5 (May): 20–21.

Article in a Journal—Two Authors

C (May and Schneider, 70)

R May, G. S., and D. K. Schneider. 1988. Reporting accounting changes: Are stricter guidelines needed? *Accounting Horizons* 2, no. 3 (September): 68–74.

Article in a Journal—More Than Two Authors

C (Barth, Landsman, and Rendleman, 75)

R Barth, Mary E., Wayne R. Landsman, and Richard J. Rendleman, Jr. 1998. Option pricing–based bond value estimates and a fundamental components approach to account for corporate debt. *Accounting Review* 73, no. 1 (January): 73–102.

Article in a Magazine

C (Blinder 1988, 25)

R Blinder, Alan S. 1988. Dithering on hill is crippling a key agency. *Business Week,* 26 September, 25.

Article in a Newspaper—Author Not Identified

C (*Wall Street Journal,* 16 July 1986)

R *Wall Street Journal*, 16 July 1986, Words count.

Article in a Newspaper—Author Identified

C (May 1987)

R May, Gordon S. 1987. No accounting for poor writers. *Wall Street Journal,* 29 May.

Annual Report for a Corporation

C (Lands' End, Inc. 1996 Annual Report, 12)

R Lands' End, Inc., *1996 annual report Lands' End Direct Merchants,* Dodgeville, Wis.

Appendix 7–D: Internal Documentation Style (cont.)

Primary Source Reprinted in a Secondary Source

C (FASB, *SFAC 1,* par. 3)

R Financial Accounting Standards Board (FASB). 1978. *Objectives of financial reporting by business enterprises, statement of financial accounting concepts no. 1.* Stamford, Conn.: FASB. Reprinted in *Accounting Standards: Original Pronouncements as of June 1, 1998,* Vol. II. New York: John Wiley & Sons, 1998.

Legal Citation

C (*Aaron v. SEC,* 446 U.S. 680, 1980)

R Aaron v. SEC, 446 U.S. 680 (1980).

Internal Revenue Code Section

C (*Internal Revenue Code* Sec. 6111(a))

R *Internal Revenue Code.* Sec. 6111(a).

Government Document

C (SEC 1995, 3)

R United States Securities and Exchange Commission (SEC). 1995. *Self-regulatory organizations; notice of filing and order granting accelerated approval of proposed rule change by the National Association of Securities Dealers, Inc., relating to an interim etension of the OTC Bulletin Board (R) service through September 28, 1995.* Securities Exchange Act Release No. 35918, 60 FR 35443. Washington, D.C. (July 7).

Federal Register

C (61 Fed. Reg. 1996, 208:55264)

R "Revision to NASA FAR supplement coverage on contractor financial management reporting." *Federal Register* 61, no. 208 (25 Oct. 1996): 55264.

World Wide Web

C (Creswell 1997)

R Creswell, Julie. 1997. Stock flow for week declines to just $1 billion. *Wall Street Journal Interactive Edition,* 8 March [on-0 line]. Available from <http://www.wsj.com>; accessed 8 March 1997.

Appendix 7–D: Internal Documentation Style (cont.)

Listserv Message

C (MONEYDAILY, 25 March 1997)

R MONEYDAILY, 25 March 1997, <moneyadm@PATHFINDER.COM>. Fed raises rates/Save on home office equipment. Available from <dailymail@listserv.pathfinder.com>; accessed 25 March 1997.

E-Mail

C (May, 28 March 1998)

R May, Gordon S., 28 March 1998, <gmay@cbacc.cba.uga.edu>. Citation style. E-mail; accessed 29 March, 1998.

More than One Work in Reference List by Same Author or Authors—Different Years

R Lang, M., and R. Lundholm. 1993. Cross-sectional determinants of analyst ratings of corporate disclosures. *Journal of Accounting Research* 31, no. 2 (Autumn): 246–271.

———. 1996. Corporate disclosure policy and analyst behavior. *Accounting Review* 71, no. 4 (October): 467–192.

More than One Work in Reference List by Same Author or Authors—Same Year

C (Frost and Pownall, 1994b, 61)

R Frost, C. A., and G. Pownall. 1994a. Accounting disclosure practices in the United States and United Kingdom. *Journal of Accounting Research* 32, no. 1 (Spring): 75–102.

———. 1994b. A comparison of the stock price response to earnings measures in the United States and the United Kingdom. *Contemporary Accounting Research* 11, no. 1 (Summer): 59–83.

Appendix 7–E

Endnotes or Footnotes and Bibliography Style

N = Endnote or footnote [Endnotes are numbered with full-sized arabic numerals in a Notes section at the end of each chapter. Footnotes are numbered with superscript numerals.]
B = Bibliographical entry

Book—Single Author
N [1]P. Pacter, *Reporting Financial Information by Segment* (London, UK: International Accounting Standards Committee, 1994), 12.
B Pacter, P. 1994. *Reporting Financial Information by Segment.* London, UK: International Accounting Standards Committee, 1994.

Book—Single Editor
N [1]J. A. Frankel, ed., *The Internationalization of Equity Markets* (Chicago: University of Chicago Press, 1994), 64.
B Frankel, J. A., ed. *The Internationalization of Equity Markets.* Chicago: University of Chicago Press, 1994.

Book—Two Authors
N [1]Timothy J. Gallagher and Joseph D. Andrew, *Financial Management: Principles and Practice* (Upper Saddle River, N.J.: Prentice Hall, 1996), 403.
B Gallagher, Timothy J., and Joseph D. Andrew. *Financial Management: Principles and Practice.* Upper Saddle River, N.J.: Prentice Hall, 1996.

Appendix 7–E: Endnotes or Footnotes and Bibliography Style (cont.)

Book—More than Two Authors

N [1]Jack E. Kiger, Stephen E. Loeb, and Gordon S. May, *Principles of Accounting,* 2d ed. (New York: Random House, 1987), 602.

B Kiger, Jack E., Stephen E. Loeb, and Gordon S. May. *Principles of Accounting,* 2d ed. New York: Random House, 1987.

Book—Author is an Association, Institution, or Organization

N [1]American Institute of Certified Public Accountants (AICPA), *The Information Needs of Investors and Creditors: A Report on the AICPA Special Committee's Study of the Information Needs of Today's Users of Financial Reporting, November, 1993.* (New York: AICPA, 1993), 2.

B American Institute of Certified Public Accountants (AICPA). *The Information Needs of Investors and Creditors: A Report on the AICPA Special Committee's Study of the Information Needs of Today's Users of Financial Reporting, November, 1993.* New York: AICPA, 1993.

Article in a Journal—Single Author

N [1]Donald Schwartz, "The Future of Financial Accounting: Universal Standards," *Journal of Accountancy* 181, no. 5 (May 1996): 20.

B Schwartz, Donald, "The Future of Accounting: Universal Standards." *Journal of Accountancy* 181, no. 5 (May 1996): 20–21.

Article in a Journal—Two Authors

N [1]G. S. May and D. K. Schneider, "Reporting Accounting Changes: Are Stricter Guidelines Needed?" *Accounting Horizons* 2, no. 3 (Sept. 1988): 70.

B May, G. S., and D. K. Schneider. "Reporting Accounting Changes: Are Stricter Guidelines Needed?" *Accounting Horizons* 2, no. 3 (Sept. 1988): 68–74.

Article in a Journal—More than Two Authors

N [1]Mary E. Barth, Wayne R. Landsman, and Richard J. Rendleman, Jr., "Option Pricing-Based Bond Value Estimates and a Fundamental Components Approach to Account for Corporate Debt," *Accounting Review* 73, no. 1 (January 1998): 75.

B Barth, Mary E., Wayne R. Landsman, and Richard J. Rendleman, Jr. "Option Pricing-Based Bond Value Estimates and a Fundamental Components Approach to Account for Corporate Debt." *Accounting Review* 73, no. 1 (January 1998): 73–102.

Article in a Magazine

N [1]Alan S. Blinder, "Dithering on Hill is Crippling a Key Agency," *Business Week*, 26 September 1988, 25.

B Blinder, Alan S. "Dithering on Hill is Crippling a Key Agency." *Business Week,* 26 September 1988, 25.

Appendix 7–E: Endnotes or Footnotes and Bibliography Style (cont.)

Article in a Newspaper—Author Not Identified

N [1]*Wall Street Journal,* 16 July 1986, "Words Count."

B *Wall Street Journal,* 16 July 1986. "Words Count."

Article in a Newspaper—Author Identified

N [1]Gordon S. May, "No Accounting for Poor Writers," *The Wall Street Journal,* 29 May 1986, Letters to the Editor.

B May, Gordon S. "No Accounting for Poor Writers." *The Wall Street Journal,* 29 May 1986, Letters to the Editor.

Annual Report for a Corporation

N [1]Lands' End, Inc. 1996 Annual Report, 12.

B Lands' End, Inc. "1996 Annual Report Lands' End Direct Merchants," Dodgeville, Wis.

Primary Source Reprinted in a Secondary Source

N [1]Financial Accounting Standards Board (FASB). *Objectives of Financial Reporting by Business Enterprises, Statement of Financial Accounting Concepts No. 1.* (Stamford, Conn.: FASB, 1978), par. 3; reprinted in *Accounting Standards: Original Pronouncements as of June 1, 1996,* Vol. II. (New York: John Wiley & Sons, 1996), 1005–1020.

B Financial Accounting Standards Board (FASB). *Objectives of Financial Reporting by Business Enterprises, Statement of Financial Accounting Concepts No. 1.* Stamford, Conn.: FASB. Reprinted in *Accounting Standards: Original Pronouncements as of June 1, 1996,* Vol. II, 1005–1020. New York: John Wiley & Sons, 1996.

Legal Citation

N [1]Aaron v. SEC. 446 U.S. 680 (1980).

B Aaron v. SEC. 446 U.S. 680 (1980).

Internal Revenue Code Section

N [1]*Internal Revenue Code* Sec. 6111(a).

B *Internal Revenue Code*. Sec. 6111(a).

Government Document

N [1]United States Securities and Exchange Commission (SEC), *Self-Regulatory Organizations; Notice of Filing and Order Granting Accelerated Approval of Proposed Rule Change by the National Association of Securities Dealers, Inc., Relating to an Interim Extension of the OTC Bulletin Board (R) Service Through September 28, 1995.* Securities Exchange Act Release No. 35918, 60 FR 35443 (7 July 1995): 3.

Appendix 7–E: Endnotes or Footnotes and Bibliography Style (cont.)

B United States Securities and Exchange Commission (SEC). *Self-Regulatory Organizations; Notice of Filing and Order Granting Accelerated Approval of Proposed Rule Change by the National Association of Securities Dealers, Inc., Relating to an Interim Extension of the OTC Bulletin Board (R) Service Through September 28, 1995.* Securities Exchange Act Release No. 35918, 60 FR 35443 (7 July 1995).

Federal Register

N [1]"Revision to NASA FAR Supplement Coverage on Contractor Financial Management Reporting." *Federal Register* 61, no. 208 (25 Oct. 1996): 55264.

B "Revision to NASA FAR Supplement Coverage on Contractor Financial Management Reporting." *Federal Register* 48, no. 208 (25 Oct. 1996): 55264.

World Wide Web

N [1]Julie Creswell, "Stock Flow for Week Declines to Just $1 Billion," *Wall Street Journal Interactive Edition,* (8 March 1997) [on–line]. Available from <http://www.wsj.com>; accessed 8 March 1997.

B Creswell, Julie. "Stock Flow for Week Declines to Just $1 Billion," *Wall Street Journal Interactive Edition,* (8 March 1997) [on-line]. Available from <http://www.wsj.com>; accessed 8 March 1997.

Listserv Message

N [1]MONEYDAILY, <moneyadm@PATHFINDER.COM>, "Fed raises rates/Save on home office equipment," 25 March 1997. Available from <dailymail@listserv.pathfinder.com>; accessed 25 March 1997.

B MONEYDAILY, <moneyadm@PATHFINDER.COM>, "Fed raises rates/Save on home office equipment," 25 March 1997. Available from <dailymail@listserv.pathfinder.com>; accessed 25 March 1997.

E-Mail

N [1]May, Gordon S., <gmay@cbacc.cba.uga.edu>, "Citation style," 28 March 1998. Accessed 29 March, 1998.

B May, Gordon S., <gmay@cbacc.cba.uga.edu>, "Citation style," 28 March 1998, E-mail; accessed 29 March, 1998.

More than One Work in Bibliography by Same Author or Authors

B Lang, M., and R. Lundholm, "Cross-Sectional Determinants of Analyst Ratings of Corporate Disclosures," *Journal of Accounting Research* 31, no. 2 (Autumn 1993): 246–271.

——. "Corporate Disclosure Policy and Analyst Behavior," *The Accounting Review* 71, no. 4 (October 1996): 467–492.

8

Letters

Accountants write many letters to clients, government agencies, fellow professionals, and so on. They may write letters seeking data about a client's tax situation, for example, or information needed for an audit. They may also write letters to communicate the results of research into a technical accounting problem. Other letters an accountant might write include engagement letters and management advisory letters.

For any letter to get the best results, of course, it must be well written.

This chapter begins with some principles of good letter writing: organization, style, tone, and format. Then we look at some letters typical of those accountants write.

PRINCIPLES OF LETTER WRITING

Effective letters have many of the characteristics of other good writing: They contain correct, complete information, and they are usually written with specific readers in mind. They are also written in an active, direct style. In other words, they are coherent, clear, and concise. They are also neat and attractive, with a professional appearance.

Planning a Letter

A letter can vary in length from one paragraph to several pages, although many business letters are no longer than a page. Whatever the length, you should be certain about what you want to include before you begin so that you won't forget something important.

As in other writing tasks, you must analyze the purpose of the letter before you write it. If you are answering another person's letter, keep that letter on hand and note any comments for which a reply is needed. Finally, jot down a brief outline to organize the material logically.

It's also important to think about the reader of your letter, especially when writing about a technical topic. The knowledge and experience of your reader determine how detailed the explanations of technical material should be.

Sometimes you must explain complex accounting procedures in words a nonaccountant can understand. Tax Research Techniques, a study published by the AICPA, discusses user needs in writing letters to clients about tax problems:

> Like a good speaker, a good writer must know the audience before beginning. Because tax clients and their staff vary greatly in their tax expertise, it is important to consider their technical sophistication when composing a tax opinion letter. The style of a letter may range from a highly sophisticated format, with numerous technical explanations and citations, to a simple composition that uses only layperson's terms. In many situations, of course, the best solution lies somewhere between the two extremes.[1]

Organization

Like other kinds of writing, a letter is organized into an introduction, a body, and a conclusion. Each section uses summary sentences to emphasize main ideas and help the reader follow the train of thought.

The *introduction* of a letter establishes rapport with the reader and identifies the subject of the letter or the reason it was written. You can mention previous communication on the subject, such as an earlier letter or phone call, or remind the reader of a recent meeting or shared interest. The introduction should also summarize briefly the main ideas or recommendations discussed in the letter. If the letter is very long, it's also a good idea to identify in the introduction the main issues or topics the letter covers.

The *body* of the letter is divided logically into discussions of each topic. Arrange the topics in descending order of importance *from the reader's point of view.* Start with the most important issue and work your way down to the least important. Begin the discussion of each issue with a summary sentence stating the main idea or recommendation.

Paragraphs should be short, usually a maximum of four or five sentences, and each should begin with a topic sentence.

The letter's *conclusion* may be a conventional courteous closing:

Thank you very much for your help.

The conclusion is also a good place to tell your correspondent exactly what you want him or her to do, or what you will do to follow up on the subjects discussed in the letter:

May I have an appointment to discuss this matter with you? I'll be in Chicago next week, October 7–11. I'll call your secretary to set up a time that is convenient for you.

If your letter is very long, the conclusion may also summarize your main ideas and recommendations.

Conciseness and Clarity

Conciseness and clarity, qualities of all good writing, are particularly important in letters. You don't want to waste your readers' time, nor do you want them to miss important ideas. Come to the point quickly and say it in a way they will understand.

A number of the techniques already presented in this handbook are useful for writing short, clear letters. For example, your writing should be unified: paragraphs with a central idea that is easy to spot. The letter should also be as brief and simple as possible, while still conveying an unambiguous, precise meaning.

Tone

One of the most important characteristics of a well-written business letter is its tone, or the way it makes the reader feel. Chapter 4 discussed writing from the point of view of your readers, emphasizing their interests and needs. Courtesy and respect are also important qualities of business letters, as they are in all forms of communication.

In general, effective letters reflect a personal, conversational tone. However, the best tone to use for a given letter depends to some extent on the purpose and reader of that letter. Review the discussion of tone in chapter 4 to see how the content of the letter and your relationship with the reader can affect the tone you choose for your correspondence.

Form and Appearance

One of the primary characteristics of an effective letter is a neat appearance. Good stationery is important: 8 1/2 × 11-inch, unlined paper of a high-quality bond, about 24-pound weight. Envelopes, 4 × 10 inches, should match the stationery. White or cream is usually the best color choice because those colors give the best appearance and do not interfere with photocopying. Word-processing programs now make it possible to design and print your own letterhead stationary. If you design your own letterhead, be conservative in the selection of font styles and sizes.

Business letters should be printed on a letter-quality printer, either laser or ink jet. Envelopes may be printed or typed.* Both the letter and the envelope should be free of errors. Neatness is essential!

A letter is usually single-spaced, with double-spacing between paragraphs, although letters can be double-spaced throughout (see the sample formats in Figures 8–1 and 8–2). Margins should be at least 1 inch on all sides and as even as possible, although the length of the letter will affect the margin width.

One-page letters should be placed so that the body of the letter, excluding the heading, is centered on the page or slightly above center. A word processor makes it easy to experiment with margins and spacing until you get the best arrangement.

Study the diagrams in Figures 8–1 and 8–2, which illustrate the parts of a letter and their proper placement for two formats, the block and the modified block styles. Remember also that formatting techniques, such as headings and set-off lists, can make your letters attractive and easy to read.

Parts of the Letter

Heading The heading contains your address (not your name) and the date of the letter. If you use stationery without a letterhead, place the heading on the left margin (for block style) or next to the right margin (for modified block style). If you use letterhead stationery, you can center the date below the letterhead or place it next to the left margin for block style.

Inside Address The inside address is a reproduction of the address on the envelope. Place the title of the person to whom you are writing either on the same line as his or her name, or on the following line:

Anna M. Soper, President
Muffet Products
516 N. 25th Street
Edinburg, TX 78539

-or-

Anna M. Soper
President
Muffet Products
516 N. 25th Street
Edinburg, TX 78539

It's usually better to address a letter to a specific person rather than to an office or title. You can find the name of the person to whom you are

*Most word processing programs contain an envelope printing feature that automatically selects and prints a business address on an envelope.

FIGURE 8–1 ***Diagram of a Letter Format—Block Style***

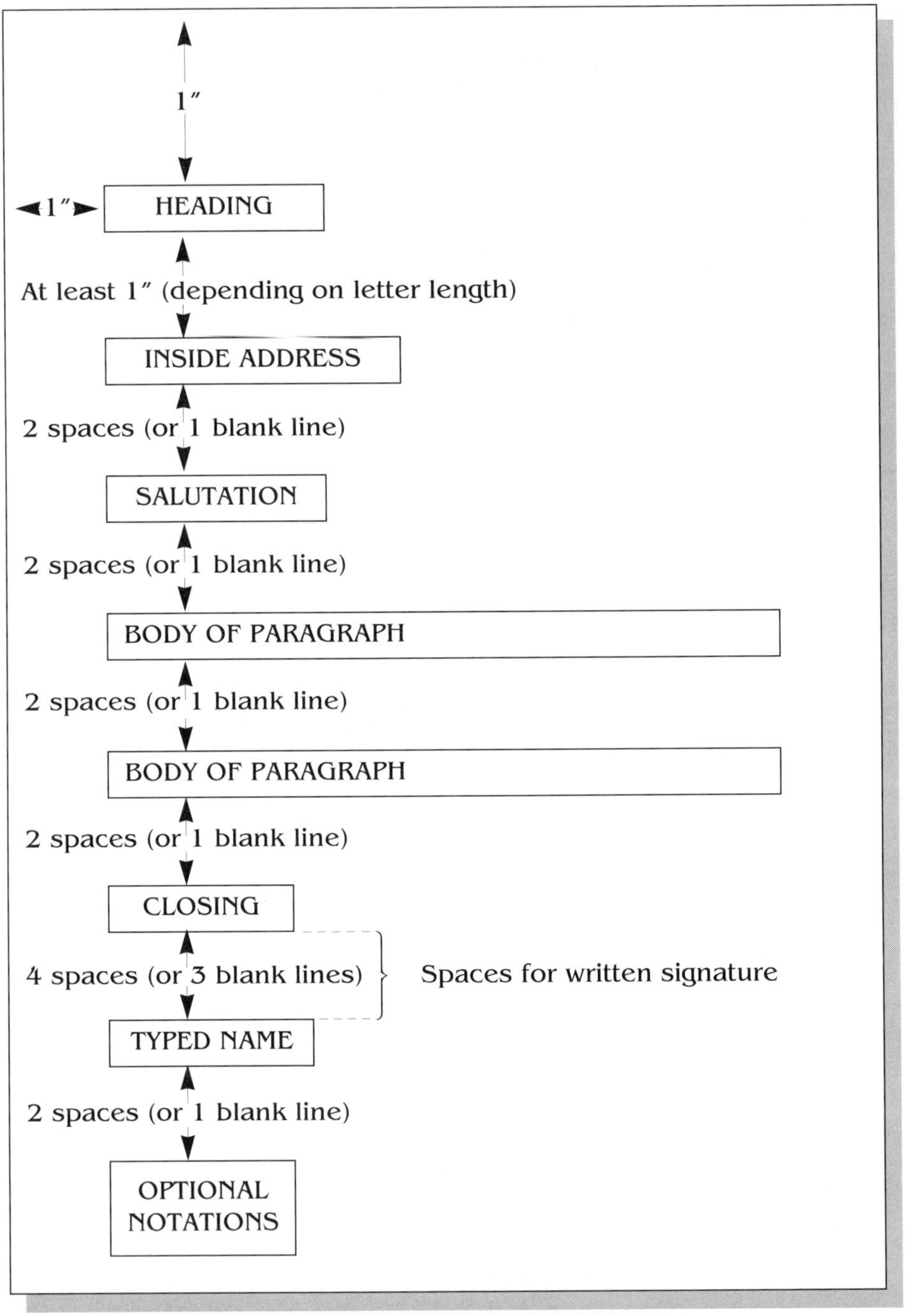

FIGURE 8–2 ***Diagram of a Letter Format—Modified Block Style***

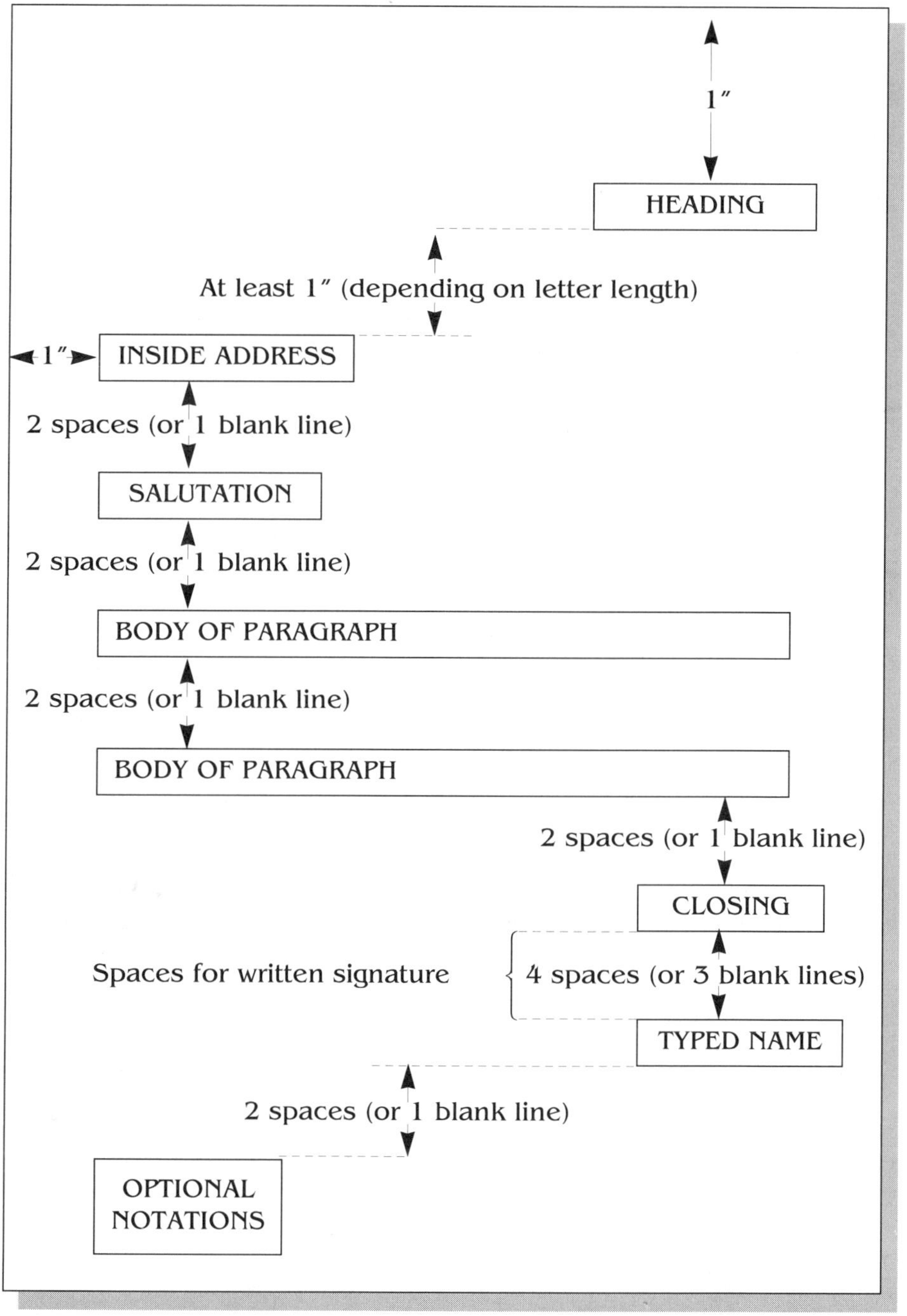

writing by phoning the company or organization. It's also a good idea to verify the spelling of the name and the gender of the person if it is not obvious.

Salutation If possible, address your correspondent by name:

Dear Ms. Soper:

or

Dear Mr. Smith:

For a female correspondent, use Ms. unless she prefers another title.

If you know your correspondent well, you may want to use his or her first name in the salutation:

Dear Anna:

Be careful with the use of first names, however, especially when writing to an older person or one in a position of greater authority than yours. In many situations, a respectful, courteous tone requires the use of a title and last name.

If you don't know the name of the correspondent, use a salutation such as the following:

Dear Director of Personnel:
Dear Registrar:

Note that a colon (:) always follows the salutation in a business letter.

Closing The formal closing of a letter is placed at the left margin for a block-style letter and next to the right margin for the modified block style. Capitalize the first word of the closing and put a comma at the end. Either of the following closings is correct:

Sincerely yours,
Sincerely,

Signature Your name should be printed four lines below the closing; your position can be placed beneath your name. The space between the closing and printed name is for your handwritten signature:

Sincerely,

Anna M. Soper

Anna M. Soper
President

Optional Parts of a Letter Sometimes you will need additional notations below the signature, at the left margin. First, if someone else types your letter, a notation is made of your initials (all capital letters) and the typist's (all lowercase):

AMS:lc

or

AMS/lc

Second, if the letter includes an enclosure, make a notation:

Enclosure(s)

Finally, if you will distribute copies of the letter to other people, note the people who will receive a copy:

cc: John Jones

Second Page Many business letters are only one page long. If you need to write additional pages, each should have a heading identifying the addressee, the date, and the page number. This information is usually printed at the left margin:

Mr. Richard Smith
November 18, 1998
Page 3

A second page (and any subsequent pages) should have at least three lines of text, in addition to the heading and closing.

RESPONDING TO CORRESPONDENCE

When you reply to a letter written by someone else, it's important to respond in a way that will build a good working relationship between you and the correspondent. Many of the techniques for effective letters already discussed apply to responses. Here is a summary of those techniques, as well as a few pointers that apply particularly when you are answering someone else's letter:

1. Respond promptly, by return mail if possible.
2. Reread carefully the letter you received, noting questions that need answers or ideas that need your comment.
3. For the opening paragraph:
   - Refer to earlier correspondence, such as the date of the letter you received.

- If your letter is good news, or at least neutral, state clearly and positively the letter's main idea.
- If your letter contains bad news, such as the denial of a request, identify the subject of the letter in the opening paragraph. State the explicit refusal later in the body of the letter, after you have prepared the reader with some buffer material.

4. Answer all your correspondent's questions fully and cover all relevant topics in sufficient detail. However, the letter should be as concise as possible.
5. End with a courteous closing.

TYPICAL ACCOUNTING LETTERS

Before we begin this section, we should note that many accounting firms have standardized letters for some situations. The management of a firm may have decided on the organization and even the specific wording that it requires its staff to use for engagement letters, management advisory letters, and the like. If your firm uses standardized letters, simply adapt the basic letter to the specific case you are concerned with, adding dates, names, figures, and other relevant facts.

Presented below are sample letters for various situations, along with some general comments on the content and organization of these letters.

Engagement Letters

Engagement letters put into writing the arrangements made between an accounting firm and a client. Engagement letters can confirm the arrangements for a variety of services: audit, review, compilation, management advisory services, or tax. The main advantage of an engagement letter is that it clarifies the mutual responsibilities of accountant and client and thus prevents possible misunderstandings.

Engagement letters can vary a great deal in content, depending on the firm writing the letter, the type of services to be provided, and the facts of the case. However, most engagement letters have three basic elements:

- A description of the nature and limitations of the service the accountants will provide
- A description of the reports the accounting firm expects to issue
- A statement that the engagement will possibly not disclose errors, irregularities, or illegal acts.[2]

In addition to these elements, an engagement letter may also include other information, such as important deadlines for the work; assistance that the client will provide, such as certain records and schedules; information about the fee; and a space for the client to indicate acceptance of the arrangements outlined in the engagement letter.

Figure 8–3 shows a sample engagement letter for an audit.

FIGURE 8–3 *Engagement Letter for an Audit*

Brown and Wynne
Certified Public Accountants
201 W. Tenth Street Austin, Texas 78712

July 15, 1998

Mr. George Smith
Heritage Manufacturing Company
301 Planters Road
Austin, Texas 78712

Dear Mr. Smith:

This letter will confirm the arrangement we discussed for the audit of Heritage Manufacturing Company for the year ended December 31, 1998.

The purpose of the audit will be to examine Heritage Company's financial statements for the year ended December 31, 1998. Our examination will be conducted in accordance with generally accepted auditing standards, and we will use the tests and procedures necessary to express an opinion on the fairness of the financial statements. As part of our audit, we will review the internal control system and conduct tests of transactions. Although these procedures may disclose material errors or illegal acts, a possibility remains that we may not discover irregularities during the course of the audit.

At the close of our examination, we will issue our report on the audit. We will also prepare your federal and state income tax returns for the year ended December 31, 1998. Both the audit report and the tax returns should be completed by March 15, 1999.

Our fees will be at our regular rates, based on the time required to perform these services. We will bill you when we have completed the work.

FIGURE 8–3 *Engagement Letter for an Audit (cont.)*

Mr. George Smith
July 15, 1998
Page 2

We are pleased that you have appointed us to be your auditor, and we look forward to working with you and your staff.

Sincerely,

Carla Brown

Carla Brown, CPA

Accepted by:
Date:

Management Advisory Letters

At the conclusion of an audit, an accountant often writes a letter to the client suggesting ways the client can improve the business. This type of letter may contain suggestions on a variety of topics:*

- Internal control
- The accounting and information system
- Inventory control
- Credit policies
- Budgeting
- Tax matters
- Management of resources
- Operating procedures

Sometimes, if the auditor includes many recommendations in the management letter, the letter may be quite long. If you write a management letter that is more than three pages long, consider organizing it into a report with a transmittal letter. Address the transmittal letter to the

*Generally Accepted Auditing Standards (GAAS) require letters to be written under certain conditions such as the presence of fraud.

president or board of directors of the client company and summarize in the letter the major recommendations made in the report.

In any case, whether the management letter is a single document or a report with a transmittal letter, remember that long letters are more attractive and easier to read if they contain headings. These headings divide the letter into logical sections.

Whatever the format of the management letter, write it so that it will be helpful to the client and build a good professional relationship between the client and your firm. The techniques for effective writing discussed so far in this book certainly apply to management letters: clear and logical organization, readable style, and specific and concrete explanation.

In an article in the *Journal of Accountancy*, Robert T. Lanz and S. Thomas Moser note that management letters often anger clients because the letters don't give enough specific information to support the accountants' suggestions.[3] Lanz and Moser stress the importance of answering three questions about each recommendation:

- Why is the change needed?
- How can it be accomplished?
- What benefits will the client receive?

In addition, Lanz and Moser note that the letter should be well organized, with key points summarized near the beginning. The authors conclude their article with a brief discussion about the style of management letters:

> Auditors may tend to write management letters in a perplexing combination of "legalese" and "accountantese." If this is what our clients are getting, we should put aside the technical jargon and verbosity and write a readable letter that makes good sense.[4]

An example of a short but effective management advisory letter appears in Figure 8–4. The recommendations included in this letter are taken from Lanz and Moser's article.[5]

Tax Research Letters

Accountants who provide tax services often write letters to their clients communicating the results of the research into some tax question. These letters can be for either tax planning or after-the-fact tax situations.

The content and organization of these letters can vary, but *Tax Research Techniques* suggests the following basic outline:

- The facts on which the research was based.
- Caution that the advice is valid only for the facts previously outlined.

FIGURE 8–4 *Management Advisory Letter*

BEASLEY AND POOLE
Certified Public Accountants
1553 W. Ellis Street
Atlanta, Georgia 30316

March 15, 1998

Mr. Robert F. Freeman, President
Southeast Manufacturing Company
24 N. Broad Street
Atlanta, Georgia 30327

Dear Mr. Freeman:

Our examination of Southeast Manufacturing's financial statements for the year ended December 31, 1997, revealed two areas where we believe you could improve your business:

- Stronger budgeting system
- Review of credit policies

The following paragraphs explain these recommendations in greater detail.

<u>Budgets</u>

Operating, selling, and general administrative expenses for 1997 as compared with 1996 increased from $1 million to $1,050,000, a change of 5 percent. Although management has been able to control expenditures, we believe efforts in this area would be assisted by implementation of a strong system of budgeting.

Under such a system, responsibility for actual performance is assigned to employees most directly responsible for the expenditures involved. (It is best that such employees have a role in establishing the budgets.) Periodic reports reflecting actual and budgeted amounts, together with explanations of significant variances, should be provided to management personnel respon-

FIGURE 8–4 ***Management Advisory Letter (cont.)***

Mr. Robert F. Freeman
March 15, 1998
Page 2

sible for approving the budgets initially. We cannot overemphasize the value of sound budgeting and planning in all areas of the company's activities.

<u>Credit Policies</u>

The history of write-offs of bad accounts over the past few years indicates that the write-off percentage has declined. Considering the low net earnings margin under which the company operates (slightly less than 0.6 percent of net sales), it is most important that this favorable record continue because a significant increase in bad debts could have a substantial negative impact on net earnings.

In view of the high cost of money for business in general, management should consider reviewing its credit policies to reasonably ensure that the risk inherent in continued sales to customers of questionable credit standing is justified. This is a delicate area of policy; it is not desirable to so restrict sales representatives that profitable sales are lost because of overly stringent credit policies. However, a reasonable amount of control should be exercised by the credit and collection department to ensure a minimum of bad accounts. For example, a limit could be set on the amount sales representatives could extend to customers whose accounts have reached a certain balance.

We will be glad to discuss these suggestions with you and help you implement them.

Sincerely,

Roger Poole

Roger Poole
Beasley and Poole
Certified Public Accountants

FIGURE 8–5 ***A Letter Reporting the Results of Tax Research—Sophisticated Client***

R.U. Partner & Company
Certified Public Accountants
2010 Professional Tower
Calum City, USA 00001

December 24, 1998

Mr. Red E. Ink, President
Ms. Judith Dixon, Vice President
120 Published Lane
Calum City, USA 00002

Dear Mr. Ink and Ms. Dixon:

This letter confirms the oral agreement of December 17, 1998, in which our firm agreed to undertake the preparation of your respective federal income tax returns along with that of Ready, Incorporated, for the next year. This letter also reports the preliminary results of our investigation into the tax consequences of the formation of Ready, Incorporated, last March. We are pleased to be of service to you and anticipate that our relationships will prove to be mutually beneficial. Please feel free to call me at any time.

Before stating the preliminary results of our investigation into the tax consequences of your incorporation transaction, I would like to restate briefly all of the important facts as we understand them. Please review this statement of facts very carefully. Our conclusions depend on a complete and accurate understanding of all the facts. If any of the following statements is either incorrect or incomplete, please call it to my attention immediately, no matter how small or insignificant the difference may appear to be.

Our conclusions are based on an understanding that on March 1, 1998, the following exchanges occurred in the process of forming a new corporation, Ready, Incorporated. Ms. Dixon transferred two copyrights to Ready, Incorporated, in exchange for 250 shares of common stock. Ms. Dixon had previously paid

FIGURE 8–5 ***A Letter Reporting the Results of Tax Research—Sophisticated Client (cont.)***

Red E. Ink
Judith Dixon
December 24, 1998
Page 2

$200 for filing the copyrights. In addition, the corporation assumed an $800 typing bill, which Ms. Dixon owed for these two manuscripts.

Mr. Ink concurrently transferred all the assets and liabilities of his former sole proprietorship printing company, Red Publishing, to the new corporation in exchange for 750 shares of Ready, Incorporated, common stock. The assets transferred consisted of $11,700 cash, $10,000 (estimated market value) printing supplies, $50,000 (face value) trade receivables, and $58,300 (tax book value) equipment. The equipment, purchased new in 1998 for $100,000, had been depreciated for tax purposes under the modified accelerated cost recovery system (MACRS) since its acquisition.

The liabilities assumed by Ready, Incorporated, consisted of the $65,000 mortgage remaining from the original equipment purchase and current trade payables of $10,000.

We further understand that Ready, Incorporated, plans to continue to occupy the building leased by Red Publishings from Branden Properties until the expiration of that lease.

Finally, we understand that Ready, Incorporated, has issued only 1,000 shares of common stock and that Mr. Ink retains 730 shares; that Mr. Ink's wife Neva holds ten shares; that Mr. Tom Books, the corporate secretary-treasurer, holds ten shares; that Ms. Dixon holds the remaining 250 shares. The shares held by Mrs. Ink and Mr. Books were given to them by Mr. Ink, as a gift, on March 1, 1998.

It is our understanding that Ready, Incorporated, will report its taxable income on an accrual method, calendar-year basis.

Assuming that the preceding paragraphs represent a complete and accurate statement of all the facts pertinent to the incorpora-

FIGURE 8–5 ***A Letter Reporting the Results of Tax Research—Sophisticated Client (cont.)***

Red E. Ink
Judith Dixon
December 24, 1998
Page 3

tion transaction, we anticipate reporting that event as a wholly nontaxable transaction. In other words, neither of you, the incorporators (individually), nor your corporation will report any taxable income or loss solely because of your incorporation of the printing business. The trade receivables collected by Ready, Incorporated, after March 1, 1998, will be reported as taxable income of the corporate entity: collections made between January 1, 1998, and February 28, 1998, will be considered part of Mr. Ink's personal taxable income for 1998.

There is a possibility that the Internal Revenue Service could argue (1) that Ms. Dixon is required to recognize $800 of taxable income and/or (2) that the corporation could not deduct the $10,000 in trade payables it assumed from the proprietorship. If either of you desire, I would be pleased to discuss these matters in greater detail. Perhaps it would be desirable for Mr. Bent and me to meet with both of you and review these potential problems prior to our filing the corporate tax return.

If Mr. Tom Books desires any help in maintaining the corporation's regular financial accounts, we shall be happy to assist him. It will be necessary for us to have access to your personal financial records no later than March 1, 1999, if the federal income tax returns are to be completed and filed on a timely basis.

Finally, may I suggest that we plan to have at least one more meeting in my office sometime before February 28, 1999, to discuss possible tax-planning opportunities available to you and the new corporation. Among other considerations, we should jointly review the possibility that you may want to make an S election and that you may need to structure executive compensation arrangements carefully and may wish to institute a pension plan. Please telephone me to arrange an appointment if you would like to do this shortly after the holidays.

FIGURE 8–5 ***A Letter Reporting the Results of Tax Research—Sophisticated Client (cont.)***

Red E. Ink
Judith Dixon
December 24, 1998
Page 4

Thank you again for selecting our firm for tax assistance. It is very important that some of the material in this letter be kept confidential, and we strongly recommend that you carefully control access to it at all times. If you have any questions about any of the matters discussed, feel free to request a more detailed explanation or drop by and review the complete files, which are available in my office. If I am not available, my assistant, Fred Senior, would be happy to help you. We look forward to serving you in the future.

Sincerely yours,

Robert U. Partner

Robert U. Partner

- The tax questions implicit in these facts.
- The conclusions, with the authoritative support for the conclusions.
- Areas of controversy that the IRS might dispute. (Tax accountants do not all agree that the letter should identify the vulnerable areas in the client's situation. *Tax Research Techniques* suggests that if the letter does identify these weaknesses, the accountant should caution the client to control access to the letter.)[6]

In addition to a logical organization, such as the one outlined here, tax research letters should be understandable to the client. Tax questions are often highly technical, and you may need to explain the conclusions in terms a businessperson will understand.

Figures 8–5[7] and 8–6[8] provide two illustrations of letters written to clients to report the results of tax research. The letter in Figure 8–5, which is written to the president of a large corporation, deals with a com-

FIGURE 8–6 ***A Letter Reporting the Results of Tax Research—Less Sophisticated Client***

September 19, 1998

M/M Dale Brown
2472 North Mayfair Road
Fillingham, SD 59990

Dear Dale and Rae:

Thanks again for requesting my advice concerning the tax treatment of your interest expenses. I am sorry to report that only part of your expenses can be deducted this year.

My research has uncovered a series of successes by the IRS in convincing several important courts that interest such as yours should not be allowed as a deduction to reduce your taxes. Unfortunately, the court whose decision initially would prevail upon us would hold against you, and a series of court hearings, over two or three years or so, would be necessary for you to win the case.

This research has been restricted to situations like yours—that is, in which the taxpayer both owns a municipal bond and owes money to the bank from an interest-bearing loan.

It seems that the IRS would rather have you purchase the municipal bonds with your own money than with the bank's. It maintains that you get a double benefit from the nontaxability of the School Board interest income and the deductibility of the interest expense that is paid to the bank. Thus, the portion of the interest that relates to the bond investment is not allowed. A business purpose for the loan salvages the deduction, however, so you can deduct the interest from the loan that relates to Dr. Rae's clinic.

You may just have to live with this situation, as the IRS has been winning cases like these for over ten years. Yours is not likely to be the one that changes their mind, so you might reconsider your investment in the municipals in the near future.

My conclusion is based on the facts that you have provided me, and on the reliability of the court cases that I found.

FIGURE 8–6 ***A Letter Reporting the Results of Tax Research—Less Sophisticated Client (cont.)***

M/M Dale Brown
September 19, 1998
Page 2

I'm sorry that this news isn't more favorable. I look forward to seeing you, though, at the firm's holiday reception!

Sincerely,

Ellen P. Morgan

Ellen P. Morgan
Tax Researcher

plicated tax issue. Although this letter is clearly written, it contains a great deal of technical information and terminology.

In contrast, the letter in Figure 8–6 is written much more simply. The topic is less complicated, and the letter contains fewer technical terms. As different as these two client letters are, they are both appropriate for their readers and the purposes for which they were intended.

STANDARDIZED LETTERS: A CAUTION

As already mentioned, many organizations have standardized letters that they use for situations that occur often, such as engagement letters. These form letters save time, and they also convey the message precisely and reliably. If your employer expects you to use these standardized letters, then of course you should do so.

With the widespread use of word processors that store documents, however, there is a danger that writers will use form letters when personalized letters would be more appropriate. If you use standardized letters, be sure that they are responsive to the reader's needs and concerns.

If you know your correspondent personally, a friendly reference to a topic of mutual interest can add warmth to your letter. The last paragraph of the letter in Figure 8–6 provides a friendly, personalized closing to a client letter:

> I'm sorry that this news isn't more favorable. I look forward to seeing you, though, at the firm's holiday reception!

EXERCISES

Exercise 8–1 (All Levels)

Suppose you received the letter shown in Figure 8–7. How would you react? What, specifically, is wrong with this letter? What about it is effective?

After you have analyzed the strengths and weaknesses of the letter as it is shown in Figure 8–7, revise it so that it would make a better impression on a reader.

Exercise 8–2 (All Levels)

You have always been close to your sister, an attorney, even though she is ten years older than you and now lives many miles away. She is quite interested in your education and career plans, so you have decided to write her a letter to explain why you are majoring in accounting. You know she will be interested in your personal reasons for choosing this career path as well as the employment opportunities that are likely to be open to you after graduation. She would also like to hear about any plans you may have for continuing your professional education and training after you receive your undergraduate degree.

Write your sister a letter that will persuade her that a major and career in accounting are good choices for you. Use the proper format, effective organization, and appropriate style. Invent any information you feel is necessary to make your letter complete.

Exercise 8–3 (All Levels)

You have prepared the federal and state income tax returns for your client, Hamilton White. Write a cover letter to Mr. White to mail with the completed returns. Use the proper format, effective organization, and appropriate style. Invent any information you feel is necessary to make your letter complete. In your letter include the following:

- A reminder for him to sign the returns on the lines checked
- The amounts he owes in both state and federal taxes
- A reminder of the filing deadline

Exercise 8–4 (All Levels)

One of your clients, Buz's Sports, has not paid for a tax return that you completed March 15. You billed the client when you completed the

FIGURE 8–7 ***Letter for Exercise 8–1***

SBB

Smith, Barnum, and Bailey
Certified Public Accountants
301 MacDonald Place
Atlanta, Georgia 36095

Members
American Institute of
Certified Public Accountants

Telephone
(306) 782-5107

May 21, 1998

Mr. John W. Simmons
234 Myers Hall, UGA
Athens, Georgia 30609

Dear John:

After considerable debate about our needs, we have decided to offer the internship to someone else. Our offer was excepted, so the position is now filled.

I enjoyed talking with you and felt you would of been a positive impact to our firm and would work well with our present staff.

Upon graduation we would be most interested in talking with you regarding full-time employment. If I can be of assistance in the near future, please feel free to call.

Sincerely,

Jason A. Smith

Jason A. Smith
JASjr/mlk
Enclosures

return and mailed a reminder in May. At the end of June, Buz's still hasn't paid the bill, and you need to write a letter to the company president, Mr. Buster Alan, requesting payment. Of course, you do not want to antagonize Mr. Alan because the company has been a client for several years and you value the business relationship.

Write the letter to Mr. Alan asking him to pay the bill. Use the proper format, effective organization, and appropriate style. Invent any information you feel is necessary to make your letter complete.

Exercise 8–5 (All Levels)

Tammy Johnson, a representative from one of your company's suppliers, Megamart Office Supplies, has called to inquire why a recent invoice hasn't been paid yet. The payment was due in 30 days, and 45 days have gone by without payment. You are aware of the situation, but your company is suffering a "cash crunch" and cannot afford to pay the invoice until after the receipt of a large cash inflow which is expected to occur in about 10 days.

Write a letter to Ms. Johnson at Megamart reassuring her that the invoice will be paid soon. Remember, your credit with this supplier is very important to your company and you don't want Ms. Johnson to have any doubts about your company's ability to pay. Use the proper format, effective organization, and appropriate style. Invent any information you feel is necessary to make your letter complete.

Exercise 8–6 (All Levels)

You are preparing the federal income tax returns for Carol and John Land and find you need some additional information: receipts for contributions to their church, the name of their youngest child, and the name of the day care center where the child is enrolled.

Write a letter to Mr. and Mrs. Land requesting this information. Use the proper format, effective organization, and appropriate style. Invent any information you feel is necessary to make your letter complete.

Exercise 8–7 (All Levels)

Shaeffer Art Supply has poor internal control over its cash transactions. Recently, Mr. G. M. Schaeffer, the owner, has suspected the cashier of stealing. Details of the business's cash position on September 30 follow.

1. The Cash account shows a balance of $19,502. This amount includes a September 30 deposit of $3,794 that does not appear on the September 30 bank statement.
2. The September 30 bank statement shows a balance of $17,924. The bank statement lists a $200 credit for a bank collection, an $8 debit for the service charge, and a $36 debit for an NSF check. The Schaeffer account has not recorded any of these items on the books.

3. September 30 the following checks are outstanding:

CHECK NO.	AMOUNT
154	$116
256	150
278	253
291	190
292	206
293	145

4. The cashier handles all incoming cash and makes the bank deposits. He also reconciles the monthly bank statement. His September 30 reconciliation follows.

Balance per books, September 3		$19,502
Add: Outstanding checks		2,060
Bank collection		200
		21,762
Less: Deposits in transit	$3,794	
Service charge	8	
NSF check	36	3,838
Balance per bank, September 30		$17,924

Mr. Schaeffer has requested that you determine whether the cashier has stolen cash from the business and, if so, how much. Mr. Schaeffer also asks you to identify how the cashier has attempted to conceal the theft. To make this determination, you perform your own bank reconciliation. There are no bank or book errors. Mr. Schaeffer also asks you to evaluate the internal controls and to recommend any changes needed to improve them.[9]

Write a letter to Mr. Schaeffer that addresses his concerns. Use the proper format, effective organization, and appropriate style. Invent any information you feel is necessary to make your letter complete.

Exercise 8–8

One morning J. Worthington Pocketmoney stormed into the offices of Apple, Altos, and Monroe, his certified public accountants. Without waiting for the receptionist to announce his arrival, he entered the office of Samuel Andrews, the partner in charge of auditing Mr. Pocketmoney's home appliance store. As usual, Mr. Andrews listened politely and calmly to the monologue delivered by Mr. Pocketmoney. An edited version follows.

> This morning at my breakfast club I spoke with my competitor, F. Scott Wurlitzer. He boasted that his accountant had saved him $19,000 in income taxes last year by recommending a switch from the FIFO to the LIFO inventory flow assumption. If he can do that, why can't I? And why haven't you

discussed this gimmick with me? I don't expect to rely on Wurlitzer for financial advice; I pay you for that.

After Pocketmoney's departure, Mr. Andrews calls you, a new staff accountant, into his office. He expresses regret at not having mentioned to Pocketmoney the possibility of change in accounting method. However, he also advises you that Pocketmoney needs new capital in his business and is trying to interest another local businessperson in becoming a limited partner. Thus, a decline in reported income could be detrimental to Mr. Pocketmoney's plans.

Mr. Andrews asks you to draft a letter to Mr. Pocketmoney. The letter should provide a balanced discussion of the advantages and disadvantages of shifting from FIFO to LIFO, with particular reference to Mr. Pocketmoney's specific situation. Although Andrews would like to provide some justification for his firm's failure to mention the possibility of a change, he cautions you to be reasonably objective and consider accounting theory.[10] Use the proper format, effective organization, and appropriate style for your letter. Invent any information you feel is necessary to make your letter complete.

Exercise 8–9 (Intermediate)

Your client, I. Seemdim, has written a letter to you. He is concerned that he has just received an offer to purchase his business for $1,000,000 more than the net carrying value of the assets on the most recent balance sheet, audited by you. He is not interested in selling the business, but he is now convinced that the value of his business is not properly reflected in the recently certified financial statements. He has been told by the prospective purchaser that the fair market value of the net separately identifiable assets is about $700,000 more than is shown in the balance sheet and that in addition there is at least $300,000 in goodwill that the would-be purchaser is willing to pay for.

Write a letter to your client explaining why the figures in the balance sheet should not be changed. Include an explanation of what goodwill is and why, even though it may exist for his company, it should not appear on the balance sheet. You may assume your client is an astute businessman but with no background in accounting. Use the proper format, effective organization, and appropriate style. Invent any information you feel is necessary to make your letter complete.

Exercise 8–10 (Intermediate)

Suppose you were the CPA to whom the letter in Figure 8–8 was written. Write a letter in reply.[11] Use the proper format, effective organization, and appropriate style. Invent any information you feel is necessary to make your letter complete.

FIGURE 8–8 *A Letter from a Client (Exercise 8–10)*

KEN-L-PRODUCTS, INC.
749 E. Peartree St.
Manhattan, Kansas 66502

May 1, 1998

Ellen Acker, CPA
331 J.M. Tull Street
Manhattan, Kansas 66502

Dear Ms. Acker:

As you well know, it is becoming impossible to conduct business without the constant threat of litigation. This year our company is faced with several lawsuits. We are unsure how these suits should be treated in our financial statements and would like clarification before you audit us this year.

Please specify the disclosure requirements for the following circumstances:

1. Several show dog owners have filed a class-action suit concerning the product "Shampoodle." The plaintiffs claim that severe hair loss has occurred as a result of product use. The suit is for a total of $2 million. However, our attorneys claim that it is probable that we will have to pay only between $500,000 and $1 million.

2. For quite sometime we have been producing a dog food called "Ken-L-Burgers." Recently we changed the formula and advertised the product as "better tasting." A consumer group known as "Spokesman for Dogs" has filed suit claiming that humans must actually eat the product in order to make the claim of better taste. Our lawyers say that the chance of losing this suit is remote. The suit is for $6 million.

3. One of our workers lost a finger in the "Ken-L-Burger" machine. Our attorneys believe that we will probably lose this suit but are unsure about the amount.

FIGURE 8–8 ***A Letter from a Client. (Exercise 8–10) (cont.)***

Ellen Acker
May 1, 1998
Page 2

4. My brother's company, House of Cats, is being sued for $4 million. His lawyers say that it is not likely that he will lose. However, Ken-L-Products, Inc., has guaranteed a debt he owes to a bank. If he loses, he will not be able to pay the bank.
5. A grain company sold us several tons of spoiled grain used as filler in our products. Because the company will not reimburse us for the spoilage, we have sued for $2 million. Our attorneys say we will probably win the case.
6. We aired several commercials that claimed Wayne Newton's dog uses our products. Mr. Newton told us that his dog hates our products and that if we show the commercials again he will probably sue us.

If each of these items is material, should we show them on the financial statements?

Thank you for your help on theses disclosures.

Sincerely,

Ken L. Price

Ken L. Price

Exercise 8–11 (Intermediate)

Carla Bryant wants to invest in an annuity for her son, Charles, who is 10 years old. She wants the annuity to pay exactly $10,000 a year for five years beginning when Charles turns 21. She wants to know how much money she will have to invest now, assuming the money will earn interest, compounded annually, of 8 percent.

Write a letter to Ms. Bryant explaining annuities and the amount she would need to invest now to set up the plan she has in mind. Use the proper format, effective organization, and appropriate style. Invent any information you feel is necessary to make your letter complete.

Exercise 8–12 (Intermediate)

At the beginning of the year, Patrick Company acquired a computer to be used in its operations. The computer was delivered by the supplier, installed by the owner, Rob Patrick, and placed into operation. The estimated useful life of the computer is five years, and its estimated residual (salvage) value is significant.

During the year, Mr. Patrick received cash in exchange for an automobile that he purchased in a prior year.

- What costs should Mr. Patrick capitalize for the computer?
- How should Mr. Patrick account for and report the disposal of the automobile?

Write a letter to Mr. Patrick in which you answer these questions.[12] Use the proper format, effective organization, and appropriate style. Invent any information you feel is necessary to make your letter complete.

Exercise 8–13 (Intermediate)

You are a senior staff accountant with the firm of Taxum and Howe in Oberlin, Ohio. Your new client, Mr. Grabmore Gusto, would like your advice. Mr. Gusto is concerned about having audited financial statements for the first time this year.

To begin operations three years ago, Mr. Gusto invested $300,000 of his own money (his life savings) and borrowed $200,000 from Oberlin Bank and Trust. The loan carries a 10 percent interest rate and has a term of 10 years from the date of issuance. Mr. Gusto set up a sinking fund immediately and has made monthly deposits to assure timely payments of interest and principal. Because of the success of his business, Mr. Gusto has been able to deposit enough money in 3 years to cover interest for the remaining 7 years as well as the principal.

Mr. Gusto has recently developed a plan to expand his business, but he needs to borrow about $500,000 to implement the plan. He is concerned, however, that Oberlin Bank and Trust will not grant him a new loan because of the existence of the original loan.

A business acquaintance, Mr. Suds, has suggested that because Mr. Gusto has deposited enough money in the sinking fund to cover principal and interest, he can simply eliminate both the sinking fund assets and the liability from his balance sheet. Mr. Suds referred to the elimination as debt defeasance.

Mr. Gusto is afraid that such an elimination or cancellation would not be in accordance with GAAP and would therefore result in a qualified audit opinion.

Write Mr. Gusto a letter explaining debt defeasance, including in your discussion a recommendation as to the conformity (or lack thereof) with GAAP. He has researched the problem and is somewhat familiar with various applications and accounting treatments of defeasance.[13] Use the proper format, effective organization, and appropriate style. Invent any information you feel is necessary to make your letter complete.

Exercise 8–14 (Auditing)

Write an engagement letter in which you agree to review the financial statements of Howard Fabricators, Inc. You may mention other services that you agree to provide. Use the proper format, effective organization, and appropriate style. Invent any information you feel is necessary to make your letter complete.

Exercise 8–15 (Auditing)

A competent auditor has done a conscientious job of auditing Brown Corporation, but because of a clever fraud by management, a material error is included in the financial statements. The irregularity, which is an overstatement of inventory, took place over several years, and it covered up the fact that the company's financial position was rapidly declining. The fraud was accidentally discovered in the latest audit by an unusually capable audit senior, and the SEC was immediately informed. A subsequent investigation indicated that Brown Corporation was actually near bankruptcy, and the value of the stock dropped from $26 per share to $1 in less than one month. Among the losing stockholders were pension funds, university endowment funds, retired couples, and widows. The individuals responsible for perpetrating the fraud were also bankrupt.

After making an extensive investigation of the audit performance in previous years, the SEC was satisfied that the auditor had done a high-quality audit and had followed generally accepted auditing standards in every respect. The commission concluded that it would be unreasonable to expect auditors to uncover this type of fraud.

One of your clients, Elizabeth Adams, is a stockholder in Brown Corporation. She has written you to express her dismay about the decline in value of the stock. She also wants to know who should bear the loss of the management fraud. Ms. Adams is an intelligent, well-educated person, but she knows very little about business or accounting.

Write a letter to Ms. Adams that will address her concerns.[14]

Exercise 8–16 (Cost)

Consider the following data of the Laimon Company for the year 1998:

Sandpaper	$ 2,000	Depreciation—equipment	$ 40,000
Material handling	40,000	Factory rent	50,000
Lubricants and coolant	5,000	Property taxes on equipment	4,000

Overtime premium	20,000	Fire insurance on equipment	3,000
Idle time	10,000	Direct materials purchased	460,000
Miscellaneous indirect labor	40,000	Direct materials Inventory, 12/31/97	50,000
Direct labor	300,000	Sales	1,260,000
Direct materials, inventory 12/31/98	40,000	Sales commissions	60,000
Finished goods, inventory 12/31/98	150,000	Sales salaries	100,000
Finished goods, inventory 12/31/97	100,000	Shipping expense	70,000
Work in process, inventory 12/31/97	10,000	Administrative expense	100,000
Work in process, inventory 12/31/98	14,000		

1. Suppose that both the direct-material and rent costs were related to the manufacturing of the equivalent of 900,000 units. What is the average unit cost for the direct materials assigned to those units? What is the average cost of the factory rent? Assume that the rent is a fixed cost.
2. Repeat the computation in requirement 1 for direct materials and factory rent, assuming that the costs are being predicted for the manufacturing of the equivalent of 1,000,000 units next year. Assume that the implied cost behavior patterns persist.

As a management consultant, explain concisely in a letter to the president why the unit costs for direct materials and rent differed in requirements 1 and 2.[15] Use the proper format, effective organization, and appropriate style. Invent any information you feel is necessary to make your letter complete.

Exercise 8–17 (Advanced Managerial or Financial)

Assume one of the following situations:

1. You are a senior member of the auditing staff of a medium-sized manufacturing corporation.

   or

2. You are a partner of a regional accounting firm.

Write a letter to the Financial Accounting Standards Board in response to a recent FASB Exposure Draft. Use the proper format, effective organization, and appropriate style. Invent any information you feel is necessary to make your letter complete.

Exercise 8–18 (Accounting Information Systems)

Parker's Shoe Store has been owned and managed by a very conservative individual who is intimidated by computers. The money from cash sales is kept in an old-fashioned cash register, and clerks keep track of the shoes sold by recording pertinent information (brand, style number, price, and size) on a yellow legal pad.

The owner of the store is planning to retire soon, and his daughter, Sue Parker, will then be the full-time manager. She believes a computer system could help her run the store more efficiently, and she hires you to evaluate the store's needs and explain how a computer system could help her manage the business.

Write a letter to Ms. Parker explaining the benefits to the store of a computer system, as well as its limitations. Remember that although she is open-minded about the usefulness of computers, she knows very little about them. Use the proper format, effective organization, and appropriate style. Invent any information you feel is necessary to make your letter complete.

Exercise 8–19 (Accounting Information Systems)

One of your clients, a small service business with 10 office employees, plans to purchase a database package for use with the office's personal computers.

Select two database packages and evaluate them for your client's needs. Consider the advantages and disadvantages of both packages, including the ease with which the staff will be able to learn the new system. You should consider basic features of the database package as well as advanced functions.

Write your evaluation in the form of a letter to the company's president, Heather Owen. Use the proper format, effective organization, and appropriate style. Invent any information you feel is necessary to make your letter complete.

Exercise 8–20 (Tax)

Elaine Harrison was divorced in 1998. Her unmarried daughter lived in her home for the entire year. To maintain her home in 1998, it cost $6,000, $2,000 of which her former husband contributed through support payments. Her former husband also provides more than half of their daughter's total support and claims her as a dependent under a written agreement with his ex-wife. What is Mrs. Harrison's correct filing status for the year?[16]

Write a letter to Mrs. Harrison in which you explain the answer to this question. Use the proper format, effective organization, and appropriate style. Invent any information you feel is necessary to make your letter complete.

NOTES

1. Ray M. Sommerfeld, G. Fred Streuling, Robert L. Gardner, and Dave N. Stewart, *Tax Research Techniques,* 3rd. ed., Revised (New York: American Institute of Certified Public Accountants, 1989), 163–164. This source provides additional information on other letters that tax accountants may write, such as tax protest letters and requests for rulings.
2. W. Peter Van Son, Dan M. Guy, and J. Frank Betts, "Engagement Letters: What Practice Shows," *Journal of Accountancy* 152, no. 6 (June 1982): 76.
3. Robert T. Lanz and S. Thomas Moser, "Improving Management Letters," *Journal of Accountancy* 149, no 3 (March 1980): 39–42.
4. Ibid., p. 42.
5. Ibid., pp. 41–42.
6. Sommerfeld et al., pp. 164–65.
7. Adapted from Sommerfeld, et. al., pp. 184–86.
8. Adapted from William A. Raebe, Gerald E. Whittenburg, and John C. Bost, *West's Federal Tax Research* (St. Paul: West Publishing Company, 1987), 259.
9. Adopted with permission from Charles T. Horngren and Walter T. Harrison, *Accounting* (Englewood Cliffs, N.J.: Prentice Hall, Inc., 1989), 306.
10. Randolph A. Shockley, "Writing Assignment for Intermediate Accounting" (unpublished class assignment, University of Georgia, 1982).
11. William R. Pasewark, "Writing Assignment for Intermediate Accounting" (unpublished class assignment, University of Georgia, 1987).
12. Adapted from American Institute of Certified Public Accountants, *Uniform CPA Exam: Questions and Unofficial Answers, November 1988* (New York: AICPA, 1989), 54.
13. George Peek, "Writing Assignment for Intermediate Accounting" (unpublished class assignment, University of Georgia, 1986).
14. Adapted with permission from Alvin A. Arens and James K. Loebbecke, *Auditing: An Integrated Approach,* 4th ed. (Englewood Cliffs, N.J.: Prentice Hall, Inc., 1988), 37.
15. Adapted with permission from Charles T. Horngren and George Foster, *Cost Accounting: A Managerial Emphasis,* 6th ed. (Englewood Cliffs, N.J.: Prentice Hall, Inc., 1987), 37.
16. Adapted with permission from Prentice Hall, *1988 Federal Tax Course* (Englewood Cliffs, N.J.: Prentice Hall, Inc., 1987), 81.

9

Memos

Memos, also called memoranda or memorandums, are often used for communication within an organization—between departments, for example, or between a supervisor and other members of the staff. Memos may be of any length, from one sentence to several pages. They may be less formal than letters written to people outside the organization, but well-written memos have the same qualities as good letters: clarity, conciseness, coherence, and courtesy.

This chapter first discusses some of the general characteristics of effective memos. Then we look at two special kinds of memos that accountants often write: memos to clients' files and memos that are part of working papers.

MEMOS: SOME BASIC PRINCIPLES

Often memos are quite short—from one sentence, perhaps, to several paragraphs. Figure 9–1 is an example. Notice the heading of the memo: the person or persons addressed, the writer, the subject, and the date. Often the writer's initials replace a formal signature.

Sometimes memos are much longer than the one in Figure 9–1; in fact, they may be used for short reports. For longer memos, organization

FIGURE 9–1 *Sample Memo*

To: Fourth-floor employees
From: Skip Waller
Subject: Scheduled painting
Date: September 12, 1998

Our painting contractors are scheduled to repaint the offices and public areas on our floor next week, September 18–22. The contractors understand that we will continue to work in the offices during this time and will try to disturb us as little as possible. But the work is bound to be somewhat disruptive, so let's all stay flexible and keep a sense of humor during this time that is bound to be somewhat inconvenient.

Thanks for your cooperation as we complete this much-needed maintenance.

and structure are more complicated, so you need to think of writing the memo in terms of the writing process discussed in chapter 2. You need to spend some time planning your memo: analyzing its purpose, considering the needs and interests of your readers, perhaps doing some research, and finally organizing the material to be covered into a good outline. Once you have planned the memo, you can then draft and revise it using the techniques covered in chapters 2 through 7.

The Parts of a Memo: Organizing for Coherence

Like most kinds of writing, a memo is organized into an introduction, a body, and a conclusion. Summary sentences are used throughout the memo to make it more coherent.

Even very short memos have this structure. The memo in Figure 9–1, which contains only two paragraphs, begins by summarizing the main idea of the memo. The remainder of the first paragraph provides additional information, and the final paragraph, which is only one sentence, concludes by thanking the readers for their cooperation.

Introduction Most introductions are from one sentence to one paragraph long, although for a longer memo the introduction may be two or three short paragraphs. The introduction should identify what the memo is about and why it was written. If the memo will discuss more than one topic or be divided into several subtopics, the introduction should identify all the most important issues to be covered. The introduction might contain a sentence such as the following to indicate the memo's contents:

> This memo explains how to account for patents, copyrights, and trademarks.

An introduction should also identify the main ideas or recommendations of your memo. Sometimes the main idea can be summarized in one or two sentences, but for longer memos, you may need an entire paragraph. If the summary of your main ideas is longer than a paragraph, it's often better to put it in a separate section immediately following the introduction. This section would have a heading such as "Summary" or "Recommendations."

Body The body of the memo can be divided into sections, each with a heading that describes the contents of that section. Remember to begin by summarizing the main idea of the section.

A section may have one or many paragraphs. Paragraphs should usually be no more than four or five sentences long, and each should begin with a topic sentence.

Conclusion Memos often end with a conclusion, which may be very brief.

> Let me know if you have any further questions about these procedures.

A conclusion such as this one brings the memo to a close and ends in a courteous, helpful tone. Here's a word of caution, though, about conclusions like the one just given: Be careful not to end all your memos with the same sentence (or some slightly altered variation). The conclusion should be a meaningful addition to the memo, not just an empty string of words added out of habit. Also, be sure your conclusion (like the rest of the memo) is appropriate to your reader. Why would the conclusion above be unsuitable for a memo you're sending to your boss?

The sample memos in this chapter show several different kinds of conclusions; all are appropriate to the content of the memo and the reader.

One misconception some people have about conclusions is that they should always repeat the memo's main ideas. For short memos, this repetition is usually not necessary, although for memos longer than about three or four pages such an ending summary may be helpful.

Whatever the length of the memo, the conclusion is a good place to tell your readers what you want them to do, or what you will do, to follow up on the ideas discussed in the memo. The memo in Figure 9–1 has such a conclusion.

Concise, Clear, Readable Memos: Style and Tone

Memos should be as concise as possible: no unnecessary repetitions or digressions and no wordiness. They should be written in clear, direct style, so that readers find them interesting and informative. Finally, memos should have flawless grammar and mechanics.

Memos can vary considerably in tone, depending on what they are about and how they will be circulated. Some memos, such as the one in Figure 9–1, are quite informal. For these memos, a conversational, personal tone is appropriate.

Other memos are more formal and may serve as short reports. Some memos, such as the one in Figure 9–4, may report the results of research or work performed, and may thus become part of the permanent records in a client's file. These memos are usually written with a more impersonal, formal tone, but whether formal or informal, all memos should be written in a vigorous, readable style.

Formats

Memos can be written in a variety of formats, as the examples in this chapter show. The memo in Figure 9–2[1] is typical of the format used in many organizations. Notice especially how the headings and set-off list make this memo attractive and easy to read.

Some organizations prefer another format that has become customary within the organization. You should prepare your memos according to your employer's expectations. The examples in Figures 9–3 and 9–4 illustrate formats some CPA firms prefer when the memos are part of a client's file.

If you are free to design the format of your memos, be conservative. Some word processing programs have memo templates that print with oversized fonts and a great deal of inked space. In many firms, these formats would be considered inappropriate.

SAMPLE MEMOS

The memo shown in Figure 9–2 was written in response to the hypothetical situation described below.

Situation:

Floyd Jones is the proprietor of the firm for which you work. Mr. Jones wants to acquire a manufacturing business. The business he wants to acquire, Sheraton Manufacturing, is insisting that Floyd pay not only for the identifiable net assets of the business but also for "goodwill." Floyd asks you: "What is goodwill? Should I pay for it? If I should pay for it, how much should I pay?"

FIGURE 9–2 *A Memo*

MEMORANDUM August 16, 1998

TO: FLOYD JONES
FROM: DENNIS SMITH DS
SUBJECT: PURCHASING SHERATON MANUFACTURING

This memo is in response to your questions concerning the purchase of Sheraton Manufacturing. The memo will first explain goodwill and then discuss how to determine its value. By determining the value of Sheraton's goodwill, you will have a dollar amount to help you determine how much you want to offer for the company as a whole.

What Is Goodwill?

Goodwill is an intangible asset made up of items that may contribute to the value and earning power of a company but that are not listed on the company's balance sheet. Here are some possible items that may make up goodwill for Sheraton Manufacturing:

1) Highly capable engineering staff
2) Strong reputation for quality work
3) Good management
4) A large number of loyal customers

These items are not listed on Sheraton's balance sheet. However, they obviously have value and, therefore, should be included in the purchase price of the business.

Determining the Value of Goodwill

The value of goodwill is established by comparing the present value of future cash earnings with the fair market value of a firm's other assets, less liabilities. The difference between the two is the value of goodwill.

The key to determining the value of goodwill is, of course, estimating the present value of future cash earnings. In the case of Sheraton Manufacturing, we can do this by accomplishing a cash-flow analysis similar to the ones we perform in our capital budgeting process.

Let me know if you have any further questions about goodwill or the Sheraton Manufacturing acquisition.

Study the memo in Figure 9–2 to see how it illustrates the principles of memo writing already discussed. Do you think Mr. Jones will be pleased with the memo?

Memos to Clients' Files

Accountants often record information about a client's situation in a memo that is placed in the client's file for later reference. Other members of the staff may refer to the information recorded in these memos months or even years later, so the information must be recorded clearly, accurately, and correctly.

For example, a client may write or call an accounting firm about a tax question. The person receiving the letter or handling the call will then write a memo to record the pertinent facts of the client's situation. Later, another member of the staff can research the question. The researcher will need adequate information to identify the issues, locate appropriate literature, and solve the client's problem.[2]

A sample memo written for a client's file appears in Figure 9–3.[3]

Memos as Part of Working Papers

When accountants prepare working papers as part of their work on a job, they usually include memos summarizing the work they've performed, what they've observed, and the conclusions they've reached. In an audit, for example, the audit staff members prepare memos describing each major area of the audit. Then a supervisor, perhaps the auditor in charge or the engagement partner, will often prepare a summary or review memo that includes comments on the entire audit process.

These memos must be clear, accurate, and complete. Other members of the firm, or lawyers on either side of a court case who review the working papers later, may need to know exactly what procedures the auditors performed. Thus, the memos should be written in a direct, active style: "I [the person writing the memo] performed a cash receipts walk-through on May 31, 1998. I used admission ticket #51065 for the test."

The memo in Figure 9–4 was written to record an inventory observation.[4] This memo has a different organization and format from the sample memos given earlier in the chapter, yet it illustrates qualities essential for effective writing: coherence, conciseness, and clarity. What specific techniques make this memo effective?

When your job requires you to write a memo, remember the techniques of effective writing stressed throughout this book. *Coherent* memos are logically organized and easy to follow; *concise* memos cover essential information in as few words as possible; and *clear* memos are precise, readable, and grammatically correct. *Courteous* memos help ensure that you maintain good relationships with your colleagues.

FIGURE 9–3 ***A Memo to a Client's File***

April 1, 1999

TO:	Files
FROM:	Tom Partner *TP*
SUBJECT:	Potential acquisition by American Rock & Sand, Inc., of Pahrump Ready Mix, Inc.

Today, Ron Jones, financial vice president of American Rock & Sand, Inc. (ARS), called to request information concerning the tax consequences of a proposed acquisition of Pahrump Ready Mix, Inc. (PRM). ARS is a Utah corporation (organized on October 1, 1962) licensed as a general contractor and specializes in road and highway construction. ARS employs the accrual method of accounting and uses a calendar year end as the basis for maintaining its books. ARS's authorized capital consists of 1,000 shares of voting common stock owned principally by the Jones family.

PRM, the target corporation, is a Utah Corporation organized on June 1, 1970. PRM is engaged in the business of making and delivering concrete. PRM employs the accrual method of accounting and uses a calendar year end as the basis for maintaining its books. PRM's authorized capital consists of 5,000 shares of voting common stock owned principally by the Smith family.

ARS has approached PRM about the possibility of acquiring the assets of PRM. PRM has expressed some preliminary interest if the deal can be structured so that the Smith family is not taxed on the initial sale of PRM. The Smith family has stated that they would consider receiving ARS stock as long as the stock will provide them with an annual income.

Due to a shortage of cash, ARS would like to accomplish the acquisition without the use of cash. Also, the Jones family has stated strenuously that they are not interested in giving up any voting power in ARS to the Smith family. John Jones has requested that we develop, if possible, a proposal of how ARS can structure the transaction to satisfy the requests of both ARS and PRM. Mr. Jones has requested that we present at their May 1, 1999, ARS board meeting our proposal for the acquisition of PRM. If we need further information, we are to contact Mr. Jones directly.

FIGURE 9–4 ***A Memo as Part of Working Papers***

Prepared by: C.J.G. Date: 1/05/99
Reviewed by: A.C.E. Date: 1/11/99

Highlight Company
Inventory Observation Memorandum—Wayne Plant A
12/31/98

1. Observing clients' inventory taking. Four members of our audit staff arrived at the Wayne plant at 7:40 a.m. on 12/31/98 for the inventory observation. All manufacturing and shipping operations had been shut down for the day. All materials had been neatly arranged, labeled, and separated by type.

   Two teams of audit staff members were assigned to different parts of the plant. Each team observed the care with which the client's personnel made the inventory counts and the control being exercised over the inventory count sheets. In every case, it appeared that the client's inventory instructions were being followed in a systematic and conscientious manner.

2. Making test counts. Each team made numerous test counts, which were recorded in our work papers (see F-2). The test counts covered approximately 22 percent of the inventory value and confirmed the accuracy of the client's counts.

3. Identifying obsolete and damaged goods. Each team made inquiries concerning obsolete, damaged, or slow-moving items. Based on our observations and inquiries, we have no reason to believe that any obsolete or damaged materials remained in inventory. We identified certain slow-moving items, portions of which on further investigation were excluded from the inventory (see F-4).

4. Observing cutoff controls. We observed that receiving reports were prepared on all goods received on the inventory date and recorded the number of the last receiving report prepared. No goods were shipped on 12/31. We recorded the number of the last shipping document used on 12/30. These numbers were subsequently used in our purchases and sales cutoff tests (see F-6 and F-7).

FIGURE 9–4 ***A Memo as Part of Working Papers (cont.)***

5. Conclusions. Based on our observation of the procedures followed by the client, it is my opinion that an accurate count was made of all goods on hand at 12/31/98 and that all obsolete, damaged, or slow-moving items were appropriately identified.

Carl Good

E-MAIL

With the explosion of information technology, many memos are now written in the form of e-mail messages. E-mail is extremely convenient; with the click of a mouse, a memo can be sent to a colleague in the next office or a business partner in Hong Kong.

A number of special considerations should be observed when you use e-mail:

- Address messages carefully. Stories of messages being sent to unintended recipients abound. This often occurs when a memo is addressed to "staff" or some other general address, when the intended recipient is an individual. The results are sometimes humorous, as when an employee sends a love note to the entire corporation; or they can be disastrous, as might occur when the plans for a new product are sent by mistake to the firm's competitors. The lesson is to "think twice and click once" when addressing e-mail messages.
- Remember that even though an e-mail message is addressed and sent to an individual it may still be read by unintended recipients. E-mail messages are not private. They are sent over computer communications networks, where they can be easily intercepted. That nasty message you sent to your friend criticizing your boss might end up on your boss's desk without your knowledge! In general, you should assume that every e-mail message you write may be read by anyone and everyone else. Compose your messages accordingly.
- Remember that all e-mail messages can be saved and used as proof that the communication took place. There are no "off-the record" e-mails. Generally this is not a problem, because presumably the reason you are sending a memo by e-mail is to record some information for the record; but occasionally people fall into the trap of treating e-mail like a phone call. For example, they may say in an e-mail something like "Steve thinks he's going to exercise his options for $4,000, but it'll never happen as long as I'm the CFO." Imagine how this CFO will feel if Steve turns up with a copy of the e-mail message. Again, the best advice is assume that every e-mail message you write will be read by everyone else. Compose your messages accordingly.

- Avoid sending junk e-mail. People, even financial professionals, constantly send e-mail to people other than their intended addressees simply because they click on group addresses out of habit. "Tom, I'll be out of town Monday. Handle the meeting, will you? Thanks, Bill." is an example of a memo that has meaning only for Tom. What may happen, however, is that Bill will send the message to "Corporate Staff," or something similar, because that is the button he is used to clicking on when he sends e-mail. Consequently, perhaps 40 people will receive Tom's message and must take time to access it and then delete it (worse—sometimes they will reply to it, perpetuating the problem).

EXERCISES

Exercise 9–1 (All Levels)

You work in the accounting department of Midsouth Corporation. The company's chief executive officer, Mary Sanders, has asked you to be in charge of your department's fundraising for the United Way campaign.

Write a memo to your coworkers asking them to contribute to this year's campaign. The memo will accompany a pledge card that they may fill in and sign. Make the memo persuasive, and add any details you think would make the memo effective.

Exercise 9–2 (All Levels)

You are newly hired as an accountant for the O-Y-Me Corporation, which is a small service business currently using the cash basis of accounting. The president of your company, Mr. Now U. Donit, has requested that you write a memo to him explaining what the accrual basis of accounting is, how it differs from the cash basis, and why O-Y-Me should switch from the cash basis to the accrual basis.

Exercise 9–3 (Intermediate)

You are newly hired as an accountant for the O-Y-Me Corporation, a small service business which has no formal capital budgeting system. The president of your company, Mr. Now U. Donit, has requested that you write a memo to him explaining what the net present value method of investment evaluation is, how it differs from the payback period method, and why O-Y-Me should use the net present value method for capital budgeting purposes instead of the payback method.

Exercise 9–4 (All Levels)

You are an accountant and loan officer at Gotham City National Bank. The proprietors of two businesses, Butler Department Store and Susan Nielsen Home Decorators, have sought business loans from you. To decide whether to make the loans, you have requested their balance sheets, which are shown in Figure 9–5. Based solely on these balance sheets, which entity would you be more comfortable loaning money to? Explain fully, citing specific items and amounts from the balance sheets.

FIGURE 9–5 *For Exercise 9–4*

Butler Department Store
Balance Sheet
August 31, 1998

Assets		Liabilities	
Cash	$ 1,000	Accounts payable	$12,000
Accounts receivable	14,000	Note payable	18,000
Merchandise inventory	85,000	Total liabilities	30,000
Store supplies	500		
Furniture and fixtures	9,000		
Building	90,000	Owner's Equity	
Land	14,000	Roy Butler, capital	183,500
		Total liabilities	
Total assets	$ 213,500	and owner's equity	$213,500

Susan Nielsen Home Decorators
Balance Sheet
August 31, 1998

Assets		Liabilities	
Cash	$11,000	Accounts payable	$ 3,000
Accounts receivable	4,000	Note payable	18,000
Office supplies	1,000	Total liabilities	21,000
Office furniture	6,000		
Land	19,000	Owner's Equity	
		Susan Nielsen, capital	20,000
		Total liabilities	
Total assets	$41,500	and owner's equity	$41,500

Write your answer in the form of a memo to the bank's vice president, Edward Barth.[5]

Exercise 9–5 (Financial)

You are the controller of Carr Corporation. One morning you receive the memo shown in Figure 9–6 from the president of your company, W. R. Pasewark. Write a memo in response to the president's questions.[6]

FIGURE 9–6 *Memo for Exercise 9–5*

CARR CORPORATION
OFFICE MEMO

To: I. N. Dunne, Controller
From: W. R. Pasewark, President *WRP*
Date: June 26, 1998
Subject: Who sets the rules for accounting?

As you know, this will be the first year that our company has issued financial statements. I am particularly concerned about what rules we must follow in preparing our financial statements to accommodate our external auditors.

Recently, I examined the audited financial statements of a company similar to ours. The auditor's opinion section mentioned that the financial statements were prepared in accordance with "generally accepted accounting principles." I suspect that these are the rules that we must follow when preparing our own financial statements.

Would you please help me by answering the following questions concerning generally accepted accounting principles?

1. Who determines generally accepted accounting principles?
2. If we violate these rules, will we be breaking the law?
3. If these rules are not law, why must we follow them?

Exercise 9–6 (Managerial)

You are the controller of Sam's Bargain Department Store. Recently, you have become aware that your company needs to evaluate and perhaps redesign its internal control system. To familiarize the store managers with the need for a good internal control system, you have decided to write a memo explaining what internal control is and why it's important to a store like Sam's. You can make up hypothetical examples to illustrate your memo.

Exercise 9–7 (Intermediate Financial)

You are the controller of the Red Mesa Ranch and are preparing the ranch's financial statements for the year. You requested information from the cattle manager, Tuf Cowan, about the value of the ranch's livestock assets. Mr. Cowan sent you the memo shown in Figure 9–7, which asks you some questions about how to classify the livestock. Write a memo to answer Mr. Cowan's questions.[7]

FIGURE 9–7 *Memo for Exercise 9–7*

RED MESA RANCH
OFFICE MEMO

To: Ian Greenberg, Controller
From: Tuf Cowan, Cattle Manager
Date: June 28, 1998
Subject: Classification of livestock on the balance sheet

I have received your request to value our livestock assets for the balance sheet for the year ending June 30, 1998. Based on available commodity prices, I can easily determine the dollar value of the livestock. However, I am unable to determine whether the following livestock categories should be shown as current inventory items or as long-term assets:

1. Bulls—kept for breeding purposes; average useful life of ten years.
2. Steers—held for approximately 15 months from birth, then sold for slaughter.
3. Heifers—most kept for breeding purposes; average useful life of five years, then sold for slaughter.
4. Calves—less than one year old, certain percentage sold as veal, others used for breeding or grazed and sold later for slaughter.

Would you please assist me by specifying how I should classify each of these categories?

Exercise 9–8 (Intermediate Financial)

You are the staff accountant for Ms. Ima Astute, who owns a small business. Ms. Astute is considering the purchase of a competing business. The sum of the fair market values of the separately identifiable assets of the business she may purchase is $350,000. Ms. Astute determined this amount by having an appraisal made before making an offer. The offer she made was equal to this amount—that is, $350,000. The owner of the business she wants to purchase has declined the offer and indicated he thinks his business is worth at least $400,000, considering the goodwill that exists. Ms. Astute cannot understand how the business can be worth more than $350,000, considering this was the amount of the appraisal.

Write a memo to Ms. Astute explaining what goodwill is, why it may exist for the business she wants to purchase, how to determine what to pay for it, and the effects on future financial statements she may expect.

Exercise 9–9 (Intermediate Financial)

Skinner Company has the following contingencies:

- Potential costs due to the discovery of a possible defect related to one of its products. These costs are probable and can be reasonably estimated.
- A potential claim for damages to be received from a lawsuit filed this year against another company. It is probable that proceeds from the claim will be received by Skinner next year.
- Potential costs due to a promotion campaign whereby a cash refund is sent to customers when coupons are redeemed. Skinner estimated, based on past experience, that 70 percent of the coupons would be redeemed. Forty percent of the coupons were actually redeemed and the cash refunds sent this year. The remaining 30 percent of the coupons are expected to be redeemed next year.

Required:

1. How should Skinner report the potential costs due to the discovery of a possible product defect? Why?
2. How should Skinner report this year the potential claim for damages that may be received next year? Why?
3. This year, how should Skinner account for the potential costs and obligations due to the promotion campaign?

You are a staff accountant at Skinner Company. Write your answer in the form of a memo the company's controller, Daniel Gordon.[8]

Exercise 9–10 (Intermediate Financial)

Daniel Gordon, the president of the Skinner Company, is considering a bond issue to raise $1,000,000 for the company. Mr. Gordon notes that long-term T–Bonds yield 6 percent, and he thinks that is a good loan rate. Before proceeding with the bond issue, however, Mr. Gordon wants to know more about it. Specifically, he wonders what the annual interest payments would be on the bonds.

You are a financial analyst at Skinner Company. Write a memo to Mr. Gordon explaining what the interest payments on a $1,000,000, 20-year bond issue would be if the bonds were issued at a 6 percent yield. Also explain in your memo why the Skinner Company would probably not be able to issue the bonds at 6 percent.

Exercise 9–11 (Auditing)

Recently, while eating lunch with your family at a local cafeteria, you observed a practice that is somewhat unusual. As you reached the end of the cafeteria line, an adding machine operator asked how many people were in your party. He then totaled the food purchases on the trays for all of your family and wrote the number of people included in the group on the adding machine tape. He handed you the tape and asked you to pay when you finished eating. Near the end of the meal, you decided you wanted a piece of pie and coffee so you returned to the line, selected your food, and again went through the line. The adding machine operator went through the same procedures, but this time he stapled the second tape to the original and returned it to you.

When you left the cafeteria, you handed the stapled adding machine tapes to the cash register operator, who totaled the two tapes, took your money, and put the tapes on a spindle.

The morning after your visit to the cafeteria, you are surprised to learn that your CPA firm has been hired to audit this cafeteria. Your job will be to evaluate the cafeteria's internal control system. As part of your evaluation, you should consider these questions:

1. What internal controls has the cafeteria instituted for its operations?
2. How can you evaluate the effectiveness of the control procedures?
3. How do these controls differ from those used by most cafeterias?
4. What are the costs and benefits of the cafeteria's system?

Write a memo to the partner in charge of the audit, summarizing your analysis of these questions.[9]

Exercise 9–12 (Auditing)

The firm for which you work, Temple and Temple, CPAs, is auditing the financial statements of Ford Lumber Yards, Inc., a privately held corporation with 300 employees and five stockholders, three of whom are active in management. Ford has been in business for many years but has never had its financial statements audited. The partner in charge of the audit suspects that the substance of some of Ford's business transactions differs from their form because of the pervasiveness of related party relationships and transactions in the local building supplies industry.

Required:

Describe the audit procedures Temple should apply to identify related party relationships and transactions.[10]

Write your answer in the form of a memo to the staff accountants who will audit Ford.

Exercise 9–13 (Tax)

Mark Rood has asked you to prepare his income tax return for the tax year ending December 31, 1998. His records indicate that he received wages and commissions of $30,000 from his job as a salesperson. The records also indicate that Rood did the following during the year:

1. Transferred one-half of his 100 shares of IMP stock, bought in 1989 for $12 a share and worth (on the date of the transfer) $26 a share, to his divorced wife as part of their property settlement.
2. Sold 50 shares of the IMP stock in March 1998 for $29 per share.
3. Bought a rare Mongolian coin to add to his collection in March of 1995 for $1,000. In August, he sold the coin for $1,800.
4. Bought a Ghanian coin for $2,500 in September and sold it in November for $1,000.

Assuming these are Rood's only capital assets transactions during the year, what is his adjusted gross income?

Write a memo to Rood's file in which you answer this question. Be sure to show the step-by-step computation of his gains and losses.[11]

Exercise 9–14 (Tax)

The George Valentine Company's current earnings and profits were $2,000,000 during the year. Has the company made a distribution of taxable dividends in any of the following transactions?

1. The company owns and rents a luxury apartment building. It rents one of its five-room apartments to its major stockholder at 30 percent less than its fair rental value.
2. The company loans $80,000 to its 50 percent shareholder to help him buy a home. In return, the shareholder gives the company a personal note as security for the loan and is charged a reasonable rate of interest (equivalent to the applicable federal rate). The company carries the loan on its books as an account receivable.
3. Mr. George Valentine was the founder and the former chairman of the board of the company. He retired 10 years ago, having been adequately compensated during the years of his active service. He still owns 100 percent of the company stock. He was paid a fee of $100,000 this year even though he has not been active in business since his retirement.

Write a memo to the client file of the George Valentine Company. Analyze each transaction and explain why it is or is not a distribution of taxable dividends.[12]

Exercise 9–15 (E-mail)

Recently you have noticed that your "in-basket" on the local area network in your company accumulates 8 to 10 messages a day that are jokes and humorous stories downloaded from the Internet. Most of these messages are not very funny, but they all take time to delete, and sometimes in the process of deleting them you delete important messages by accident. Clearly the situation has gotten out of hand. Write a memo to the staff about the problem and ask that the practice of distributing humorous e-mail messages be discontinued. Be sure to explain your reasoning so you won't come across as dictatorial. You expect to send your memo as an e-mail message.

NOTES

1. Adapted from Pete Wardlaw, "Purchasing DCL Broadcasting" (unpublished student paper, University of Georgia, 1987).
2. Ray M. Sommerfeld, G. Fred Streuling, Robert L. Gardner, and Dave N. Stewart, *Tax Research Techniques*, 3rd ed., Revised (New York: American Institute of Certified Public Accountants, 1989), 160-62.
3. Adapted from Sommerfeld et al., p. 161.
4. Reprinted by permission, from pp. 490–91 in *Modern Auditing* by Walter G. Kell and Richard E. Ziegler. Copyright © 1980 by John Wiley & Sons, Inc.
5. Adapted with permission from Charles T. Horngren and Walter T. Harrison, *Accounting,* 2nd ed. (Englewood Cliffs, N.J.: Prentice Hall, Inc., 1989), 36–37.
6. William R. Pasewark, "Writing Assignment for Intermediate Accounting" (unpublished class assignment, University of Georgia, 1987).
7. Ibid.
8. Adapted from American Institute of Certified Public Accountants, *Uniform CPA Exam: Questions and Unofficial Answers, November 1988* (New York: American Institute of Certified Public Accountants, 1989), 55.
9. Adapted from Alvin A. Arens and James K. Loebbecke, *Auditing: An Integrated Approach,* 6th ed. (Englewood Cliffs, N.J.: Prentice Hall, Inc., 1994), 307. Reprinted by permission.
10. Adapted from American Institute of Certified Public Accountants, *Uniform CPA Exam: Questions and Unofficial Answers, November 1988* (New York: American Institute of Certified Public Accountants, 1989), 34.
11. Adapted with permission from Prentice-Hall, *1988 Federal Tax Course* (Englewood Cliffs, N.J.: Prentice-Hall, Inc. © 1987), 279.
12. Ibid., p. 279.

10

Reports

Sometimes accountants prepare formal reports, such as a report for a client that a CPA in public practice might prepare. Managerial accountants might prepare reports for other departments in their firm or perhaps for a group of managers with a particular need.

A report usually involves analysis of an accounting problem and application of accounting principles to a particular situation. It may also require some research of professional literature or other material, so the research techniques discussed in chapter 7 are often part of report preparation.

Reports vary in length, but all reports should meet certain basic criteria. The accounting content should be accurate, the organization should be coherent, the report should be presented attractively, and the writing style should be clear and concise. Like all forms of writing, a report should be designed and written with the readers' needs and expectations in mind.

PLANNING A REPORT

If you are preparing a report on the job, your company may have an established format for you to follow for all reports. Be sure to find out the expectations and policies of your organization before you begin work on your report. Even if the organization doesn't require employees to follow a certain report format, you may find your job easier if you use several well-written reports as models.

If you are free to design your own report format, or if you are preparing the report for a class assignment, the format presented in this chapter can serve as a model. It is a generic model, typical of those used in business and industry.

In planning the report, you must also consider the purpose of the report and who its readers will be. The analysis of purpose and audience for a report may be more difficult than it is for letters and memos. A report may have many groups of readers, and each group will have different interests and needs.

For example, a report recommending that a firm invest in a new computer system might be circulated to the Management Information Systems (MIS) department, the accounting department, the departments that would actually use the system, and senior management. Of course, the accounting department would be interested in the accounting aspects of the acquisition as well as how the system could be used for various accounting tasks. The MIS department would be interested in the technical features of the system and how it would affect MIS personnel. Other departments would want to know how the system would make their work easier or more difficult, whether it would affect their budgets, and whether their personnel would have the training to use the system. Senior management, on the other hand, would be interested in a bigger picture, such as how the system would affect the firm's efficiency, competitiveness, and cash flow.

To write this report, you would need to identify clearly who the readers are and what information they want the report to include. You would obviously be writing to readers with different degrees of knowledge about technical features of the new system and with different interests and concerns as well. The way to handle this complicated situation is to write different parts of the report for different groups of readers.

Fortunately, many reports are not as difficult to plan and write as this one would be, but this example shows how important it is to analyze carefully the needs and expectations of different groups of readers.

Most reports require a great deal of research. They may report the results of empirical studies or pilot projects, or report research involving technical literature or generally accepted accounting principles. Organizing this research into a coherent outline is essential. Review the principles of organization discussed in chapter 3, and then apply the following questions to your report as you are planning the outline and structuring your draft.

1. Is the subject covered adequately?
   - Background information when necessary
   - Adequate explanations, supporting data, and examples

- Citations from GAAP and other authorities, as needed
- Application to the specific needs and interests of the readers

2. Is the report too long?
   - Digressions—off the subject
   - Too much explanation or detail
   - Repetitions or wordiness
3. Is the report organized logically?
   - In order from most to least important—from the readers' point of view
   - Summary sentences where helpful
   - Transitions to link ideas
   - Short, well-organized paragraphs with topic sentences

The format of a report—how its various parts are put together—also determines how coherent the report is.

THE PARTS OF A REPORT

Reports can be presented in a variety of formats, but they are all designed to make the report easy to read. The format presented in this handbook is typical of the ways in which reports are structured.

A report may include these sections:

Transmittal document
Title page
Table of contents
List of illustrations
Summary section
Introduction
Body of the report
Conclusion
Appendices
Notes
Bibliography
Graphic illustrations

Transmittal Document

The transmittal document can be either a letter or memo, depending on whether you are sending your report to someone outside your organization or within it. This document is a cover letter or memo: It presents the report to the people for whom it was written and adds any other information that will be helpful.

The transmittal document will not be long, but it should include essential information: the report's title, its topic, and its purpose. It's usually a good idea to summarize the main idea or recommendation of the report if you can do so in about one or two sentences. You may want to add other comments about the report that will be helpful to the readers, but always end with a courteous closing.

Whereas the style of the actual report is usually formal and impersonal, the transmittal document can usually be more conversational, including the use of personal pronouns.

Title Page

In a professional report, the title page may look something like this:

Title of Report
Prepared for . . .
Prepared by . . .
Date

For a student's report, the instructor may prefer information such as this:

Title of Report
Student's Name
Course and Period
Instructor
Date

Table of Contents

The table of contents should be on a separate page and should have a heading. The contents listed are the major parts of the report, excluding the transmittal document, with the appropriate page numbers.

List of Illustrations

The list of illustrations, if applicable, includes titles and page numbers of graphs, charts, and other illustrations.

Summary Section

All formal reports should have a section at the beginning of the report that summarizes the main ideas and recommendations. This section can vary in length from one paragraph to several pages, and it can come either immediately before or immediately after the introduction. The summary section may be called an executive summary, abstract, synopsis, summary, or some other term.

An executive summary is especially helpful for long reports. This section gives the readers an overview of the report's contents without the technical detail. Busy managers may read the executive summary to decide whether they should read the entire report.

The executive summary identifies the purpose and scope of the report and possibly the methods used for research. It includes the major findings of the research, the conclusions of the researcher, and the recommendations, if any.

The length of an executive summary varies with the length of the report, but it is generally about one to three pages long. It should begin on a separate page following the table of contents or list of illustrations, and should be titled *Executive Summary*. The sample report at the end of this chapter uses this kind of summary.

For shorter reports, a section right after the introduction can provide a summary of the report's main ideas and recommendations. This section should be labeled *Summary;* it is usually one or two paragraphs long.

Introduction

The introduction of a formal report is longer than that of a letter or memo. It is usually at least two or three short paragraphs, and for long reports may even be longer than a page.

The introduction should identify the subject of the report and may state why it was written—who requested or authorized it, or for whom it was prepared. The introduction should state the purpose of the report in specific terms:

> The purpose of this report is to discuss the feasibility of offering a stock bonus plan to employees of Gulf Coast Industries.
>
> NOT: The purpose of this report is to discuss stock bonus plans.

Sometimes an introduction includes additional information to help the reader. For example, it may give a brief background of the report's topic. However, if it's necessary to include very much background information, this material should be presented in a separate section in the body of the report.

Finally, the introduction of a report should end with a plan of development that gives the reader an overview or forecast of the topics the report covers and the order in which they are presented. A simple plan of development may be in sentence form:

> This report describes the proposed pension plan and then discusses its costs and benefits.

Sometimes a set-off list makes the plan of development easier to read:

> This report discusses the following topics related to the proposed pension plan:
>
> - Major provisions
> - Benefits to employees
> - Benefits to the corporation

- Cost
- Accounting for the plan

Body of the Report

The body of the report should be divided into sections and possibly subsections, each with an appropriate heading. Remember to begin each section with a statement that summarizes the main idea to be covered in that section.

The body of the report may also contain graphic illustrations, as discussed below.

Conclusion

In addition to the summary section at the beginning, a report should have a conclusion to remind the reader of the report's main ideas and recommendations. This section may be from one paragraph to several pages.

Appendices (Optional)

Depending on the report's audience and purpose, you may want to place technical information and statistics in appendices at the end of the report. If you use an appendix, give it a title and refer to it in the body of the report.

Notes and Bibliography

What to put at the end of the report depends in part on the style of documentation you use. If you use endnotes, they should begin on a separate page and be labeled *Notes.*

Almost all reports have some sort of bibliography or reference list. This list identifies the sources you cited in your paper, and it may also include additional references the reader might wish to consult. This section should begin on a separate page following the notes (if any), and should have a title such as *Bibliography* or *References.*

Chapter 7 demonstrates the proper form for endnotes and bibliographical entries.

Graphic Illustrations

Sometimes graphic illustrations, such as graphs or tables, make a report easier to read and more interesting, especially if you are presenting statistical or numerical data or if the subject of the report concerns a process. You can place graphic illustrations either in an appendix or in the body of your report, just after the place in the text where they are discussed.

Graphic illustrations are discussed more fully in chapter 6.

APPEARANCE

It's important to present your report as attractively as possible. Use good quality paper and be sure that the report is printed with a letter-quality printer.

Reports may be single-spaced or double-spaced, depending on the situation. Student's reports are usually double-spaced to provide space for annotations when they are graded. In all reports the transmittal document and any set-off material are single-spaced. Pages should be numbered, using lowercase Roman numerals for front matter (table of contents, list of illustrations, executive summary) and Arabic numerals for the remainder of the report, from the introduction through the end matter.

STYLE AND TONE

The tone of a formal report should usually be just what its name implies: formal, and therefore impersonal. For example, you probably would not use personal pronouns or contractions. However, a formal style should still be readable and interesting, so you should use the techniques of effective style discussed in chapter 4. Even a formal document can be written simply, clearly, and concretely.

Unlike the actual report, the transmittal document may be written in a personal, more informal style.

The report in Figure 10–1 illustrates many of these techniques of effective report writing.[1]

FIGURE 10–1 *A Report*

B&H Financial Consultants
125 Easy Street
Athens, Georgia
August 8, 1998

Mr. Sam Hamilton
Hamilton Manufacturing
1890 Meerly Avenue
Atlanta, Georgia 30306

Dear Mr. Hamilton:

Enclosed is the report about convertible bonds that you requested in your letter of July 21. The report, titled *Convertible Bonds: Financial and Accounting Considerations*, examines the nature of convertible debt, the pros and cons of such an issue, and the accounting treatment of the securities.

The report shows that convertible bonds may represent a relatively less expensive method of raising capital than nonconvertible bonds. Another advantage is that should the convertible bonds be converted, the existing shares of common stock will not be diluted as severely as they would be if common stock had been issued. However, as the report makes clear, these effects are by no means certain.

I believe the report will provide you with the information you need. If you have any further questions, however, don't hesitate to give me a call.

Sincerely yours,

Joyce Byran

Joyce Byran

jhw

FIGURE 10–1 *A Report (cont.)*

CONVERTIBLE BONDS:
FINANCIAL AND ACCOUNTING CONSIDERATIONS

Prepared for Hamilton Manufacturing

by

JOYCE BYRAN

AUGUST 8, 1998

FIGURE 10–1 *A Report (cont.)*

CONTENTS

i

FIGURE 10–1 *A Report (cont.)*

EXECUTIVE SUMMARY

This report provides information about convertible bonds for the managers of Hamilton Manufacturing. Included is information about the nature of convertible bonds, financial advantages and disadvantages of issuing such bonds, and their accounting treatment.

A convertible bond is a debt security that carries the option of exchange for an equity security, usually common stock. The bond indenture specifies when the bonds may be converted and a conversion price or ratio. The conversion price is usually 10 to 20 percent above the market price of the common stock at the time of issue. Both the issuer and the investor expect the market price of the stock to rise above the conversion price; therefore, bondholders are likely to convert the bond into equity.

Convertible bonds would offer Hamilton three advantages:

- The company could issue the bonds at a premium or at a low stated interest rate, which investors would accept because of the conversion privilege.
- The company could avoid another stock issue now, when the price of Hamilton's stock is low.
- Management would avoid possible conflict with its major stockholder.

There are also potential disadvantages management should consider before issuing the convertible bonds:

- The uncertain conditions of the economy make a future increase in the market price of the company's stock uncertain. If conversion does not occur, Hamilton may have difficulty meeting the debt requirements.
- Bond conversion will reduce earnings per share and operating leverage. Conversion will also increase Hamilton's income tax liability because of the loss of interest expense.
- The required accounting treatment of convertible bonds may have an unfavorable effect on the company's financial statements: a high level of debt may be presented alongside a lowered diluted earnings per share (DEPS).

ii

FIGURE 10–1 *A Report (cont.)*

CONVERTIBLE BONDS:
FINANCIAL AND ACCOUNTING CONSIDERATIONS

Introduction

The purpose of this report is to provide information for the management of Hamilton Manufacturing about an increasingly popular form of financing: convertible debt. Convertible debt is an issue of debt securities (bonds) that carry the option of exchange for equity securities (usually common stock).

Three major topics make up the report: (1) The nature of convertible bonds, (2) financial advantages and disadvantages Hamilton could expect if it issues the bonds, and (3) accounting treatment for the bonds.

Nature of Convertible Bonds

When convertible bonds are issued, the bond indenture specifies a period of time after issuance during which the bonds may be converted. The indenture also specifies a conversion price, "the amount of par value of principal amount of the bonds exchangeable for one share of stock" (Bogen 1968, 31). If a conversion ratio, rather than a conversion price, is specified, the effective price of stock to the bondholder may be determined by dividing the par value of the bond by the number of shares exchangeable for one bond.

The conversion price, which is determined when the bonds are sold, is usually from 10 to 20 percent above the prevailing market price of the common stock at the time of issue. Both the issuing firm and the investor expect that the market price of the stock will rise above the conversion price and that the conversion privilege will then be exercised by most or all bondholders.

The indenture typically includes a call provision so that the issuing firm can force bondholders to convert. Therefore, it is evident that firms issuing convertible debt often truly want to raise equity capital. The reasons that they choose convertible debt are discussed below.

1

FIGURE 10–1 *A Report (cont.)*

Financial Advantages and Disadvantages

Advantages

Use of convertible debt would offer Hamilton advantages over straight debt or stock issues.

Bonds that are convertible into stock are in demand. Therefore, bond buyers are willing to accept a low stated interest rate on such bonds, to pay a premium and accept a lower yield, or to accept less restrictive covenants. Hamilton could thus obtain funds at a lower cost than would be possible if it issued bonds without the conversion privilege.

The advantages of a convertible bond issue over a common stock issue relate to timing. Although Hamilton might be willing to take on more equity in the future, current economic conditions make this an unfavorable time to sell stock. One authority has explained this advantage as follows:

> To sell stock now would require giving up more shares to raise a given amount of money than management thinks is necessary. However, setting the conversion price 10 to 20 percent above the present market price of the stock will require giving up 10 to 20 percent fewer shares when the bonds are converted than would be required if stock were sold directly (Brigham 1978, 532).

Another possible advantage to Hamilton of issuing convertible bonds is that the company could avoid creating a possible conflict with the major stockholder, who would probably want to maintain his controlling interest. The stockholder might vote against a large issue of stock. However, the bond issue could be convertible into a number of shares small enough not to injure significantly the stockholder's interest.

Disadvantages

Most of the disadvantages of convertible bonds are related to the uncertainty of the conversion and its timing. If Hamilton's stock price does not rise, conversion will not occur and the company will not obtain the equity financing it desires. Hamilton might then have difficulty meeting the unplanned-for obligations of debt.

Other disadvantages arise, however, if the conversion does occur. When the debt becomes equity, basic earnings per share (BEPS) is reduced, operating leverage is reduced, and income taxes increase because interest expense is reduced.

2

FIGURE 10–1 *A Report (cont.)*

Accounting Treatment

The Accounting Principles Board (APB) has ruled that convertible bonds "which are sold at a price or have a value at issuance not significantly in excess of the face amount" must be treated in the same manner as other bonds (1969, par. 1). That is, "no portion of the proceeds from the issuance . . . should be accounted for as attributable to the conversion feature" (par. 10). The expectation that some or all of the bonds will be converted into stock is not recognized in the accounts.

Because convertible bonds are normally sold at a premium, the amount of the cash proceeds from the issue is greater than the face value of the bonds. The premium is amortized over the life of the bonds. The effect of the amortization is that the interest expense recorded by Hamilton each period would not equal the amount of the interest payment, but would reflect the effective yield to the bondholders.

When the bonds are converted, Hamilton will remove from the accounts the balance associated with those bonds. Two methods can be used to record the common stock issued in exchange for the bonds. Under one method, the stock is assigned a value equal to the market value of the stock or the bonds. If this value differs from the book value of the bonds (the balance associated with the bonds, mentioned above), then a gain or a loss is recorded. Under the other method, which is more widely used, the value assigned to the stock equals the book value of the bonds and no gain or loss is recognized or recorded (Chasteen, Flaherty, and O'Connor 1995, 693).

If Hamilton decides to retire its convertible bonds for cash before their maturity date, the transaction will be recorded in the same way as the early bonds and the cash paid to retire them will be a gain or a loss on the income statement.

Although convertibles are accounted for solely as debt, Hamilton must also consider the equity characteristics of such issues in computing diluted earnings per share (DEPS). The Financial Accounting Standards Board (FASB) requires that corporations having issued securities that are potentially dilutive of EPS, such as convertible bonds, must present both basic earnings per share (BEPS) and diluted earnings per share (DEPS) in their financial statements (1997, par. 36).

The DEPS figure represents EPS as if the bonds had been converted into stock. If they had been converted, the removal of the bonds would have caused a reduction of interest expense, which would have increased earnings. However, the positive effect of the earnings adjustment may not offset the negative effect of the shares adjustment. Thus, convertibles reduce reported DEPS.

3

FIGURE 10–1 *A Report (cont.)*

Conclusion

In the decision whether to finance with convertible debt, Hamilton must consider whether it would benefit from using convertibles rather than straight debt or stock issues and whether it can meet the debt requirements, should conversion not occur as expected. In addition, management should analyze carefully the effect of the issue on readers of the financial statements, because until the bonds are converted, a possibly high level of debt will exist alongside a lowered presentation of DEPS.

WORKS CITED

Accounting Principles Board. 1969. *Accounting for convertible debt and debt issued with stock purchase warrants.* Opinion no. 14. New York: AICPA.

Bogen, J. I., ed. 1968. *Financial handbook,* 4th ed. New York: Ronald Press.

Booker, J. A., and B. D. Jarnagin. 1979. *Financial accounting standards: Explanation and analysis.* Chicago: Commerce Clearing House.

Brigham, E. F. 1978. *Fundamentals of financial management.* Hinsdale, Ill.: Dryden Press.

Chasteen, L. G., R. E. Flaherty, and M. C. O'Connor. 1995. *Intermediate accounting,* 5th ed. New York: McGraw-Hill.

Financial Accounting Standards Board. 1997. *Earnings per share. Statement of financial accounting standards no. 128.* Stamford, Conn.: FASB.

4

EXERCISES

Exercise 10–1 (All Levels)

One of your clients, Albert P. Moneybags, III, has recently inherited a portfolio of stocks in various Fortune 500 companies. He has received the annual reports of these companies, which of course include the income statement, balance sheet, statement of cash flows, and statement of owners' equity.

Mr. Moneybags knows very little about these statements. He has asked you to write a report that explains the statements so that he can use them to manage his investments.

Prepare the report for your client. Supplement your discussion with sample financial statements that you construct yourself or find in the annual report of an actual company. Invent any details you need to make the report complete.

Exercise 10–2 (Intermediate)

A client, Robert Gutierrez, has just inherited some money and has decided to begin investing in a stock portfolio. He is not interested in mutual funds because he prefers to have personal control over his stock investments. He also realizes that over time he will need to have a diversified portfolio, but for now he wants to begin his investment strategy by purchasing stock in one company. Your client wants to invest about $10,000, but he is very concerned to keep his risk as low as possible.

Mr. Gutierrez has asked you to evaluate the annual reports of several corporations as possible investment options. Choose three corporations whose stock is listed on the New York Stock Exchange or the NASDAQ and whose annual reports you can study. Compare the information found in these reports and then write a report for Mr. Gutierrez that explains which of the companies is likely to be his best investment. Explain your conclusions thoroughly, quoting from the annual reports as necessary.

Exercise 10–3 (Intermediate)

You have received an inquiry from a prospective client, Lasy Sofa, Inc., concerning the accounting for investments. Betty Jason, owner of Lasy Sofa, is considering investing some of her company's idle cash in either equity or debt securities. Write a report for Ms. Jason, explaining briefly how the types of investments and her purpose for investing might affect the accounting methods used. Remember that your client is not an accountant and knows very little about accounting.

Exercise 10–4 (Intermediate)

Carol Loudermilk and Russell Williams are planning to open a new mall music store that will carry CDs, tapes, posters, and T-shirts. They have heard of the FIFO, LIFO, specific identification, and lower-of-cost-or-market methods of valuing inventory, but do not understand them. Because you will be the accountant for the new business, they have asked you to prepare a report about these inventory valuation methods. They are interested in the advantages and disadvantages of all these methods for their business, as well as your recommendation of the best method for their store.

Exercise 10–5 (Intermediate or Auditing)

Write a report in response to the letter in Figure 10–2.[2]

Exercise 10–6 (Intermediate)

Select a publicly traded company from the business references in the library. Write a report analyzing the financial aspects of the business including (1) liquidity, (2) profitability, (3) productivity, and (4) debt management. If your analysis uncovers any problems, include recommendations on how they may be overcome.

Exercise 10–7 (Accounting Information Systems)

Select a small business in your community that plans to improve its accounting system. Analyze the business's needs for an accounting system, including the possibility of a microcomputer.

This project will probably require you to interview the business's management so that you understand how the business operates, what its systems needs are, and the budgetary constraints within which management will be working.

You may decide, after evaluating the business's needs, that it does not need a microcomputer at the present time. If this is the case, write a five- or ten-year systems plan based on projected growth of the business.

If you do conclude that the business should purchase a microcomputer, what hardware and software do you recommend?

If the business already has a computer system, should it scrap the present system or update it?

Write your evaluation and recommendation in the form of a report to the business's manager or owner.

Exercise 10–8 (Professional Issues)

James Bienville, the managing partner of the local CPA firm, Bienville & Dusquene, for which you work, is concerned about the future growth of

FIGURE 10–2 *Letter for Exercise 10–5*

Office of the Controller
Southern Cement
1021 Peachtree Ave.
Atlanta, GA 30309

January 10, 1999

Mary L. De Quincy
Auditor-in-Charge
Lewis and Clark, CPAs
111 Baxter St.
Athens, GA 30605

Dear Ms. De Quincy:

Last year's fiscal year will be the fifteenth year that you have audited our financial statements. I appreciate the work you have done for us.

As you know, the company has been growing steadily since our inception 75 years ago. The last 10 years have been particularly good because of Atlanta's tremendous growth in condominiums. Continued growth has required us to purchase at a rapid rate machinery to mix and pour cement at construction sites. Almost all of our machinery has been financed by Confederate National Bank. Until now, the bank has been eager to lend us money at the prime rate when using the machines as collateral.

Southern Cement usually makes large down payments from contract proceeds on equipment purchases. Lately we have experienced equipment purchasing problems because our contracts do not require payment until the contract is complete. We have recently accepted some long-term contracts that will be quite lucrative, but we will not receive payment for two years. There is no reason to believe that we will not be paid eventually.

Confederate National refused to make additional equipment loans to us because it believes we are over-leveraged. The loan officer supports this refusal by calling attention to our debt-to-equity ratio, which is higher than those of our customers.

FIGURE 10–2 ***Letter for Exercise 10–5 (cont.)***

Mary L. DeQuincy, Lewis and Clark, CPAs
January 10, 1999
Page 2

Southern Cement's liabilities are higher than the liabilities of our competitors due to one account—deferred taxes. The deferred taxes account is higher for Southern Cement for two reasons:

(1) Our company is older than the competitors and deferred taxes have accumulated over a number of years.
(2) Tax advantages from accelerated depreciation on equipment purchases in the last 10 years have allowed us to defer large amounts of tax payments.

I do not expect this account to decline in the future because our company continues to require additional equipment. Quite frankly, I have never seen the need to include deferred taxes in the liability section of the balance sheet because it is highly unlikely that these amounts will ever be paid to the federal government. Deferred taxes that become due have always been replaced by a greater amount that will be deferred. The deferred tax account has continued to grow at a steady rate. Removal of deferred taxes that will not become due would significantly reduce Southern Cement's debt-to-equity ratio enough to convince any banker to make an additional equipment loan to us.

In the last three years, several other CPA firms have approached me to solicit our account. Because I am reluctant to change accountants, is it possible for you to prepare the financial statements without including deferred taxes? The absence of deferred taxes would provide the following advantages.

(1) Eliminate a "false liability" that misleads our creditors and stockholders.
(2) Reduce our debt-to-equity ratio, thereby allowing us to obtain our desperately needed loan.

FIGURE 10–2 ***Letter for Exercise 10–5 (cont.)***

Mary L. DeQuincy, Lewis and Clark, CPAs
January 10, 1999
Page 3

I have never fully understood the disclosure requirements for deferred taxes. I do believe, however, that the elimination of this account from our balance sheet would result in a more accurate representation of our financial position. I would appreciate a detailed analysis of your position on this proposal.

Sincerely,

Sandy Loam

Sandy Loam
Controller

the firm. He is aware that many CPA firms are rapidly beginning to provide various types of assurance services to clients. He has asked you to do some research on the topic of assurance services and what kind of services Bienville & Dusquene might be able to provide. You are aware that much has been written about this topic in the *Journal of Accountancy* and other practitioner magazines and that the AICPA has published information on this topic on its web site (http://www.aicpa.org). Research the topic of assurance services and write a report for Mr. Bienville.

NOTES

1. Adapted from Jean Bryan, "Financial and Accounting Considerations of Issuing Convertible Debt" (unpublished student paper, University of Georgia, 1980).
2. Adapted from William R. Pasewark, "Writing Assignment for Intermediate Accounting" (unpublished class assignment, University of Georgia, 1986).

Part III WRITING AND YOUR CAREER

11

Writing Essay Exams: Academic Courses and Professional Certification Exams

One of the more interesting developments to affect the accounting profession in recent years is the decision of professional organizations to evaluate the writing skills of candidates seeking professional certification. For example, writing skills are now evaluated explicitly on the CPA exam.

This chapter discusses strategies you can use to answer essay exams successfully. Because you may also encounter essay or discussion questions in accounting courses, the chapter suggests ways to prepare for and answer those questions.

ACADEMIC ESSAY EXAMS

Essays or discussion questions that appear on school exams may cause you some anxiety, but they give you a chance to practice for the professional examinations you may take later in your career. You can learn how to study for an essay exam as well as strategies for writing your answer and managing the pressure. You can also learn how to write an answer that ensures that you receive full credit for what you know.

Preparation

Although much of your studying for an objective examination will also help prepare you for essay questions, you need to do a different kind of studying as well. Remember that a discussion or essay question requires that you show mastery of ideas. You may be asked to explain a concept, compare or contrast two methods of doing something, evaluate alternative treatments for a given situation, or justify a recommendation. Therefore, when you are reviewing your class notes and assigned reading material, you should note concepts and explanations that would lend themselves to this type of question.

One good way to prepare is to outline notes given in class, especially lecture notes. It's also a good idea to highlight and then outline key ideas and explanations from assigned readings.

Once your notes and outlines are ready, review them and try to guess questions that might appear on the exam, paying particular attention to concepts the instructor has stressed in class or important discussions in the text. Then make outlines of the information you would include in answers to those questions. With any luck, you will predict at least a few of the questions that appear on the exam, especially after you have taken the first exam given by your instructor and have a better idea of the kinds of questions usually asked.

It is also helpful to study in a small group of students, after all of you have prepared your notes and outlines. This group can brainstorm possible questions and answers and check that everyone in the group understands the material that will be covered on the exam.

Taking the Exam

Actually writing the answer to an essay or discussion question is easier if you have a strategy for using your time and composing your answer.

Budget Your Time Managing your time well is a crucial part of your strategy. You may not have as much time as you would like to plan in detail, revise extensively, and then copy your answer over to create a perfect paper. Make the time you do have work to your advantage by following the three steps of the writing process: planning, writing, revising.

First, take a few minutes to read the question carefully to be sure you know what is being asked. It may be helpful to underline key phrases in the question so that your answer won't overlook something important. Then jot down the main ideas you want to include in the answer. Put numbers by these ideas or draw arrows to arrange them in the most effective order. If you have 30 minutes to answer a question, planning your answer, the first step in the writing process, should take about five minutes.

The next step, writing your answer, should take most of the remaining time. Write as legibly as possible, and write on every other line of your paper to allow room for editing. Write as well as you can, but don't spend much time looking for the perfect word or phrase if it doesn't come quickly. The most important objective is to get the ideas down on paper in order to get credit for what you know.

Finally, allow at least five minutes to edit your answer. When you edit, check that all words are correctly spelled and that sentences are grammatically correct and clearly constructed. It's acceptable to cross out words and write your revisions in the line above as long as the essay remains legible.

Time is a big factor in answering essay and discussion questions, so use it wisely. Budget your time so that you can plan, write, and then revise.

Organize Your Answer The goals in organizing your answer are to help the instructor read it easily and to receive full credit for what you know. Thus, you should apply one of the primary recommendations emphasized throughout this book: Use summary sentences so that main ideas stand out. In an essay or discussion question, the key is to begin the answer with a thesis statement and to use topic sentences at the beginning of each paragraph.

The thesis statement should echo the question and summarize the main ideas of your answer. Suppose you find this question on an exam:

> Explain the matching concept in accounting.

Your answer to this question might begin this way:

> The matching concept is used to determine what expense amounts should appear in the income statement for a particular period.

For short discussion questions, your answer might be only one paragraph long. In this case, the thesis statement for the answer would also function as the topic sentence for the paragraph. For more extensive questions, organize your answer into several paragraphs, each discussing one aspect of your answer. Each paragraph will have a topic sentence that provides a transition from the last paragraph, where needed, and that summarizes the main idea to be discussed in the new paragraph. Suppose you're asked this question on an exam:

> Discuss how the definition of an asset has changed since the Accounting Principles Board was replaced by the Financial Accounting Standards Board.

Your answer might be organized like this:

Thesis (first paragraph of your answer):

> When the Financial Accounting Standards Board replaced the Accounting Principles Board, it switched the focus of income determination from the Expense/Revenue View to the Asset/Liability View.

Topic sentence for paragraph 2:

Under the Expense/Revenue View previously taken by the Accounting Principles Board, assets were merely debit balances left over after deciding the proper amount of expenses to match with revenues in the income statement.

Topic sentence for paragraph 3:

Under the Asset/Liability View favored by the Financial Accounting Standards Board, net income is determined by directly measuring changes in the value of net assets adjusted for changes resulting from owners' equity transactions.

One final reminder about organization: In deciding how many paragraphs to use for your answer, remember that readers usually find shorter paragraphs easier to read, as long as you provide adequate transitions so that they can follow your train of thought.

For further discussion of organization, review chapter 3.

Use Document Design Sometimes the best way to include a number of points in your answer in a minimum amount of time is to use the principles of document design explained in Chapter 6, especially set-off lists and headings. The sample question and answer given in Figure 11–1[1] shows how to use a list to organize the answer to a short question.* For a longer essay, headings may be a good way to divide your answer into its main components.

Qualities of a Good Essay

The discussion so far has already suggested several qualities of an effective answer to an essay or discussion question. Here is a summary of those qualities, plus a few additional pointers:

- Your handwriting should be legible and your pages neat and easy to read. Corrections, additions, and deletions should be made as neatly as possible.
- Main ideas should be easy to identify; the flow of thought should be easy for the grader to follow.
- Answer the question directly and completely. Supply adequate details and examples to support your assertions.
- Sentences should be concise, clear, and readable. Grammatical and mechanical errors should not distract the reader.

These qualities of a good essay and the strategy you use to prepare for and write an academic essay exam also apply to professional examinations, with a few modifications.

*This question and answer are from an old CMA exam. The CMA exam no longer includes essay questions. We use this question and answer only to illustrate the use of lists in organizing an answer.

FIGURE 11–1 *Sample Question and Answer*

QUESTION NUMBER 2

Estimated time 30 minutes
(A required question)

In recent years, there has been considerable competition for clients among public accounting firms. Auditor changes arise for a variety of reasons including mergers and acquisitions, expanded professional services requirements, dissatisfaction with current external auditors, and the desire to reduce audit fees. An important step in establishing the relationship between the audit firm and the client is the preparation and acceptance of the engagement letter.

During the audit engagement, the external auditors may work closely with the client's internal audit staff; however, care must be taken to develop the proper relationship. Prior to the conclusion of the audit, the external auditors are required by the third standard of field work to obtain a representation letter from the client's management. In addition, at the conclusion of the audit engagement, auditors generally issue a management letter which has become an integral part of the services rendered by many auditors.

REQUIRED:

A. Identify at least three reasons why external auditors prepare an engagement letter.
B. Explain the relationship that should exist between external auditors and a client's internal audit staff.
C. Identify at least three reasons why external auditors require management to issue a representation letter.
D. Identify at least three reasons why a management letter is prepared by the external auditors.

QUESTION NUMBER 2 (D2)

A. At least three reasons why external auditors prepare an engagement letter include
- clarifying the nature of the audit and the responsibilities assumed by the auditor.

FIGURE 11–1 ***Sample Question and Answer (cont.)***

- indicating how the audit fee will be determined, and estimating the time that will be spent, including a staffing schedule.
- identifying any restrictions that will be put on the audit.

B. The relationship between the internal auditor staff and the external auditors is usually a close and professional one. Although the internal auditor's work cannot be used as a substitute, it can serve as an important complement to the external audit engagement and minimize duplication of effort. Before the external auditor can rely on the internal auditor's work, the objectivity and competence of the internal audit staff, as well as the quality of their work, should be evaluated.

C. At least three reasons why external auditors require management to prepare a representation letter are that it
- confirms oral and written representations made by management.
- emphasizes the client management's prime responsibility for the records and the data included in the financial statements.
- represents that all related party transactions, contingencies, compensating balances,
- and material events subsequent to the balance sheet date have been disclosed.

D. At least three reasons a management letter is prepared by external auditors are to
- make recommendations for improving efficiency and effectiveness.
- demonstrate the auditors' interest in the continuing welfare of the client.
- encourage management's follow-up on matters such as internal control weaknesses, tax-related matters, and management of resources such as cash, inventories, and investments.

PROFESSIONAL CERTIFICATION EXAMS

A number of professional certification exams require candidates to write answers to essay or short answer questions. As we mentioned earlier, the professional associations sponsoring these exams recognize that it is not enough for professional accountants to be able to "crunch numbers." They must be able to communicate their findings to others as well.

Since May 1994, the writing skills of candidates for professional CPA certification have been explicitly evaluated on certain essay questions in three sections of the exam: Auditing, Financial Accounting and Reporting, and Business Law and Professional Responsibilities. The quality of the writing on any professional exam affects whether candidates receive credit for what they know. You are more likely to receive full credit for the content of your answer if the grader has an easy time reading and understanding what you've written.

Even when an answer is not evaluated explicitly for writing skills, how well it is written can influence the score. Graders of these exams have a lot of work to do in a short amount of time. Their job is to determine whether the candidates know the answers to the questions asked. Thus, graders appreciate essays that enable them to spot main ideas quickly and easily. They also appreciate sentences that are clear and readable.

Like readers of business documents, graders of professional exams want essays to be coherent (main ideas easy to identify, flow of thought easy to follow), concise (no wasted words), and clear (no guesswork about meaning, no distractions by nonstandard English). Thus, the writing skills emphasized in this book apply to professional exams as well as to more common forms of business writing.

Preparing For and Taking the Exam

Preparing for professional examinations is much more involved than studying for an exam in a course. You will study many long hours, perhaps with the help of an exam review text or course. However, the types of questions you are asked may resemble those in your course exams: to explain a concept, describe a process, or analyze a situation, for example.

Manage Your Time The pressure of time constraints in a professional examination may be even greater than the stress you feel during a course exam because your ability to be a certified accounting professional depends on how well you do. However, the strategies for managing this stress remain the same regardless of what kind of exam you're taking. The keys are to budget your time so that you can plan your answer, draft the essay, and edit what you've written.

Use the Question to Organize Your Essay As with the essays and discussion questions you write for your accounting courses, you can help graders of professional exams identify your main ideas by writing in short paragraphs with strong topic sentences. The question itself can suggest the wording of the topic sentences. Sample questions and answers from past exams show how this strategy works. Figures 11–2, 11–3, and 11–4 contain CPA exam questions and unofficial answers suggested by the AICPA.[2]

Part **a** of an auditing question (Figure 11–2) states this requirement:

> In what ways may Tyler's work be relevant to North, the independent auditor?

The answer begins with a variation of the question:

> Tyler's work may be relevant to North in obtaining . . .

The answer then continues with a discussion of several specific ways Tyler's work may be relevant to North. Notice how the discussion is divided into short paragraphs, each beginning with a strong topic sentence.

Another question from a past CPA exam, this time from the Business Law and Professional Responsibilities section, is shown in Figure 11–3. For this question, the requirements specify the organization of the answer:

> In separate paragraphs, determine whether Suburban's positions are correct, and state the reasons for your conclusions.

Notice how each paragraph of the answer begins with a topic sentence that summarizes the main idea of the paragraph.

The CPA exam question shown in Figure 11–4, which comes from the Financial Accounting and Reporting section of the exam, contains two parts. Part **a** requires a schedule of interest expense, and part **b** requires an essay presented in the form of a memo.

Use Formatting Techniques to Make Your Essays Easy to Read Good document design makes it easier for graders to read your essays and give you full credit for them. Although you are obviously limited to what you can accomplish quickly with a paper and pen, formatting techniques such as bullets and set-off lists may make it easier for graders to spot main ideas and follow your train of thought.

For example, Part A of the answer to the exam question shown in Figure 11–1 uses a set-off list with bullets to identify reasons why external auditors prepare an engagement letter.

FIGURE 11–2 *Sample Question and Answer, CPA Exam*

Number 4 (Estimated time—25 to 35 minutes)

North, CPA, is planning an audit of the financial statements of General Co. In determining the nature, timing, and extent of the auditing procedures, North is considering General's internal audit function, which is staffed by Tyler.

REQUIRED:

a. In what ways may Tyler's work be relevant to North, the independent auditor?

b. What factors should North consider and what inquiries should North make in deciding whether to use Tyler's work?

ANSWER 4 (10 POINTS)

a. Tyler's work may be relevant to North in obtaining a sufficient understanding of the design of General's internal control structure policies and procedures, in determining whether they have been placed in operation, and in assessing risk, Since an objective of most internal audit functions is to review, assess, and monitor internal control policies and procedures, the procedures performed by Tyler in this area may provide useful information to North.

Tyler's work may also provide direct evidence about material misstatements in assertions about specific account balances or classes of transactions. Therefore, Tyler's work may be relevant to North in planning substantive procedures. Consequently, North may be able to change the nature, timing, or extent of certain procedures.

North may request direct assistance from Tyler. This direct assistance relates to work North specifically requests Tyler to perform to complete some aspect of North's work.

b. If North concludes that Tyler's work is relevant to North's audit of General's financial statements, North should consider whether it would be efficient to consider how Tyler's work might affect the nature, timing, and extent of North's

FIGURE 11–2 *Sample Question and Answer, CPA Exam (cont.)*

audit procedures. If so, North should assess Tyler's competence and objectivity in light of the intended effect of Tyler's work on North's audit.

North ordinarily should inquire about Tyler's organizational status within General and about Tyler's application of the professional internal auditing standards developed by the Institute of Internal Auditors and the General Accounting Office. North also should ask about Tyler's internal audit plan, including the nature, timing, and extent of the audit work performed. Additionally, North should inquire about Tyler's access to General's records and whether there are any limitations on the scope of Tyler's activities.

Qualities of a Good Answer

The definition of effective writing provided by the AICPA gives the qualities you should strive for in the essays you write, not only for the CPA exam, but for other professional certification exams, because these qualities apply to any well-written essay. (See Figure 11–5.) According to the AICPA, effective writing meets these criteria:[3]

- Coherent organization
- Conciseness
- Clarity
- Use of standard English
- Responsiveness to the requirements of the question
- Appropriateness to the reader

As you probably realize, these criteria are stressed throughout this book.

When you are studying for a professional certification exam, you may find it helpful to review the chapters of this book that discuss these qualities of effective writing. These chapters, listed at the bottom of page 228, would probably be the most useful to you:

FIGURE 11–3 *Sample Question and Answer, CPA Exam*

NUMBER 5 (ESTIMATED TIME—15 TO 25 MINUTES)

Suburban Properties, Inc. owns and manages several shopping centers. On May 4, 1993, Suburban received from Bridge Hardware, Inc., one of its tenants, a signed letter proposing that the existing lease between Suburban and Bridge be modified to provide that certain utility costs be equally shared by Bridge and Suburban, effective June 1, 1993. Under the terms of the original lease, Bridge was obligated to pay all utility costs. On May 5, 1993, Suburban sent Bridge a signed letter agreeing to share the utility costs as proposed. Suburban later changed its opinion and refused to share in the utility costs.

On June 4, 1993, Suburban received from Dart Associates, Inc. a signed offer to purchase one of the shopping centers owned by Suburban. The offer provided as follows: a price of $9,250,000; it would not be withdrawn before July 1, 1993; and an acceptance must be received by Dart to be effective. On June 9, 1993, Suburban mailed Dart a signed acceptance. On June 10, before Dart had received Suburban's acceptance, Dart telephoned Suburban and withdrew its offer. Suburban's acceptance was received by Dart on June 12, 1993.

On June 22, 1993, one of Suburban's shopping centers was damaged by a fire, which started when the center was struck by lightning. As a result of the fire, one of the tenants in the shopping center, World Popcorn Corp., was forced to close its business and will be unable to reopen until the damage is repaired. World sued Suburban claiming that Suburban is liable for World's losses resulting from the fire. The lease between Suburban and World is silent in this regard.

Suburban has taken the following positions:

- Suburban's May 5, 1993, agreement to share equally the utility costs with Bridge is not binding on Suburban.
- Dart could not properly revoke its June 4 offer and must purchase the shopping center.
- Suburban is not liable to World for World's losses resulting from the fire.

FIGURE 11–3 ***Sample Question and Answer, CPA Exam (cont.)***

REQUIRED:

In separate paragraphs, determine whether Suburban's positions are correct and state the reasons for your conclusions.

ANSWER 5 (10 POINTS)

Suburban is correct concerning the agreement to share utility costs with Bridge. A modification of a contract requires consideration to be binding on the parties. Suburban is not bound by the lease modification because Suburban did not receive any consideration in exchange for its agreement to share the cost of utilities with Bridge.

Suburban is not correct with regard to the Dart offer. An offer can be revoked at any time prior to acceptance. This is true despite the fact that the offer provides that it will not be withdrawn prior to a stated time. If no consideration is given in exchange for this promise not to withdraw the offer, the promise is not binding on the offeror. The offer provided that Suburban's acceptance would not be effective until received. Dart's June 10 revocation terminated Dart's offer. Thus, Suburban's June 9 acceptance was not effective.

Suburban is correct with regard to World's claim. The general rule is that destruction of, or damage to, the subject matter of a contract without the fault of either party terminates the contract. In this case, Suburban is not liable to World because Suburban is discharged from its contractual duties as a result of the fire, which made performance by it under the lease objectively impossible.

Chapter 2: Writing appropriately for the reader and responding to the requirements of the questions
Chapter 3: Organizing for coherence
Chapter 4: Writing with a style that is clear and concise
Chapter 5: Writing in standard English
Chapter 6: Formatting techniques

FIGURE 11–4 *Sample Question and Answer, CPA Exam*

NUMBER 5 (ESTIMATED TIME—30 TO 40 MINUTES)

Chris Green, CPA, is auditing Rayne Co.'s 1993 financial statements. The controller, Dunn, has provided Green with the following information.

- At December 31, 1992, Rayne had a note payable to Federal Bank with a balance of $90,000. The annual principal payment of $10,000, plus 8% interest on the unpaid balance, was paid when due on March 31, 1993.
- On January 2, 1993, Rayne leased two automobiles for executive use under a capital lease. Five annual lease payments of $15,000 are due beginning January 3, 1993. Rayne's incremental borrowing rate on the date of the lease was 11% and the lessor's implicit rate, which was known by Rayne, was 10%. The lease was properly recorded at $62,500, before the first payment was made.
- On July 1, 1993, Rayne received proceeds of $538,000 from a $500,000 bond issuance. The bonds mature in 15 years and interest of 11% is payable semiannually on June 30 and December 31. The bonds were issued at a price to yield investors 10%. Rayne uses the effective interest method to amortize bond premium.
- For the year ended December 31, 1993, Rayne has adopted Statement of Financial Accounting Standards No. 109, *Accounting for Income Taxes*. Dunn has prepared a schedule of all differences between financial statement and income tax return income. Dunn believes that as a result of pending legislation, the enacted tax rate at December 31, 1993, will be increased for 1994. Dunn is uncertain which differences to include and which rates to apply in computing deferred taxes under FASB 109. Dunn has requested an overview of FAS 109 from Green.

REQUIRED:

a. Prepare a schedule of interest expense for the year ended December 31, 1993.

b. Prepare a brief memo to Dunn from Green:
  - identifying the objectives of accounting for income taxes,
  - defining temporary differences,

- explaining how to measure deferred tax assets and liabilities, and
- explaining how to measure deferred income tax expense or benefit.

ANSWER **5 (10** POINTS)

a.

Rayne Co.
SCHEDULE OF INTEREST EXPENSE
For the Year Ended December 31, 1993

Note Payable	$ 6,600 [1]
Capital lease obligation	4,750 [2]
Bonds payable	26,900 [3]
Total interest expense	$38,250

[1] 1,800 (90,000 × 8% × 3/12) + 4,800 (80,000 × 8% × 9/12)
[2] 10% × 47,500 (62,500 – 15,000)
[3] 538,000 × 10% × 1/2

b.

To: Dunn
From: Green
Re: Accounting for income taxes

Below is a brief overview of accounting for income taxes in accordance with FASB 109.

The objectives of accounting for income taxes are to recognize (a) the amount of taxes payable or refundable for the current year, and (b) deferred tax liabilities and assets for the estimated future tax consequences of temporary differences and carryforwards. Temporary differences are differences between the tax basis of assets or liabilities and their reported amounts in the financial statements that will result in taxable or deductible amounts in future years.

Deferred tax assets and liabilities are measured based on the provisions of enacted tax law; the effects of future changes in the tax laws or rates are not anticipated. The measurement of deferred tax assets is reduced, if necessary, by a valuation allowance to reflect the net asset amount that is more likely than not to be realized. Deferred income tax expense or benefit is measured as the change during the year in an enterprise's deferred tax liabilities and assets.

FIGURE 11–5 ***The AICPA's Definition of Writing Skills***

DEFINITION OF WRITING SKILLS

Answers to selected essay questions will be used to assess a candidate's writing skills. Effective writing skills include the following characteristics:

- Coherent organization
- Conciseness
- Clarity
- Use of standard English
- Responsiveness to the requirements of the question
- Appropriateness to the reader

The following are general descriptions of the six characteristics of writing skills.

1. *Coherent organization.* Responses should be organized so that ideas are arranged logically and the flow of thought is easy to follow. Generally, knowledge is best expressed by using short paragraphs composed of short sentences. Moreover, short paragraphs, each limited to the development of one principal idea, can better emphasize the main points in the answer. Each principal idea should be placed in the first sentence of the paragraph, followed by supporting concepts and examples.
2. *Conciseness.* Conciseness requires that candidates present complete thoughts in as few words as possible, while ensuring that important points are covered adequately. Short sentences and simple wording also contribute to concise writing.
3. *Clarity.* A clearly written response prevents uncertainty concerning the candidate's meaning or reasoning. Clarity involves using works with specific and precise meaning, including proper technical terminology. Well-constructed sentences also contribute to clarity.
4. *Use of standard English.* Responses should be written using standard English. *The Business Writer's Handbook*[4] describes standard English as follows:

FIGURE 11–5 ***The AICPA's Definition of Writing Skills (cont.)***

> There are two broad varieties of written English: standard and non-standard. These varieties are determined through usage by those who write in the English language. Standard English . . . is used to carry on the daily business of the nation. It is the language of business, industry, government, education, and the professions. Standard English is characterized by exacting standards of punctuation and capitalization, by accurate spelling, by exact diction, by an expressive vocabulary, and by knowledgeable usage choices.

5. *Responsiveness to the requirements of the question.* Answers should directly address the requirements of the question and demonstrate the candidate's awareness of the purpose of the writing task. Responses should not be broad expositions on the general subject matter.
6. *Appropriateness for the reader.* Writing that is appropriate for the reader takes into account the reader's background, knowledge of the subject, interests, and concerns. The requirements of some essay questions may ask candidates to prepare a written document for a certain reader, such as an engagement memorandum for a CPA's client. When the intended reader is not specified, the candidate should assume the intended reader is a knowledgeable CPA.

EXERCISES

Exercise 11–1

The question in Figure 11–6 comes from a past CMA exam.[5] Write an answer to this question, using the techniques discussed in this chapter. You should plan, write, and revise your answer in about 30 minutes. (Note: The CMA exam no longer includes essay questions.)

Exercise 11–2

The question in Figure 11–7 is adapted from from a past CPA exam.[6] Plan, write, and revise an answer to this question in the suggested time of 15 to 25 minutes.

FIGURE 11–6 *Question for Exercise 11–1*

QUESTION NUMBER 2
13 POINTS-ESTIMATED TIME 30 MINUTES
(A REQUIRED QUESTION)

Adult Recreation Inc. (ARI) manufactures games for sale to the adult marketplace. This is a very competitive industry that continually requires modification to existing games and the introduction of new games to meet customer desires. Bill James, vice president of marketing, and Charlene Scott, vice president of design, have been discussing the challenges facing ARI as a result of the continued worldwide recessionary climate.

James and Scott noted that the current economic conditions may present a unique opportunity if ARI could design and promote sales of games that meet expended family recreational needs. The recession is causing customers to turn away from more expensive types of entertainment and spend their disposable income on less expensive entertainment.

These discussions then turned to the establishment of a group of diverse company personnel to coordinate customer input and identify new ideas. Questions were raised about who should participate in this group and whether or not this should be an ongoing effort. Their discussions also revolved around the needs of this group to assure that it has the appropriate power and authority to make it effective.

REQUIRED:

A. In a business environment,
   1. define what constitutes a group, providing at least two examples.
   2. describe at least two advantages and two disadvantages of groups.

B. Describe the general reasons why authority is delegated.

FIGURE 11–6 ***Question for Exercise 11–1 (cont.)***

C. For groups to perform effectively, they need to hold certain types of power.

   1. Define each of the following types of power.
      - Legitimate.
      - Referent.
      - Expert.

   2. Why should each of these specific types of power be represented when selecting group members for Adult Recreation, Inc.?

FIGURE 11–7 *Question for Exercise 11–2*

NUMBER 4 (ESTIMATED TIME—15 TO 25 MINUTES)

Best Aviation Associates is a general partnership engaged in the business of buying, selling, and servicing used airplanes. Best's original partners were Martin and Kent. They formed the partnership on January 1, 1997, under an oral partnership agreement which provided that the partners would share profits equally. There was no agreement as to how the partners would share losses. At the time the partnership was formed, Martin contributed $320,000 and Kent contributed $80,000.

On December 1, 1998, Best hired Baker to be a salesperson and to assist in purchasing used aircraft for Best's inventory. On December 15, 1998, Martin instructed Baker to negotiate the purchase of a used airplane from Jackson without disclosing that Baker was acting on Best's behalf. Martin thought that a better price could be negotiated by Baker if Jackson was not aware that the aircraft was being acquired for Best. The agreement provided that Jackson would deliver the airplane to Baker on January 2, 1999, Jackson attempted to deliver the used airplane purchased for Best by Baker. Baker, acting on Martin's instructions, refused to accept delivery or pay the purchase price.

On December 20, 1998, Kent assigned Kent's partnership interest in Best to Green. On December 31, 1998, Kent advised Martin of the assignment to Green. On January 11, 1999, Green contacted Martin and demanded to inspect the partnership books and to participate in the management of partnership affairs, including voting on partnership decisions.

On January 13, 1999, it was determined that Best had incurred an operating loss of $160,000 in 1998. Martin demanded that Kent contribute $80,000 to the partnership to account for Kent's share of the loss. Kent refused to contribute.

On January 28, 1999, Laco Supplies, Inc., a creditor of Best, sued Best and Martin for unpaid bills totaling $92,000. Best had not paid the bills because of a cash shortfall caused by the 1998 operating loss.

FIGURE 11–7 ***Question for Exercise 11–2 (cont.)***

Jackson has taken the following position:

- Baker is responsible for any damages incurred by Jackson as a result of Best's refusal to accept delivery or pay the purchase price.

Martin has taken the following positions:

- Green is not entitled to inspect the partnership books or participate in the management of the partnership.
- Only the partnership is liable for the amounts owed to Laco, or, in the alternative, Martin's personal liability is limited to 50% of the total of the unpaid bills.

Kent has taken the following positions:

- Only Martin is liable for the 1998 operating loss because of the assignment to Green of Kent's partnership interest.
- Any personal liability of the partners for the 1998 operating loss should be allocated between them on the basis of their original capital contributions.

REQUIRED:

a. Determine whether Jackson's position is correct and state the reasons for your conclusions.
b. Determine whether Martin's positions are correct and state the reasons for your conclusions.
c. Determine whether Kent's positions are correct and state the reasons for your conclusions.

NOTES

1. Institute of Certified Management Accountants, *Certified Management Accountant Examination: June 1993 Questions & Unofficial Answers* (Montvale, N.J.: Institute of Certified Management Accountants, 1993), 23, 29. The CMA exam no longer includes essay questions. We use this question and answer only to illustrate the use of lists in organizing an answer.
2. American Institute of Certified Public Accountants, *Uniform CPA Examination: May 1994 Questions and Unofficial Answers* (New York: American Institute of Certified Public Accountants, 1994), 15, 34, 69, 72, 75, 82.
3. American Institute of Certified Public Accountants, "Definition of Writing Skills" (New York: American Institute of Certified Public Accountants, 1990).
4. Charles T. Brusaw, Gerald J. Alred, and Walter E. Oliu, *The Business Writer's Handbook,* 3rd ed. (New York: St. Martin's Press, 1987), 220.
5. Institute of Certified Management Accountants, *Certified Management Accountant Examination: June 1993 Questions & Unofficial Answers* (Montvale, N.J.: Institute of Certified Management Accountants, 1993), 7.
6. American Institute of Certified Public Accountants, *Uniform CPA Examination: May 1994 Questions and Unofficial Answers* (New York: American Institute of Certified Public Accountants, 1994), 14.

12

Writing for Employment: Résumés and Letters

One of the greatest concerns for most accounting students is the need to find a job after graduation. Your communication skills can be your greatest asset in finding that job. A study discussed in chapter 1 pointed out that an applicant's communication skills are the *single most important factor* in employers' hiring decisions. This chapter focuses on several important skills you will need to get a good job: researching a targeted company, preparing a résumé and letter of application, and writing a thank-you letter to follow an interview.

STARTING THE JOB SEARCH: RESEARCHING POSSIBLE EMPLOYERS

How you begin your job search depends to some extent on where you are when you begin. If you are still a student in a large university, for example, you will probably work with your school's job placement office, its faculty, and the recruiters who visit your campus. If you are a student in a small school, opportunities for on-campus interviews may be more limited, and you may find it helpful to work with accounting faculty to identify potential employers. If you have already graduated, then you may be on your own in locating potential jobs and establishing initial contacts with employers, although the placement office of the school from which you graduated may still work with you.

Regardless of how you begin your job search, you will need to write certain documents to secure the job, including a letter of application, a résumé, and a thank-you letter after you have had an interview. For all these documents, knowledge of the targeted employer is important because you will want to tailor what you write to the potential employer's needs. You will also want to show the people who read these documents that you are familiar with the company and that you did the preparation necessary to make a good impression. (By now, you probably recognize the strategy that underlies this preparation: analyze your reader's interests and needs.)

Once you have decided to apply for a job at a particular company or organization, you need to find as much information as possible about both the organization as a whole and the particular job for which you are applying.

If there is a specific job opening, you will probably have general information about the position in a job announcement. Read the announcement carefully so that you learn as much as possible about the requirements of the position and the credentials for which the employer is looking. This information can guide you when you prepare your résumé and letter of application.

You will also need general information about the organization that is doing the hiring. If you are working with your school's job placement office, it may have a file of information on the company. You can also visit the library or search the Internet to look for articles and news items that may have been in the financial press, and you can talk with business faculty about the organization. Perhaps also you will be fortunate enough to meet recruiters from the organization on campus at meetings of accounting clubs or job fairs. If you have this opportunity, listen carefully to what the recruiters say about their organization and ask any questions that seem appropriate. Show in your polite, attentive listening that you are interested in what the recruiters have to say. And remember the names of the people you meet!

All this information about the organization or company, the names of individuals you have met, and the requirements for particular job openings will be important as you write your letter of application and edit your résumé.

Preparing A Résumé

Preparing a résumé may be one of the most important steps you take in finding a good job. A tongue-in-cheek saying actually has some truth when applied to résumés: "An ounce of image is worth a pound of performance." Of course your performance in school and in previous jobs is essential; but if the résumé doesn't project a professional, competent image, your performance won't be considered seriously. So take the time and the care necessary to do a good job.

The résumé in Figure 12–1 is an illustration of an effective résumé, and you may want to use it as a model for preparing your own. You should realize, however, that this example is not the only way to prepare a good résumé; you may find other models in business communication texts or in materials supplied by your school's job placement office. We will consider the résumé in Figure 12–1 to be a generic model that you can adapt to your own situation.

Using a Word Processor As with all business documents, you should prepare your résumé on a word processor and use a letter-quality printer. A word processor allows you to experiment with layout, headings, and fonts, as well as the wording and organization of your résumé's text. Another advantage of using a word processor is that you can tailor the résumé for a particular job. For example, you may want to emphasize the experience you have that fits the employer's requirements.

Some applicants have their résumé s printed professionally if they don't have access to excellent equipment that produces flawless copy. If you decide to have your résumé printed professionally, you may also receive advice on the design and content. You can find professional help with your résumé at a copy center or at an agency that prepares résumés.

Even if you use professional help, keep the following guidelines in mind to check that your résumé is properly prepared.

Format First of all, look at the document design of the résumé in Figure 12–1. Notice the placement of text on the page and the pleasing use of white space, headings, fonts, and bullets. The résumé is arranged so that it has an attractive, professional appearance; it is also easy to read because it's not crowded and important information is easy to find. We'll see how these design techniques can be used with the various parts of a résumé.

Name and Address Center your name in bold print at the top of the page. On the next line, put your address at the left margin and your phone number (including your area code) at the right margin as shown in Figure 12–1. If you have a fax number or an e-mail address list them with your phone number. Then place a horizontal line under this portion to separate your identifying data from your qualifications.

Career Objective Be as specific as possible about the kind of job you're looking for so that the employer will see if your goals match available openings. For example, you might indicate an accounting specialty such as tax, auditing, or systems. At the same time, you don't want to close any doors you will later wish you had left open, so consider describing your objective in a way that will allow for all reasonable possibilities of employment for which you're qualified. As an alternative, you might

FIGURE 12–1 *Sample Résumé*

Shane W. Brown

1324 Horsetooth Road Fort Collins, Colorado 80125	Phone: (970) 435-1234 e-mail: sbrown@csu.edu

CAREER OBJECTIVE	An accounting position that will allow me to build on my academic and employment background and provide opportunities for professional growth and development. Willing to travel.
SUMMARY OF QUALIFICATIONS	Degree in accounting; honor student; experience with corporate staff; experienced in customer service; computer literate.
EDUCATION	Bachelor of Business Administration, University of Georgia, June 1998. Major: Accounting GPA: 3.55/4.0
WORK EXPERIENCE:	
June 1997– September 1997	**Jaymart, Inc.; Executive Offices,** Norcross, Ga. *Accounting Internship* • Assisted in the preparation of year-end audit work papers. • Worked on depreciation schedules; updated property, plant, and equipment accounts. • Participated in the preparation of the 1997 corporate tax return work papers, and set up schedules for the 1998 corporate return. • Prepared 1998 income tax projections for individual corporate officers.
March 1996– June 1997	**University of Georgia Language Laboratories,** Athens, Ga. *Laboratory Assistant* • Supervised foreign language students using the laboratory.
June 1995– September 1995	**AT&T Information Systems,** Atlanta, Ga. *Support Services* • Assisted AT&T employees with their mailroom needs.
June 1994– September 1995	**Food Giant,** Atlanta, Ga. *Courtesy Clerk, Produce Department* • Promoted to Produce Department in July 1994. Assisted customers.

FIGURE 12–1 *Sample Résumé (cont.)*

HONORS AND ACTIVITIES	Association of Students of Accounting; Beta Alpha Psi Initiate (Accounting Fraternity); University Honors Program, Recipient of Junior Division Honors; Program Certificate; Beta Gamma Sigma (Business Honor Society); Dean's List (Seven of eleven quarters); Phi Eta Sigma; Tau Epsilon Phi (Social Fraternity); Finance Club; College Republicans; Intramural Softball, Volleyball.
INTERESTS	Racquetball, current events, travel, music.

edit your résumé so that your objective fits specific openings for which you're applying.

Summary of Qualifications Employers who receive a large number of résumés (and that covers just about everyone) do not have time to study the detailed information the résumés contain. Therefore it is important to provide a "snapshot" of your qualifications that will immediately catch the employer's eye. Notice Shane Brown's Summary of Qualifications section in Figure 12–1. In one quick phrase she sums up why the employer should pick her for the job.

Education Beginning with your most recent degree or school, provide information in reverse chronological order about your education to show your qualifications for employment. You will need to include much of this information:

- Degree(s) you have completed or are working on.
- Complete name of the school granting this degree.
- Date of the degree, or expected graduation date.
- Major and, if applicable to the job, your minor.
- Grade point average, if it is above 3.0 on a 4.0 scale. (Figure your GPA several ways to try to reach at least a 3.0—cumulative GPA, GPA in your major coursework, GPA in upper level courses, etc., and then label it accordingly.)
- Approximate percentage of your college expenses you financed yourself, if this amount is significant.

If you have attended several colleges or universities, include information about all of them, especially if you received a degree. If you attended schools without completing a degree, give the dates of your attendance.

You probably would not include information about your high school education, unless that information would be relevant to a potential employer. If you're applying for summer employment but still have some time before you graduate from college, then it may be a good idea to list your high school and date of graduation.

Work Experience Again in reverse chronological order, provide information about the jobs you have held, both full- and part-time. You can even list volunteer work if it is relevant to the job for which you're applying. For each job you list, provide the following information:

- Dates of employment. You may decide to put the dates in the left margin, as in the sample résumé.
- Name and location of the organization for which you worked.
- Your position.
- A description of your responsibilities, with emphasis on the ones that show you are qualified for the job you are now seeking. Note any promotions or honors you received. Whenever possible, describe your responsibilities using active voice verbs, such as *assisted, completed, prepared,* and *supervised.*

Honors and Activities List the organizations you belonged to, the honors you received, and any other activities that would show you to be a well-rounded, active person. List these activities from most important to least important, *from the point of view of your employer.* If you held an office in an organization or had significant responsibilities, add this information as well. Finally, if an organization or honor is not self-explanatory, give a brief explanation of its significance. You might, for example, explain the importance of honorary societies.

Interests Information about your hobbies and interests is optional on a résumé. The advantage of including this information is that it also can show that you are a well-rounded person with interests that might help you relate to other people, such as your co-workers and clients.

References Whether to list your references on your résumé is sometimes a difficult decision. If you provide the names, addresses, and phone numbers of your references, the employer can contact them easily. On the other hand, you run the risk that an employer will call your reference at an inconvenient time, or that the reference will not immediately recall detailed information about you. As a general rule, do not include references unless they are specifically requested. However, you will normally be asked for references when you fill out a formal job application, so it is important to have some.

If you don't include references on your résumé, it's a good idea to indicate on your résumé that references are available on request. The best solution, if you are enrolled or recently graduated from a college or university, is to have letters on file with your school's job placement office. Then your résumé can have a line such as this one:

References available upon request from

Placement Office
University of Manhattan
Manhattan, Georgia 30678

One final word about references. Never list people as references without first asking their permission. You would also ask people to be references who are likely to remember you well and have favorable things to say about you. Former instructors and employers are good candidates.

What *Not* to Put on a Résumé

Remember that there are laws against hiring discrimination on the basis of age, sex, race, religion, marital status, or national origin, so do not put information of this nature on a résumé. Also, when preparing résumés try to avoid phrases such as

- gets along well with coworkers
- pleasant disposition
- always eager to please

These phrases make you sound as if you were applying to be a pet rather than an employee! "Fluff" in the form of phrases like these is guaranteed to send your résumé straight to the bottom of the pile.

Generally, employers considering hiring someone for an accounting position are interested in two things: what you know and what you can do. Therefore, your résumé should specifically state what you know and what you can do.

Writing a Letter of Application

Often you will mail your résumé to a potential employer with a formal letter of application or to follow up some earlier communication. Like the résumé, the letter must be professional and well researched.

Your letter should follow the general advice for letters discussed in chapter 8, including these guidelines:

- Address the reader by name. Get the appropriate name over the telephone or by other means, if possible.
- Give your letter an attractive, professional appearance. Use good stationery and a letter-quality printer. The letter and résumé should be printed on matching paper.
- Write in short, concise paragraphs and clear sentences. A courteous, conversational tone is best.
- The spelling, grammar, and mechanics of your letter should be perfect.

The content of your letter will depend on your particular situation. If you have already discussed the job or possible employment with an employee of the company, you should refer to this person by name and say exactly why you're sending the résumé. You might write a sentence such as this one:

> Sara Evans suggested that I write you about a possible opening in your auditing department. I had the pleasure of meeting Ms. Evans at a meeting of our Accounting Club here at the University of Central California.
>
> As you will see in my enclosed résumé, . . .

For a formal letter of application, you might begin with a sentence such as this:

> I would like to apply for the position of staff accountant that you advertised in the June 25, 1998, issue of the *Denver Press Register*. My résumé is enclosed.

After the introduction to your letter, you will need to show the reader two things: that you are familiar with the organization doing the hiring and that you have the credentials they are looking for. Thus, you can refer briefly to what you've learned about the company from your research and highlight the information on your résumé that shows you to be especially interested in and qualified for the position. In other words, you use the letter of application to sell yourself as the best person for the job. You will probably write from one to three short paragraphs for this purpose. The following paragraphs show examples from two different letters.

> As you will see on my enclosed résumé, I will graduate from the University of Northern Idaho in June of this year with a Master of Accounting degree and a specialty in tax, so my training should qualify me for an entry-level position in your tax department. In addition, I have experience as a tax assistant with the Smith Company, a position I held during the past two summers.
>
> During the years I have studied for my accounting degree here at the University of Tempe, I have worked an average of twenty hours a week to pay approximately half my college and living expenses. At the same time I have managed to maintain a cumulative GPA of 3.3 and have been active in a number of campus organizations, as you can see from my résumé. I believe this record shows that I am a conscientious worker with an ability to organize my time and achieve goals in a deadline-intensive environment.

The final paragraph should include a courteous closing and suggest a response from the reader or follow-up action you will take. You might suggest that you will call in a week or so to see if the employer needs additional information. At the least, express enthusiasm for the position and a hope that you will hear from the employer soon:

> I hope that you will find my education and experience suitable for this position and that we can set up an interview soon to discuss the position further. I look forward to hearing from you.

Figure 12–2 shows a letter of application.

FIGURE 12–2 *Letter of Application*

2134 Roxboro Road
Atlanta, GA 30378
January 15, 1999

Ann Bradbury, Partner
Bradbury, Ellis, and Gomez, CPAs
33 Hightower Building
Atlanta, GA 30391

Dear Ms. Bradbury:

It was a pleasure meeting you and Mr. Ellis last week at the Accounting Club meeting here at Fulton University. As you suggested, I am sending you my résumé because you anticipate having an opening soon for which I would be qualified.

As my résumé shows, I will graduate from Fulton in May of this year with an MACC degree and a speciality in auditing. I also have on-the-job experience as an intern with Brown and Hill, CPAs. My work there last summer enabled me to participate in several audits in the north Georgia area. I hope you will find that my education and experience make me a good candidate for an auditing position with Bradbury, Ellis, and Gomez.

I would very much appreciate the opportunity to talk with you further about possible future employment. I look forward to hearing from you.

Sincerely,

Carla Brown

Carla Brown

Enclosure

Writing a Thank-You Letter

With an impressive résumé and letter of application and good credentials to support them, as well as a little luck, you will probably have one or more interviews for jobs. After the interviews you need to write letters to the people who met with you to thank them for their hospitality

FIGURE 12–3 *Thank-You Letter*

2134 Roxboro Road
Atlanta, GA 30378
April 23, 1998

Ann Bradbury, Partner
Bradbury, Ellis, and Gomez, CPAs
33 Hightower Building
Atlanta, GA 30391

Dear Ms. Bradbury:

Thank you very much for meeting with me last week to discuss the possibility of my working for Bradbury, Ellis, and Gomez after my graduation next month. I certainly enjoyed the opportunity to visit your office and meet the other members of your auditing staff. The lunch with June Oliver and Richard Wang was particularly pleasant and informative because they were able to share their experiences as first-year auditors.

I would very much welcome the opportunity to work as an auditor with your firm, so I hope that you will decide that my qualifications meet your needs. Please let me know if I can provide any additional information.

Thank you once again for your hospitality. I look forward to hearing from you.

Sincerely,

Carla Brown

Carla Brown

and to show enthusiasm for what you learned about the organization and the position for which you're applying.

This letter need not be long; two or three short paragraphs will usually be long enough. Again, you need to address your readers by name and refer specifically to your meeting and to one or two of the topics you discussed. If you met any of the firm's other employees, it would be good to express pleasure at having that opportunity. End your letter with a courteous closing and express your hope that you will be hearing from your reader soon.

This letter, like the letter of application, should follow the guidelines for letters covered in chapter 7. A sample thank-you letter is shown in Figure 12–3.

EXERCISES

Exercise 12–1

Imagine that you are an employer who received the résumé shown in Figure 12–4. What would be your reaction to the résumé? Would you be likely to give the applicant an interview? Why or why not?

Examine the résumé closely, noting the applicant's accomplishments and experience. Does this person indeed have credentials that might make him a good employee?

Rewrite this résumé so that the applicant's credentials show to good advantage. You may have to make up some details so that the résumé is complete.

Exercise 12–2

Draft your own résumé on a word processor. Then show it to a variety of your colleagues for helpful feedback. You might show it to several of your instructors as well as other accounting students and, if possible, to recent graduates who have been successful in finding jobs.

Evaluate the suggestions you receive and revise your résumé so that it looks professional and shows your qualifications effectively.

Exercise 12–3

Imagine that you find the following advertisement in your hometown newspaper, the *Metropolitan Reporter*. Prepare a letter of application for this position to accompany your résumé.

> ACCOUNTANT Entry-level staff accountant for small manufacturing firm. Degree required. Send résumé to Robert Damico, Controller, Bay State Alarm Systems, Gulf Shores, AL 35598. An equal opportunity/affirmative action employer.

FIGURE 12–4 ***Résumé to Accompany Exercise 12–1***

William H. Bonney

PRESENT ADDRESS	PERMANENT ADDRESS
745 Main St.	1634 Scaffold Lane
Athens, GA 30600	Highnoon, Ga. 31200
(706-512-6947)	(912-867-9361)

EDUCATION	GRAD. DATE	DEGREE MAJ. GPA	CUM. GPA
University of Georgia	6/98	3.4	3.5
Oconee Springs High School	6/94		3.9

MAJOR COURSES

Principles of Accounting I and II; Financial Accounting I, II, III; Systems I.

WORK EXPERIENCE	TITLE	FROM	TO
Telemarketing, Inc. Athens, Ga.	Telemarketer	7/97	Present
Esops, Inc. Athens, Ga.	Office/Customer svc.	6/96	10/96
Sam's Market Athens, Ga.	Salesperson	11/95	1/96
Tulips Discount Stores Roosevelt, Ga.	Clerk	6/95	9/95
Hamilton's Coldwater, Ga.	Cashier	5/93	9/94
Auto Stores, Inc. Clarkstown, Ga.	Cashier	7/94	9/94

HONORS AND ACTIVITIES

Honors Program
Dean's List
Golden Key
Outstanding College Students of America
Phi Chi Theta Business Fraternity
Association of Students in Accounting
James E. Cassidy Scholarship

PERSONAL

Date of Birth- October 20, 1976; excellent health; prefer to work in the Atlanta area.

Exercise 12–4

The letter of application you prepared for Exercise 12–3 was so effective and your résumé looked so impressive that you had an office interview with Bay State Alarm Systems. At the interview you met the company's president, George Owen, and several other accountants in the accounting department. You had lunch after the interview with Mary Wilson, a senior accountant in the firm, as well as the controller. You learned that the company has been in business for several decades but that it is now expanding into a larger market and adding a research and development department in order to offer technologically advanced equipment to its customers.

Write a thank-you letter to follow up on your interview.

13

Writing for Publication

As a practicing accountant, you may decide at some point in your career to write an article for publication. This might be a short article for publication in a newsletter, perhaps one published by the organization for which you work; or it might even be a longer article for publication in a professional journal, such as the *Journal of Accountancy* or *The CPA Journal*. The techniques discussed in this book apply to writing for publication, but in this chapter we consider some additional pointers.

PLANNING YOUR ARTICLE

To plan your article, start by considering the publication for which you want to write and the topic you want to write about. Most likely, you'll be writing about your experience in practice, such as a better way to approach an accounting procedure or solve an accounting problem. You may also write a position paper or essay to express your opinion on some controversial accounting or business issue currently under discussion in the profession.

Whatever the topic you've chosen, target what you write to the editorial practices and readers of the publication to which you're submitting the article. Keep in mind that one of the best ways to ensure publication of an article is to write on a subject that is interesting and relevant to a wide range of the publication's readers.

One consideration is the type of writing typically published by the targeted publication. Do the editors prefer articles on scholarly research? *The Accounting Review* is an example of this kind of publication. Other journals prefer practical articles about the practice of accounting. *The Journal of Accountancy* publishes practical articles on public accounting, and *The Practical Accountant,* as its title suggests, publishes articles about practical concerns shared by accountants. Journals and newsletters published on the state or local levels might publish articles of general interest to accounting professionals, but they also include articles of local interest.

Here are other questions to consider about the publication where you hope to publish your writing:

- Who are the readers of the publication? What are their interests and concerns? How much technical expertise on your topic are they likely to have?
- What format, organization, and length do the publication's editors prefer? You can learn this either from a statement of editorial policy or by studying articles already published.
- What style for documentation of sources does the publication use?
- What writing style do the editors prefer? Articles in professional accounting journals may be written either in a serious, scholarly style or in a light, conversational one. All publications, however, prefer prose that is clear, readable, and concise and that is written in a style that avoids accounting jargon as much as possible.

RESEARCH

Once you have chosen a topic and publication to target, it may be a good idea to find out what else has been written on the topic lately, especially if you are hoping to publish the article in a national or regional journal. You can search the Internet and visit a good library to find out this information. This research will help in several ways:

- You will find out what has been published recently on the topic so your article will not repeat what has already been done.
- You will find out what issues or approaches are of current interest in the profession.
- You may find references that you can use in your article to support your position. Alternatively, you may find positions taken by other people that you want to refute.

In addition to this background research to find out what has already been published on the topic, you may need to do some original research so that what you write will be backed up by sound observations and reasoning, and perhaps by authoritative accounting pronouncements as well. You may find it helpful to review chapter 7 of this handbook, which discusses accounting research in more detail.

DRAFTING AND REVIEWING THE ARTICLE

After you have planned the article and done any necessary research, you're ready to begin writing. Draft and revise your article according to the guidelines discussed throughout this book. When you feel reasonably satisfied with the article, ask colleagues to critique it. People who have successfully published may be particularly helpful.

For the final manuscript you will submit for publication, pay particular attention to a professional presentation, including an accurate and complete documentation of any sources you have used, prepared according to the guidelines of the journal to which you're sending the article. Professional appearance of the document pages is also important, and grammar and mechanics should be flawless.

SUBMITTING THE ARTICLE

When you're finally ready to submit your article to the targeted publication, send it along with a cover letter addressed to the editor by name. This letter should be concise and courteous, and it should mention the title of your article. You might also explain briefly why you think it would interest the publication's readers.

Double-check to make sure you have complied with the submission requirements of the publication to which you are applying. For example, if the publication requirements state that you must write your article in Microsoft Word® and submit it on 3-inch diskettes, then make sure you have done so.

After all this preparation, your article should have a good chance of acceptance for publication. However, be prepared for the possibility that your article will be rejected by the first journal you send it to.

If your article is rejected, turn it around and send it somewhere else. However, be sure to revise it to suit the readers and editorial policies of the new journal: type of articles published, interests and needs of the readers, length and style of writing, and style of documentation.

Writing for publication can be a rewarding component of your professional accounting career, but like all the writing discussed in this book, it requires planning and attention to detail, including a concern for the readers.

EXERCISE

Obtain a recent issue of several professional publications. For each of these publications, answer the following questions:

1. What type of writing does this publication publish? Possibilities include academic research, practical accounting applications for public or managerial accountants, articles of organizational or local interest, or articles addressed to some special-interest group.
2. Who writes the articles for these publications? They may be written by members of a sponsoring organization, professional writers, professors, or other accounting professionals.
3. Analyze the specific articles published. Are they all the same length, format, and style? Some publications may publish a variety of articles, such as short notes and longer essays and articles.
4. What are standard editorial practices, such as article length and style of documentation?

14

Oral Presentations

Speaking before a group, like writing, is often an important part of an accountant's professional responsibilities, yet public speaking creates anxiety for many people. If you learn a few strategies for public speaking, however, and practice as often as possible, your fear of these situations will diminish. With guidance and practice comes mastery, and with mastery comes control.

In this chapter, you will see that effective oral presentations, like writing, result from a process: preparation, practice, and delivery. This chapter shows you how to prepare for speaking before a group. We begin by discussing the first step in any important communication: analyzing the purpose of the presentation and the needs and interests of the audience.

PLANNING THE PRESENTATION: ANALYZING PURPOSE AND AUDIENCE

The first step in planning your presentation is to analyze its purpose. Perhaps you need to inform the listeners about the progress you've made on a project or propose that the decision makers in the group approve a new project. You may be convincing senior management to invest in a new system or explaining to coworkers how to implement the system already adopted. Remember that no matter what the primary purpose of your presentation, it has an important secondary purpose as well: your desire to impress your listeners as a competent professional.

As you analyze the purpose of the presentation, think also about the audience. How many people will you be speaking to? Will they be a fairly homogeneous group, or will you be speaking to people with different degrees of knowledge about your topic and different interests? An important consideration about the audience is which decision makers will be present. In planning your presentation, the needs and interests of these decision makers should be a primary concern.

Think in advance about the questions the audience will have about the topic, whether or not there will be a formal question-and-answer session as part of the presentation. By anticipating listeners' questions, you can explain your ideas in a convincing way. Anticipating listeners' questions and having the information ready to answer them also shows the audience that you are thoroughly prepared, credible, and professional.

Throughout the planning and preparation of the speech, think always about the audience: what they know about your topic, what they need to know, what their concerns and interests are, and what their attitudes may be toward your point of view and the information you'll present.

OTHER THINGS TO CONSIDER

In addition to analyzing your purpose and audience, you need to determine how much time you'll have for the presentation. In addition, find out how you will be speaking to your audience, whether formally from a podium or informally, perhaps from your seat in a conference setting.

Yet another consideration is whether to illustrate your speech with visual aids, such as charts or other graphic material. If you decide to use visual aids, consider the room where the presentation will be made. Will the space and facilities allow you to use the visual aids you prefer? A later section of this chapter discusses how to prepare effective visual aids. For now, the important point to remember is that you need to start planning visual aids early.

Finally, budget your time so you can complete the work needed to gather information, compose the speech, make notes, prepare visual aids, and practice the presentation. All of these steps take time, particularly if your topic requires much underlying research.

The key to handling all these tasks is to make a schedule with dates for the completion of each step. It's important to plan the work you have to do and budget your time.

GATHERING INFORMATION

The next step in preparing the presentation is to gather the necessary information. Be thorough in your research so that you can answer any questions the audience has. When you are thoroughly prepared, you will seem competent and professional, and your presentation will have an excellent chance of success.

Before you begin the research for your presentation, you may want to review chapter 2, which discusses how to generate ideas, and chapter 7, which covers accounting research.

COMPOSING THE SPEECH

Once you've gathered the information you need, organize the material into an outline. Keeping in mind the purpose of the speech and the interests of your audience, identify the main points you want to make: *Your speech should contain no more than three to five main points.* These main points, with an introduction and conclusion, are the outline of your presentation. Let's look now at how to fill in that outline.

Introduction

The introduction should do two things: It should get the listeners' attention and preview for them the main points you will cover.

When you plan the opening sentences of the presentation, consider the listeners' point of view. Why should they listen to what you have to say? Will your speech be meaningful to them, perhaps helping them solve a problem or accomplish a goal? What do you and your listeners have in common that would make them interested in your presentation? What makes your topic particularly timely and relevant to your listeners? Questions such as these can help you compose the opening sentences of your presentation to get your audience's attention. Here are a few additional suggestions:

- Begin with an interesting story or example to introduce your topic.
- Cite a startling statistic.
- Ask a rhetorical question—one that you don't expect your audience to answer but that will start them thinking about the topic.

These are just a few examples of ways to begin the presentation.

After your opening sentences, the next important part of the presentation is a preview of what the speech will cover. If you tell the audience what the main points will be, you'll help them remember what's important as you progress through your presentation.

Body of the Presentation

In the body of the presentation, you present again your main points and develop them in detail. Be specific and concrete: Use facts, examples, and, where appropriate, statistics.

As you move from one main point to the next, you can help your listeners remember main ideas with two techniques: internal summaries of what you've already said and clear transitions that lead into the next main topic. For example, you might say something like this:

> So one advantage of this new system is that it would reduce the time needed to process customer accounts. [This is an internal summary. We know it's a summary because of the word *so*.] The second advantage is that the system would provide us with better records for our sales managers. [This sentence provides a transition into the next major section of the speech and identifies for the listeners the second main point.]

By providing internal summaries and obvious transitions, you can help your listeners remember main ideas as you give your presentation.

Conclusion

The last part of the formal presentation is the conclusion. Once again, you will help the listeners if you summarize the main ideas you want them to remember. Your presentation will be most effective, however, if you end with a forceful closing. Here are some suggestions:

- Ask your audience to do something. This call to action may be low key—a request that they consider your recommendation, for example. You may want to be more forceful and sometimes even dramatic if you think the topic warrants this approach and if this tone is suitable for your audience.
- Refer again to the opening sentences of your presentation. For example, if you used a story, example, or statistic, suggest how the ideas expressed in your speech relate to these concepts.
- Remind your audience of the benefits they will receive if they follow your recommendations.

For additional help in composing your speech, you will find it useful to review chapter 3, which covers the principles of coherent organization.

MAKING NOTES

Once you have gathered your material and completed the outline, you are ready to put your notes in final form—the form from which you will actually speak. Notice that this section is *not* called "Writing Your Speech," and for a very good reason. Most experienced speakers find it unnecessary to write down every word they want to say. In fact, having a word-for-word manuscript of your speech could lead you to make two mistakes in your presentation: reading the speech or trying to memorize it. (More about these pitfalls later.)

The most helpful way to prepare notes is in outline form. You should already have this outline because you prepared it as you gathered information and organized your materials. Your job now is to put this outline into notes you can speak from. Here are a few pointers:

- Transfer the outline to note cards or standard-sized paper. Write large enough that you can see what you've written at a glance.
- Include main points, as well as supporting details and examples.
- Write out the opening sentences and the conclusion. (This is the exception to the advice not to write out the speech word-for-word.)
- Indicate in your notes where you will use your visual aids.
- As you review your notes, highlight or underline key phrases in a contrasting color of ink. When you make the presentation, these underlined phrases will remind you of the points you want to make.
- Number the notecards or pages and clip them together.

When we discuss practicing and delivering your presentation, you will see how notes prepared in this way will help you make a smooth presentation.

PREPARING VISUAL AIDS

To appreciate how visual aids can contribute to an effective presentation, consider your audience's point of view.

When people read, they have a number of visual cues to help them identify and remember main ideas. They have titles and headings, paragraph breaks to signal a shift in topic, and often graphic illustrations. If they need to review something that has already been covered, they have only to turn back the page to see that material again.

Listeners to an oral presentation have none of these visual cues to help them follow the flow of thought, unless the speaker provides them with visual aids. A major advantage of visual aids is that they help listeners identify and remember main ideas. They offer another advantage as well, because well-constructed, attractive visual aids make the presentation more interesting.

Visual aids appeal to the audience by making the presentation easier to follow and more interesting. What are the best kinds of aids to use?

To some extent, your choices depend on where you'll be speaking. If you are making a classroom presentation, for example, you can prepare handouts, write on the chalkboard, prepare posters and charts, and probably use an overhead projector. In some settings, you may also have access to more sophisticated equipment, such as videocassette players and projection equipment that can be run by computers.

You may decide to use more than one kind of visual aid. For example, handouts give your listeners something to take with them to reinforce what you've said especially when you want to give them lengthy or detailed information. You don't want them reading the handout instead of looking at you when you speak, so it may be a good idea to illustrate your presentation with posters or overhead transparencies and distribute the handouts after the presentation.

Let's look more closely at guidelines for preparing visual aids such as posters and overhead transparencies:

- Keep your aids simple. Use key words and phrases rather than sentences, and limit each aid to about ten lines.
- Be sure the writing is legible and large enough to be read from the back of the room. It's much better to prepare the aid using a software package, but if you must write by hand, write clearly in a dark or bright color so that the writing is easy to see.
- If possible, use bright colors to make your aids more attractive.
- Make your aids neat and professional-looking. A computer with a graphics package will help you achieve a professional appearance. You might even consider having the aids prepared professionally.

You can include any information on your visual aid that will help your listeners understand and remember your message, but visual aids are particularly helpful in identifying your main points, summarizing your recommendations or conclusions, or providing a vivid illustration. You can also summarize statistical information in a table or graph. Yet another technique is to reproduce cartoons to amuse your listeners as you illustrate a point.

Once you have prepared your visual aids and notes, you are ready for the next important step in the preparation of the oral presentation: practice.

PRACTICING THE PRESENTATION

Practicing the presentation is essential for several reasons. For one thing, the more often you review the speech, the more familiar you become with it, so that when you speak before an audience you will appear knowledgeable and convincing. You will also feel more confident that you have mastered the ideas you want to present. When you practice, especially before other people, you also identify in advance any potential problems that could occur, such as a presentation that is too long or too short for the allotted time.

Here are some strategies that will make your practice time most useful:

- Practice the speech out loud. Pay attention to your voice, posture, and gestures.
- Time the presentation to make sure it is the appropriate length.
- Practice using the visual aids, including any equipment you will be using, such as an overhead projector or Power Point™ presentation.
- If possible, practice in the actual room you will be using for the presentation.
- Practice before a live audience, such as friends, family, or coworkers. Ask them to be critical of the content and delivery of the speech.
- If you have access to video equipment, ask someone to make a videotape of the presentation so that you can identify and correct any problems.

Finally, avoid this common pitfall:

Never read or try to memorize your speech!

The only exception to this guideline is that you may find it helpful to memorize the opening and closing sentences.

CHECKING THE ARRANGEMENTS

For some oral presentations, preparations will include arranging for a room and equipment. Even if someone else is responsible for these duties, it may be a good idea to check thoroughly. For example, be sure that the room will be unlocked in time for the early arrivals at the presentation and that equipment will be delivered and set up in working order.

Check again on these arrangements a little while before the presentation begins. If there is some unforeseen problem, such as malfunctioning equipment, you'll have time to correct it.

APPEARANCE AND DRESS

A final consideration in the preparation for your presentation is appearance and dress. As in any professional situation, your grooming should be impeccable. The clothing you wear will depend to some extent on the situation, but professional styles and colors are almost always preferable. If you are in doubt, it's usually better to err on the side of conservatism.

In summary, thorough preparation for the presentation—your appearance, the arrangements, your visual aids, and the speech itself—will help you ensure good results when you speak before a group.

MAKING THE PRESENTATION: POISE AND CONFIDENCE

Earlier we discussed the steps of preparing an oral presentation before you actually give it: planning, composing, and practice. Now we'll look at the qualities of effective delivery and strategies to help you become an accomplished public speaker.

The effect you should create on your audience is one of poise and confidence. With adequate practice and preparation, you are well on your way to reaching this goal. Let's look at techniques of actual delivery that contribute to an effective presentation.

Eye Contact

One of the secrets of public speaking is eye contact between the speaker and the audience. When you look your listeners in the eye, you involve them in the topic and help ensure that they listen carefully.

Establish eye contact when you first stand before the audience: Stand straight, smile, and look around the room. Look directly at various people at different locations. This initial eye contact should probably last for a total of two or three seconds.

As you begin the presentation and progress through it, continue to maintain this eye contact. Hold the eye contact with each person for several seconds, perhaps the length of a complete phrase. Shift the contact from one side of the room to the other, front to back, and at various points in the middle. If your audience is small, you may be able to make eye contact with everyone in the room several times.

Regardless of the size of your audience, though, it's essential to establish eye contact with one important group of listeners: the decision makers. They will be judging the ideas you present and your effectiveness as a speaker. Good eye contact will help you keep their attention. You'll also seem confident and in control of the situation.

You may also find it helpful to look frequently at the listeners who seem most interested and supportive of what you are saying. You can recognize this group by their expressions of interest and attention, perhaps even nods and smiles. Their enthusiasm can give you extra energy and confidence.

When you think about the importance of maintaining good eye contact with the audience, it becomes obvious why you shouldn't read your speech and why you should be so familiar with your notes that you only glance at them from time to time.

Body Movement and Gestures

Poised, natural use of your body and gestures also contributes to an effective presentation. Stand still, with good posture, and look directly at the listeners. Don't move about, except to use your visual aids (for example, to point to something on a chart or to change a transparency on the overhead projector).

Natural, expressive use of your hands is an effective way to emphasize ideas and feelings. For this reason, it is better to place your notes on a table or lectern so that your hands are free for gestures.

Voice

Three elements of your voice contribute to the effectiveness of a presentation: pitch, volume, and speed. Pitch is how high or low one speaks. Most people's natural pitch is fine and requires no modification for public speaking. A few people need to pitch their voices a little lower than normal, especially if they are nervous when they speak.

Volume and speed may require more attention. The key to speaking at the correct volume is to speak loudly enough so that people in the back of the room can hear you. Be consistent; don't let your voice drop at the ends of sentences, for example, so that your audience misses the last words or must strain to hear you.

When you practice the presentation, pay particular attention to the speed at which you are speaking. You should speak slowly enough to enunciate each word clearly. Some speakers have a tendency to speak more rapidly when they are nervous. If you fall into this category, make a conscious effort to slow down.

Managing Stage Fright

Now that we've introduced the topic of nervousness, let's think for a minute about how to manage what for many speakers is the worst part of public speaking: stage fright. Notice that the heading for this section is "*Managing* Stage Fright," not "*Eliminating* Stage Fright." Even the most experienced, effective speakers usually have some stage fright; furthermore, they use this heightened emotion to help them make a more effective presentation. The emotion, if kept in control, can give you the extra charge to make an energetic, enthusiastic, and convincing presentation.

Of course, too much stage fright is counterproductive. Let's look at some strategies you can use to manage stage fright before and during presentation.

Prepare Well in Advance One advantage of thorough preparation and practice is that they help prevent stage fright. When you know you thoroughly understand the topic, and when you have thought in advance about the questions and interests of the listeners, you will *feel* prepared, and thus competent. A feeling of competence, in turn, gives you confidence in your ability to do a good job.

Actual practice, especially before a live audience, will also increase your confidence.

Just Before You Speak Two tricks may be helpful in the last few minutes before you are scheduled to speak. The first is to use this time to go over your notes one last time, to be sure your main points, as well as your opening and closing sentences, are fresh in your mind. The second trick is this:

Don't think about how you're feeling!

If you think about being nervous, you'll only increase the feeling. Instead, think about something pleasant that is completely unrelated to your presentation. Perhaps you can think about something nice you will do later in the day.

During the Presentation Most speakers find that their stage fright goes away after the first few minutes of their presentation. When you are speaking, look directly at your listeners with poise and confidence: They'll probably reflect these positive feelings back to you. Notice which of your listeners are most interested and receptive to what you're saying, and make frequent eye contact with these people. Their enthusiasm will add to your feelings of confidence and ensure that your presentation is effective.

SPECIAL CONSIDERATIONS IN PRESENTATIONS OF FINANCIAL INFORMATION

The standard techniques for presentations given in this chapter apply to accounting presentations as well, of course, but there are a number of special considerations to bear in mind when you are presenting financial information. Most of the time, presentations of financial information contain numbers, tabular data, and charts that will be shown on slides or overhead transparencies. The following points apply in this type of presentation:

- Make sure your numbers are consistent. If "Sales are expected to reach $7.25 million in 1999" appears on one slide, make sure your other slides don't contain some other number.*
- Make sure your numbers "add up." If your presentation includes a statement such as "Sales are expected to grow 20 percent from their 1998 level of

*It's easier to make this error than you might think. When a presentation is developed, it tends to be revised several times before a final version is produced. When numbers are changed during the revisions, it is sometimes difficult to find all the places in the presentation where they appear. As a result, conflicting numbers end up in the final presentation.

$7 million, reaching $8.4 million in 1999," make sure that $7,000,000 × 1.20 does in fact equal $8,400,000 (which it does in this case).

- Make sure the audience can read the charts in your presentation. This applies to the size of charts as well as their design. For example, many members of the audience would have difficulty making out the slide in Figure 14–1. While the slide illustrates where the company's funds came from and where they went, the labels on the pie slices are too small to read. Also, there is a bit too much information on the slide to take in at once. In this case the presenter should probably separate the charts into two slides.
- Try to use computer-assisted presentations wherever possible. Presentations developed in graphics programs such as Microsoft PowerPoint™, Corel Draw™, or Lotus Freelance™ look very professional, and they may well make the difference between your recommendations' being accepted or rejected. An example of a financial presentation created in Microsoft PowerPoint™ is shown in Figure 14–2. Although the presentation is reproduced here in black-and-white, you can imagine how the addition of color (accomplished automatically in PowerPoint™) would bring the presentation to life.

A Final Word

Public speaking may always fill you with some apprehension. With practice and the mastery of technique, however, you will become much more sure of yourself and your ability to be an effective oral communicator. For that reason, it's a good idea to take advantage of every opportunity to practice your public speaking. The payoff will be greater professional success.

FIGURE 14–1 *Example of a Poor Slide*

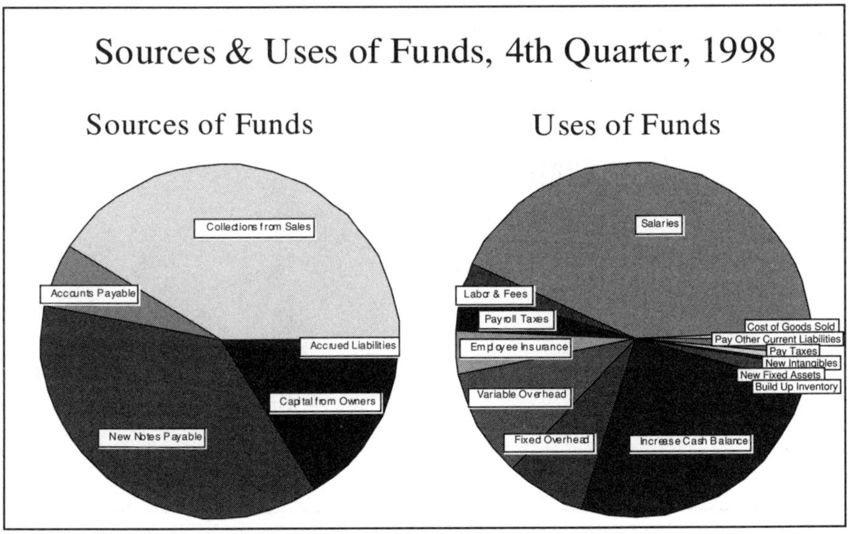

FIGURE 14–2 *A Financial Presentation Created in Microsoft PowerPoint™*

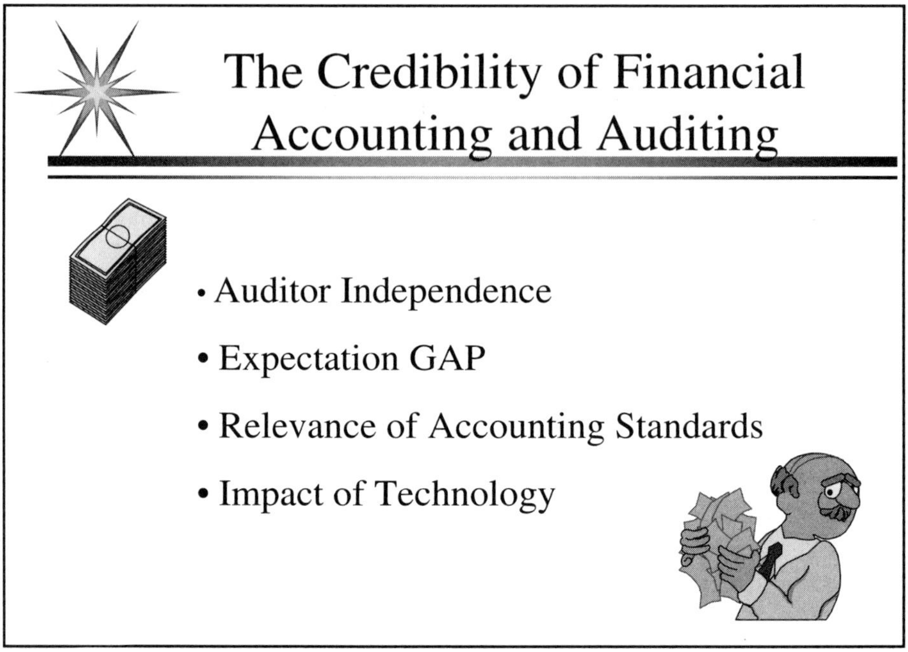

FIGURE 14–2 ***A Financial Presentation Created in Microsoft PowerPoint™ (cont.)***

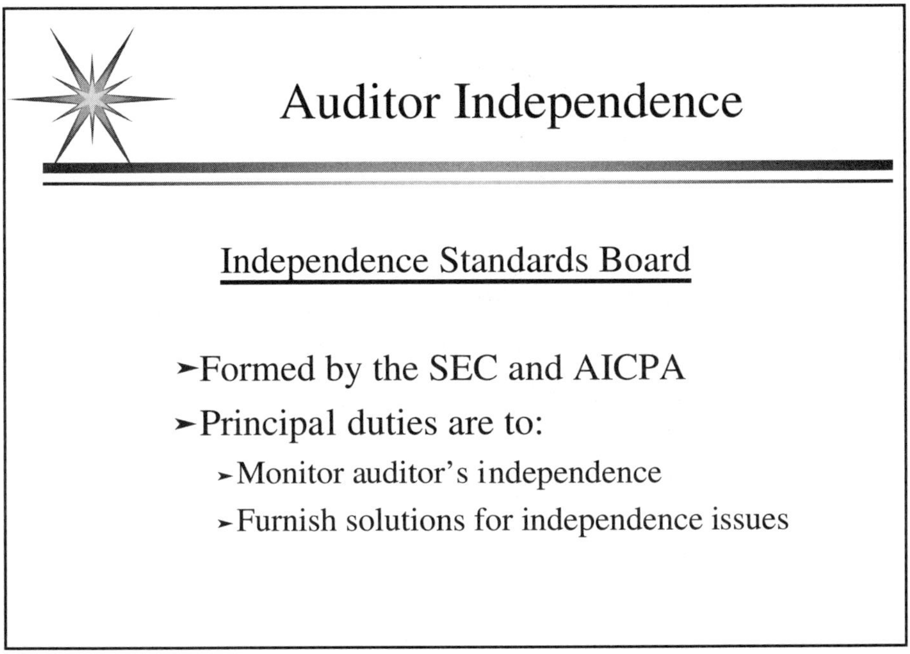

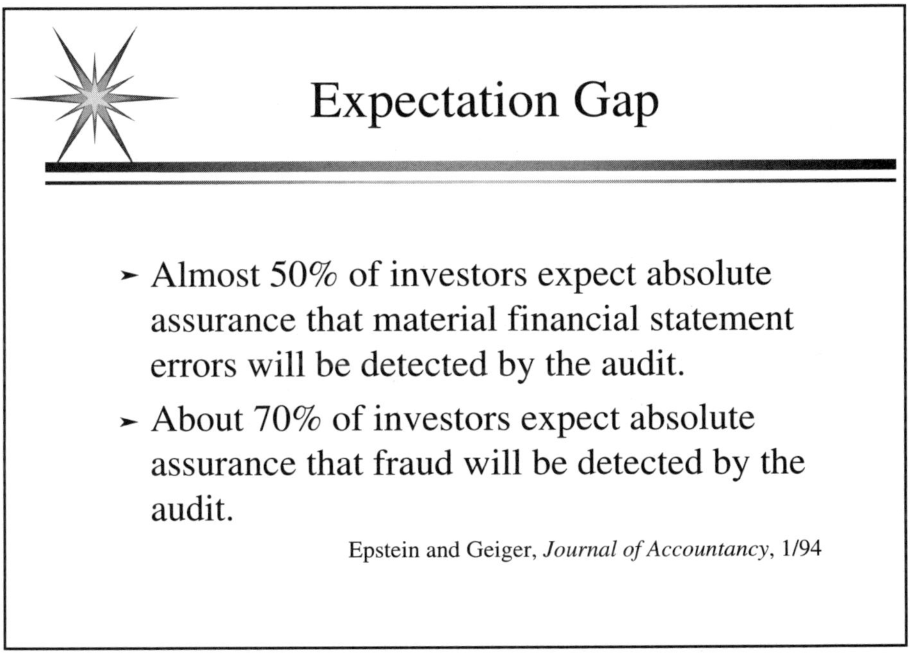

FIGURE 14–2 *A Financial Presentation Created in Microsoft PowerPoint™ (cont.)*

Relevance of Accounting Standards

"I think financial accounting and reporting have lost some of their credibility, and we need to improve their relevance."

Walter Schuetz, Chief Accountant of the SEC, 1992

Relevance of Accounting Standards

Recommendations of Walter Schuetze:

- Simplify accounting rules.
- Make standards more responsive to the information needs of investors and creditors.

FIGURE 14–2 *A Financial Presentation Created in Microsoft PowerPoint™ (cont.)*

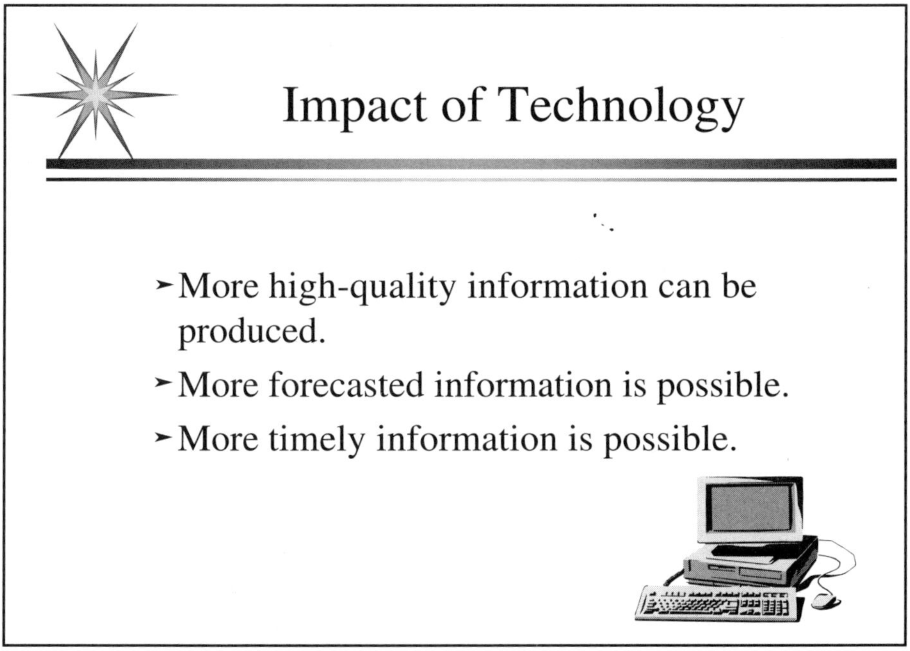

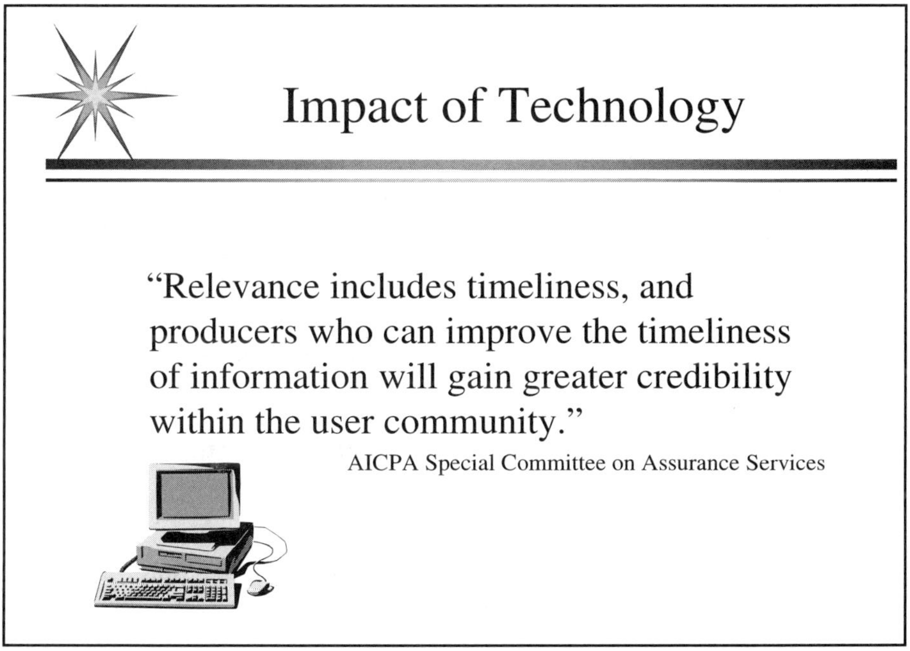

FIGURE 14–2 *A Financial Presentation Created in Microsoft PowerPoint™ (cont.)*

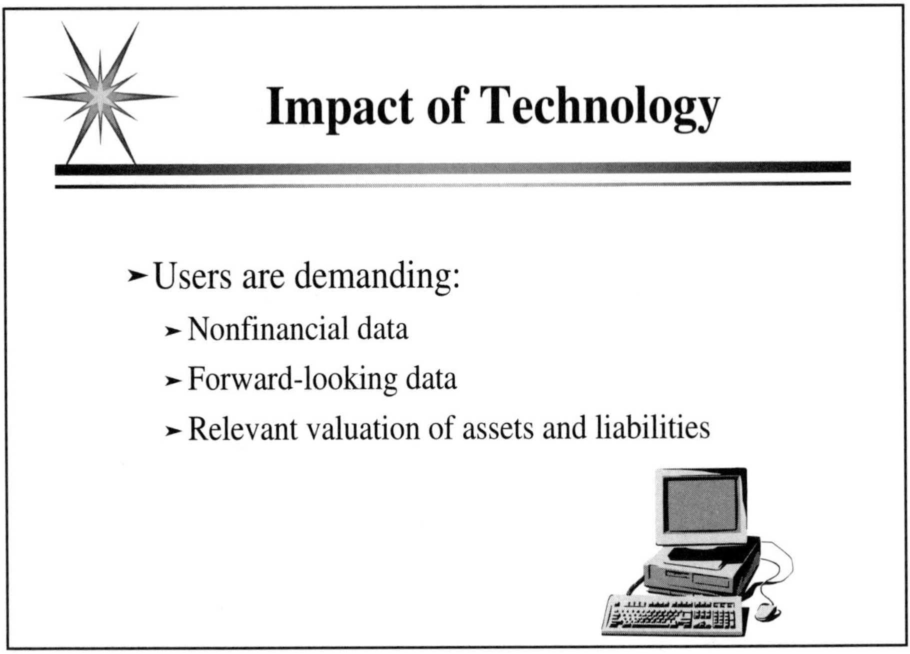

EXERCISES

Exercise 14–1

Select as a partner for this exercise one of your classmates. Imagine that you have been asked to introduce your classmate before a professional meeting of your peers. Interview your classmate, taking notes as you ask questions. Then review your notes for accuracy and organize them into an outline that you can use for a two- or three-minute introduction.

(*Hint:* Analyze the interests of your audience as the basis for the questions you ask in your interview.)

After you have completed one interview, you and your partner can switch roles so that you are interviewed for an introduction your partner will make.

Exercise 14–2

Select one of the following topics and prepare a five-minute presentation to give before your class:

- Career opportunities in accounting
- Tips for studying accounting

- Stereotypes about accountants
- The accounting profession in the next decade
- The users of accounting information

Exercise 14–3

Prepare an oral presentation of the report you wrote for chapter 10. Assume the audience for the oral presentation is the same as that for the written report. If necessary, condense the material in the written report, prepare additional visual aids, or make any other changes needed for an effective oral presentation. Reminder: Do not read the report to the audience.

Your presentation should be about 20 minutes long.

Exercise 14–4

The more opportunities you have to speak before a group of people, the more confident you'll be of your abilities. With your instructor's approval, make these informal oral presentations:

1. Introduce the classmate you interviewed for Exercise 14–1.
2. Explain to the class how to work an accounting problem that was assigned for homework.

Exercise 14–5

Present to your class the presentation prepared for Exercise 14–2 or 14–3. After the presentation, ask your classmates and instructor to identify what you did well and to suggest ways you could improve.

Exercise 14–6

Have someone videotape a presentation you make before your class. Then review the tape to identify what you did well and what areas you need to improve.

Exercise 14–7

Learn to be a good listener. When classmates give oral presentations, listen politely and attentively. Then for each speaker, identify

- At least two strengths of the presentation
- Two suggestions for improvement

Write your evaluations on 3 × 5-inch cards, which you can give to the speakers at the end of class.

Index